Marriage and Health

The Politics of Marriage and Gender: Global Issues in Local Contexts

Series Editor: Péter Berta

The Politics of Marriage and Gender: Global Issues in Local Contexts series from Rutgers University Press fills a gap in research by examining the politics of marriage and related practices, ideologies, and interpretations, and addresses the key question of how the politics of marriage has affected social, cultural, and political processes, relations, and boundaries. The series looks at the complex relationships between the politics of marriage and gender, ethnic, national, religious, racial, and class identities, and analyzes how these relationships contribute to the development and management of social and political differences, inequalities, and conflicts.

Joanne Payton, *Honor and the Political Economy of Marriage: Violence against Women in the Kurdistan Region of Iraq*

Rama Srinivasan, *Courting Desire: Litigating for Love in North India*

Sara Smith, *Intimate Geopolitics: Love, Territory, and the Future on India's Northern Threshold*

Hui Liu, Corinne Reczek, and Lindsey Wilkinson, eds., *Marriage and Health: The Well-Being of Same-Sex Couples*

Marriage and Health

The Well-Being of Same-Sex Couples

EDITED BY
HUI LIU
CORINNE RECZEK
LINDSEY WILKINSON

RUTGERS UNIVERSITY PRESS

NEW BRUNSWICK, CAMDEN, AND NEWARK, NEW JERSEY, AND LONDON

Library of Congress Cataloging-in-Publication Data

Names: Liu, Hui, 1977– editor. | Reczek, Corinne E., editor. | Wilkinson, Lindsey, 1982– editor.
Title: Marriage and health : the well-being of same-sex couples / edited by Hui Liu, Corinne Reczek, Lindsey Wilkinson.
Description: New Brunswick, New Jersey : Rutgers University Press, [2019] | Series: The politics of marriage and gender: global issues in local context | Includes bibliographical references and index.
Identifiers: LCCN 2019024575 | ISBN 9781978803480 (paperback) | ISBN 9781978803497 (hardback) | ISBN 9781978803503 (epub) | ISBN 9781978803510 (mobi) | ISBN 9781978803527 (pdf)
Subjects: LCSH: Gay couples—Health and hygiene. | Married people—Health and hygiene. | Gay couples—Social conditions. | Married people—Social conditions.
Classification: LCC HQ76.34 .M38 2019 | DDC 306.84/8—dc23
LC record available at https://lccn.loc.gov/2019024575

A British Cataloging-in-Publication record for this book is
available from the British Library.

♾ The paper used in this publication meets the requirements of the American National Standard for Information Sciences—Permanence of Paper for Printed Library Materials, ANSI Z39.48-1992.

www.rutgersuniversitypress.org

Manufactured in the United States of America

CONTENTS

PART TWO
Health Behaviors

PART THREE
Physical Health, Mortality,
and Health Care

PART FOUR
Relationship Quality, Experience, and Identity

SERIES FOREWORD

The politics of marriage (and divorce) is an often-used strategic tool in various social, cultural, economic, and political identity projects as well as in symbolic conflicts between ethnic, national, or religious communities. Despite having multiple strategic applicabilities, pervasiveness in everyday life, and huge significance in performing and managing identities, the politics of marriage is surprisingly underrepresented both in the international book publishing market and in the social sciences.

The Politics of Marriage and Gender: Global Issues in Local Contexts is a series from Rutgers University Press examining the politics of marriage as a phenomenon embedded into and intensely interacting with much broader social, cultural, economic, and political processes and practices such as globalization; transnationalization; international migration; human trafficking; vertical social mobility; the creation of symbolic boundaries between ethnic populations, nations, religious denominations, or classes; family formation; or struggles for women's and children's rights. The series primarily aims to analyze practices, ideologies, and interpretations related to the politics of marriage, and to outline the dynamics and diversity of relatedness—interplay and interdependence, for instance—between the politics of marriage and the broader processes and practices mentioned earlier. In other words, most books in the series devote special attention to how the politics of marriage and these processes and practices mutually shape and explain each other.

The series concentrates on, among other things, the complex relationships between the politics of marriage and gender, ethnic, national, religious, racial, and class identities globally, and examines how these relationships contribute to the development and management of social, cultural, and political differences, inequalities, and conflicts.

The series seeks to publish single-authored books and edited volumes that develop a gap-filling and thought-provoking critical perspective, that are well-balanced between a high degree of theoretical sophistication and empirical richness, and that cross or rethink disciplinary, methodological, or theoretical boundaries. The thematic scope of the series is intentionally left broad to encourage creative submissions that fit within the perspectives outlined previously.

Among the potential topics closely connected with the problem sensitivity of the series are "honor"-based violence; arranged (forced, child, etc.) marriage; transnational marriage markets, migration, and brokerage; intersections of marriage and religion, class, and race; the politics of agency and power within marriage; reconfiguration of family: same-sex marriage or union; the politics of love, intimacy, and desire; marriage and multicultural families; the (religious, legal, etc.) politics of divorce; the causes, forms, and consequences of polygamy in contemporary societies; sport marriage; refusing marriage; and so forth.

Marriage and Health: The Well-Being of Same-Sex Couples is an original, path-breaking, and stimulating volume, examining various dimensions of the health and well-being of individuals in same-sex unions (legal marriage, civil unions, cohabitation, and so on). Demonstrating and insightfully analyzing contemporary opportunities, challenges, and constraints faced by same-sex unions, the chapters cover a wide range of timely and underexplored topics such as minority stress experienced by same-sex couples prior to the legalization of same-sex marriage; the association between same-sex union status and adult mortality risk; health care access; lesbian couples' experiences of childbirth and (gendered) parental identities; and the likelihood of dissolution for gay and lesbian couples. The novelty of this volume derives, on the one hand, from the new theoretical perspectives and newly available population-based data used, and, on the other, from the fact that the authors investigate not only same-sex marriage and civil unions but also dating and cohabiting relationships as well as same-sex sexual experiences outside of relationships. This volume is a landmark study in a relatively new and growing area of research, and also offers nuanced critical perspectives on how some key systems in the wider context of same-sex unions—such as health care and the law—work and how individuals can or cannot navigate within "institutional mazes" relating to these systems. Consequently, the new research findings presented in this volume will certainly have far-reaching policy implications for the health of sexual minorities—making these chapters essential reading not only for academics but also for practitioners and policy makers.

PÉTER BERTA
University College London
School of Slavonic and East European Studies

LIST OF ABBREVIATIONS

ACASI	audio-computer assisted self-interviewing
AME	average marginal effects
ANOVA	analysis of variance
AOR	adjusted odds ratios
ATL	Greater Atlanta metropolitan area
ATT	average treatment effect among the treated
ATUS	American Time Use Survey
BMI	body mass index
BRFSS	The Behavioral Risk Factor Surveillance System
CDC	Centers for Disease Control and Prevention
DOMA	Defense of Marriage Act
DSM-IV	*Diagnostic and Statistical Manual of Mental Disorders*, version 4
EPDS	Edinburgh Postnatal Depression Scale
ESI	employee-sponsored insurance
FE	fixed effects
GED	General Educational Development
GSS	General Social Survey
IHIS	Integrated Health Interview Series
IOM	Institute of Medicine
IPUMS-NHIS	International Public Use Microdata Series National Health Interview Surveys
IRR	Incidence Rate Ratio
ISMW	"invisible" sexual minority women
K6	Kessler Six-Item Psychological Distress Scale
LGBTQ	lesbian, gay, bisexual, transgender, and queer
MOS	Medical Outcomes Study
MPC	Minnesota Population Center
NCHS	National Center for Health Statistics
NHIS	National Health Interview Surveys
NHIS-LMF	National Health Interview Survey Linked-Mortality Files
NIH	National Institutes of Health
NIMHD	National Institute on Minority Health Disparities

NSFG	National Survey of Family Growth
NSHAP	National Social Life, Health, and Aging Project, Int.-8
NSMW	non-sexual minority women
OR	odds ratio
PPD	postpartum depression
RE	random effects
SAF	Sample Adult files
SES	socioeconomic status
SESSP	sexual experiences with same-sex partners
SF	San Francisco Bay area
SJSP	Social Justice Sexuality Project
SMI	serious mental illness
SMW	sexual minority women
SSC	same-sex contact
STAI	State-Trait Anxiety Inventory
TPIF	Texas Pride Impact Funds
VSM	visible sexual minorities
VSMW	visible sexual minority women

Marriage and Health

Introduction

The Health and Well-Being of Sexual Minority Couples

HUI LIU

CORINNE RECZEK

LINDSEY WILKINSON

The number of individuals identifying as sexual minorities (e.g., lesbian, gay, bisexual, transgender, and queer [LGBTQ], or LGBTQ identified) and living in sexual minority households worldwide continues to rise given ongoing social and political changes. Across the globe, countries have been debating whether same-sex couples should be given access to the marriage and family rights available to heterosexual couples (Merin 2010), with many countries in Europe and the Americas legalizing same-sex marriage at national or jurisdictional levels (Masci, Sciupac, and Lipka 2017). Most recently, in 2017, Australia and Malta legalized same-sex marriage at the national level. Yet opposition to same-sex marriage and rights for LGBTQ individuals remains strong in many Pacific Rim, Asian, Middle Eastern, and African countries (Felter and Renwick 2017).

In the United States, same-sex marriage was legalized at the national level in 2015, yet U.S. state variation in legal access to same-sex unions and marriages characterized much of the 1990s and 2000s. In the United States, same-sex couple households are increasing at a faster rate than other household types: there were an estimated 646,464 same-sex couple households in 2010, an increase of 80 percent from 2000 (Gates 2012). The growing number of sexual minority households in the United States and access to new data sources that now incorporate questions on sexual orientation and union status have led to a new and growing field of study, attracting both public and academic attention: the health and well-being of sexual minority couples.

Given the robust empirical link between union status and health, the social changes surrounding LGBTQ families, and the increased data sources available to researchers, particularly in the United States, this edited volume seeks to do the following: (1) present emerging empirical research and theoretical perspectives on the health and well-being of individuals in sexual minority couples; (2) examine the experiences and outcomes of individuals in sexual minority couples in multiple areas of well-being, including physical and mental health, health behaviors, and relationship quality, often in comparison with their heterosexual counterparts; and (3) to offer a broad view of sexual minority couples by focusing not only on those in legal marriages and civil unions but also on sexual minority individuals inside and outside of dating and cohabiting relationships.

By addressing these aims, this edited volume takes a step forward in understanding the critical and complex questions of whether and how union status matters for health and well-being, primarily in the context of the United States. Scholars and policy makers have contended that marriage, a fundamental social institution, promotes individual health and well-being in a way that other types of unions such as cohabitation do not. This previous body of work shows that married people have better mental and physical health than unmarried people, including both cohabiting and single people (Waite and Gallagher 2000). Yet, this finding is primarily based on evidence among different-sex, or heterosexual, cisgender couples. Because marriage has been legally denied to sexual minority couples throughout the majority of U.S. history, our understanding of union status and health has been primarily limited to dynamics in heterosexual couples. In fact, prior to the 1990s, scholars had not regularly asked the empirical question of what marriage would be like for same-sex or sexual minority couples due to the deeply held belief that marriage was fundamentally between one man and one woman.

The increase in the number of U.S. states with legal same-sex marriage over the past decade, along with the recent legalization of national same-sex marriage, means we now, for the first time, have access to new population-based data with which to assess the health of the sexual minority population. Very recent data and methodological developments have allowed for the identification of sexual minority unions in a small number of U.S. population-based national survey data sets, and a growing body of research has begun to examine the health and well-being of individuals in sexual minority couples. The majority of the chapters within this book draw on evidence from such large-scale, nationally representative, U.S.-based data sets. As one of the first efforts to showcase developments in innovative research and data sources, this edited volume includes work at the cutting edge of sexual minority health research. In this sense, this book is unique in its unprecedented ability to promote knowledge of population health patterns among sexual minority couples. In order to orient the reader to this comprehensive edited volume on sexual minority unions and health, we first briefly review what we know about how marriage matters for health and well-being among heterosexual couples. We then discuss in more detail the previous evidence on how marriage and cohabitation matter for sexual minority couples. We conclude this introduction by detailing the organization of the book.

Marriage, Health, and Well-Being among Heterosexuals: What We Know

Hundreds of empirical studies have demonstrated that married people have better health, both mental and physical, than unmarried people, especially those who are divorced or widowed (Liu and Umberson 2008; Umberson and Montez 2010; Waite and Gallagher 2000). This marital advantage in health, primarily documented in heterosexual marriages, is often presumed to be due to the protective resources that people obtain when they participate in this privileged institution (Waite and Gallagher 2000) and/or the selection of people with greater access to economic and psychosocial resources into marriage (Musick, Brand, and Davis 2012). Heterosexual marriage is found to be related to unique economic, social, and psychological resources that cannot be obtained, at least to the same extent, from other types of relationships (such as cohabitation); these resources in turn affect health and well-being (Umberson, Thomeer, and Williams 2013). In terms of economic resources, marriage may lead to an increase in economic resources through specialization, economies of scale, and the pooling of wealth (Becker 1981). Economic resources may enhance health by improving nutrition, providing care in the event of illness, and allowing the purchase of medical care or other health-enhancing resources. In terms of social and psychological resources, marriage increases access to social support (i.e., providing love, advice, and care), social integration (i.e., feeling connected to others), and social control of health behaviors (i.e., the deliberate efforts of others to control one's health and health behaviors) (Liu and Umberson 2008). Marriage reinforces social integration by extending involvement in social relationships (Umberson and Montez 2010) and by increasing access to social support and perceived security (Liu and Umberson 2008). Moreover, marriage also provides external regulation and facilitates self-regulation of health behaviors (e.g., diet, smoking, and exercise), which affects health.

Sexual Minority Unions and Well-Being: What We Know

At the turn of the twenty-first century, a fundamental empirical and theoretical question emerged: does marriage matter for the well-being of those in sexual minority unions in similar ways as it does for heterosexual unions? On one hand, leading scholars and policy makers have theorized—and to some extent shown empirically—that same-sex marriage enhances health in analogous ways as heterosexual marriage (Buffie 2011; Cherlin 2013; Herek 2006; Liu, Reczek, and Brown 2013; Reczek, Liu, and Spiker 2014). Yet, most same-sex couples are historically restricted from legal marriage and have maintained other types of unions (such as cohabitation and civil unions). Restricted access to legal marriage may facilitate poorer health and lower levels of well-being among same-sex and other sexual minority couples compared with their heterosexual peers. Legal scholars suggest that if given equal access to the same institution—with all the same *financial* and *legal* benefits—sexual minority couples should experience the same health benefits as heterosexuals do given increased resources, less stress, and greater relationship security that come with legal marriage.

On the other hand, sexual minority marriage may confer different *social* benefits, and thus have differential effects on health among sexual minority couples, relative to heterosexual couples. For example, the vast majority of the current cohort of LGBTQ individuals who make up sexual minority couples today grew up in a context where same-sex marriage was not only illegal but also socially unacceptable. Rapid social change and legalization of same-sex marriage opened up new possibilities, but they also presented challenges: social stigma and minority stressors associated with nonheterosexuality may carry over into same-sex marriages and obscure the advantages of marriage for sexual minority couples. Family and social support and feelings of belonging and acceptance, for example, may be lower among sexual minority couples relative to heterosexual couples, and the "minority stress" model suggests that even if sexual minority couples can marry, they may not experience all of the benefits of marriage due to the stress associated with being a sexual minority (Meyer 1995). In fact, it is remarkable that while public opinion on sexual minority status is more favorable than ever before, there remains significant stigma faced by sexual minorities. Recent debates about protection for sexual minorities in the workplace, for example, suggest that our social institutions remain resistant to fully accepting the legitimacy of sexual minorities and same-sex families. Thus, if individuals in sexual minority couples face higher levels of discrimination and minority stress than those in heterosexual couples, this may have negative implications for relationship quality and overall health and well-being of sexual minority unions, regardless of the legal marital status of these unions (Cao et al. 2017; Frost et al. 2017). Structural stigma at the macro level, such as laws banning same-sex marriage, has been found to compromise the health of sexual minorities (Hatzenbuehler et al. 2014).

Moreover, the historical body of work on marriage and health has relied on assumptions of heteronormativity (i.e., the belief that everyone should be heterosexual), heterosexism (i.e., discrimination based on someone not being heterosexual), and the notion that men and women—husband and wife—are distinct and opposite forces that inherently shape marriage (i.e., gender traditionalism). Yet, there may be fundamentally different forms of gender dynamics among sexual minority couples that therefore change the very fabric of what marriage is and how it influences health. In fact, many sexual minority adults reject marriage altogether because it is inherently based on heterosexual marriage norms. Thus, marriage may mean very different things to sexual minority couples depending on their stance on marital norms. As evidence of the importance of this dynamic for health, research suggests that heterosexual married women, but not men, attempt to promote healthy behavior in their spouses, while in gay and lesbian couples both spouses simultaneously work to improve one another's health (Reczek and Umberson 2012). This qualitative evidence suggests a more egalitarian approach to relationships that may shape health and well-being in alternative ways across couple type.

Previous studies on well-being of sexual minorities have been historically dominated by qualitative research based on small, community, and nonrepresentative samples. Quantitative research on sexual minority relationships and health is much more limited, primarily due to data limitations. It was not until recent years that quantitative scholars started to move to this area. The majority of the quantitative work in this line was done prior to marriage equality; thus, we are limited in our ability to fully understand the health implications of same-sex marriage. Instead, population-level scholarship has focused on examining health and well-being among same-sex cohabiting unions, as an alternative format to marriage, prior to marriage equality. It is much easier to examine same-sex cohabitations using existing data, in part because information on same-sex cohabiting couples could be collected prior to same-sex marriage equality. The question, however, is whether cohabitation is institutionalized to the same degree that marriage is and thus whether it protects health to the same degree that marriage could. As a whole, previous limited quantitative studies suggest that same-sex cohabiting relationships are less beneficial to health than different-sex marriage relationships, but are either similar or more beneficial to health than being single or in a different-sex cohabiting relationship (Gonzales and Henning-Smith 2015; Liu, Reczek, and Brown 2013). For example, in research using data from the National Health Interview Surveys (NHIS), scholars have determined that same-sex cohabiting adults report poorer health (Denney, Gorman, and Barrera 2013; Liu, Reczek, and Brown 2013) and a higher smoking risk (Reczek, Liu, and Brown 2014) than different-sex married adults, while same-sex cohabitors experience some advantages in these outcomes relative to different-sex cohabitors and singles, mostly due to their relatively higher socioeconomic status (Liu, Reczek, and Brown 2013).

More recently, scholars have started to move beyond data on same-sex cohabitors to test the relationship between same-sex marriage and health. This early work shows that on the whole, when examining health behaviors, the impacts of same-sex and different-sex marriages are fairly similar (Reczek, Liu, and Spiker 2014; Wight, LeBlanc, and Lee Badgett 2013); marriage may benefit same-sex couples in a similar way as it does different-sex couples. For example, in a study using state-level data in California, married gay, lesbian, and bisexual people experienced less psychological distress than unmarried gay, lesbian, and bisexual people (Wight, LeBlanc, and Lee Badgett 2013). However, our study (Reczek, Liu, and Spiker 2014) shows that same-sex married and cohabiting people have similar levels of alcohol use as do different-sex married people, suggesting less of a marriage effect among sexual minorities. Given that same-sex marriage was not legalized at the federal level until recently, there is still a long way to go to understand the health benefits and costs of same-sex marriage. Previous studies represent a nascent state of knowledge on the health and well-being of sexual minority couples in part due to a lack of reliable and valid population-based, nationally representative data. So far, there is not a definitive consensus on the relationship between sexual minority unions and health (Institute of Medicine 2011).

Organization of This Book

This book is composed of seventeen chapters written by leading and emerging scholars in the field of sexual minority families and health. We organize the book into four parts. In part I, we open with four chapters that focus on the mental health of sexual minority couples—a health outcome underexplored in previous work. In chapter 1, Brown and colleagues compare serious mental illness incidence (SMI) of individuals in same-sex cohabiting, different-sex married, different-sex cohabiting, previously married, and never married relationships using pooled cross-sectional data from the 1997–2016 NHIS. This chapter demonstrates that individuals in different-sex marriages have lower odds of SMI, relative to individuals in all other union status groups, and individuals in same-sex and different-sex cohabiting unions have similar odds of SMI when socioeconomic attributes are not controlled. Importantly, this chapter implies that differential access to socioeconomic resources helps explain differences in SMI between same-sex cohabitors and different-sex married persons. In chapter 2, Flood and Genadek examine momentary well-being (happiness, stress, and meaning), a unique health outcome collected through diaries as individuals spent time with their same-sex partners. The authors analyzed data from the well-being module of the American Time Use Survey (ATUS 2010, 2012, 2013) and found that men in same-sex couples are happier when they are with, rather than without, a partner, and that women are less stressed when they are with, rather than without, a partner. In chapter 3, Alston-Stepnitz and colleagues analyze qualitative data from a large-scale, mixed-methods study of same-sex couples. Their analysis provides insight into the minority stress experienced by same-sex couples in the Atlanta and San Francisco Bay areas prior to the national legalization of same-sex marriage. Finally, in chapter 4, Goldberg and colleagues examine postpartum depression and anxiety among male-partnered and female-partnered sexual minority women, finding that male-partnered sexual minority women experience higher levels of postpartum depression and anxiety than female-partnered sexual minority women and non–sexual minority women.

Part II includes four chapters that move beyond mental health outcomes, exploring health behaviors across same-sex and different-sex union types. In chapter 5, Denney and colleagues analyze data from nine years of the NHIS

(2008–2016) to examine weight status, cigarette smoking, and alcohol use among same-sex coupled, different-sex cohabiting, and different-sex married adults with and without children. Findings reveal important variations in health and behavioral outcomes by union type, the presence or absence of children, and gender. In chapter 6, Fan demonstrates how the relationships between couples' conjoint work hours and health behaviors (smoking and sleep) are shaped by gender and sexual identity, drawing on unique couple data (different-sex and same-sex married or cohabiting couples) constructed from NHIS 1997–2003 and 2008–2017 data. In chapter 7, Oyarvide and colleagues use data from the 2010 Social Justice Sexuality Project (SJSP) to examine how union status relates to overweight/obesity among sexual minorities, finding that being in a legal union with men or women is positively associated with overweight/obesity among sexual minority women. Findings indicate that union status is not significantly associated with overweight/obesity among sexual minority men, however. Chapter 8 examines differences in alternative medicine usage among sexual minority and heterosexual older adults, using lifetime experience of same-sex contact as a measure of sexual orientation. In this chapter, using data from the National Social Life, Health, and Aging Project (NSHAP), Ritter and Ueno show that older adults who reported any same-sex contact in their lifetime had higher levels of alternative medicine usage in the past year than respondents who did not report same-sex contact.

Part III further explores health outcomes, addressing the physical health, mortality, and health care of sexual minority couples and their heterosexual counterparts—with several studies using NHIS data. In chapter 9, Spiker examines activity limitations across different-sex married, different-sex cohabiting, same-sex male cohabiting, and same-sex female cohabiting couples using data from the 1997–2015 NHIS. Findings indicate that sexual minority status is associated with activity limitations and that same-sex female cohabitors are at higher risk of activity limitations than individuals in other type of couples. In chapter 10, Fenelon and colleagues document the association between same-sex union status and adult mortality risk using 1997–2009 NHIS data linked to mortality files. In chapter 11, Ruther and Hsieh, also analyzing NHIS data, find important disparities in health care access between same-sex and different-sex partnered individuals. Moving beyond NHIS data, in chapter 12, Kazyak and Finken analyze twenty-one qualitative in-depth interviews with lesbian women, examining lesbian couples' experiences of childbirth and the navigation of health care settings in which childbirth occurs. Finally, in chapter 13, Sutton and Scotch examine a wide range of outcomes, including socioeconomic status, physical and mental health, and health care utilization, of sexual minorities across relationship status, using survey data collected from LGBTQ communities across Texas. They find that married and cohabiting respondents are older, have greater economic security, report fewer personal problems, and encounter less discrimination than single respondents.

The final chapters, in part IV, focus on topics that fall outside the narrow range of union status and health outcomes. These topics include the quality of same-sex relationships, first sexual experiences with a same-sex partner, and maternal identity of lesbian mothers. In chapter 14, Joyner and colleagues analyze data on romantic and sexual relationships from the National Longitudinal Study of Adolescent to Adult Health (Add Health), comparing the likelihood of dissolution for gay, lesbian, and heterosexual couples. Results provide new evidence that gay couples, but not lesbian couples, exhibit a significantly higher likelihood of relationship dissolution than different-sex couples, yet there is geographic variation in this trend. In chapter 15, Mernitz and colleagues analyze dyadic data from 295 same-sex and 165 heterosexual married couples in Massachusetts. Results show that positive dimensions of marital quality are associated with fewer depressive symptoms, while negative dimensions of marital quality are associated with more depressive symptoms. These associations are found among both same-sex and different-sex couples. In chapter 16, using data from the 2011–2015 National Survey of Family Growth (NSFG), Brewster and colleagues examine the timing and correlates of first same-sex sexual experience, finding that risk of first same-sex sexual experience peaks between the ages of sixteen and eighteen and then declines thereafter. Gender and birth cohort variations are also considered in this study. Finally, in chapter 17, Henry uses qualitative interviews with eleven lesbian mothers to explore how the sexual identity of lesbian mothers is associated with parental identity. Henry finds that the lesbian and motherhood identities are not incongruent and that these mothers do significant work to maintain the salience of both identities.

We conclude this book by pointing to future directions for research on the health and well-being of sexual minority couples. In doing so, we look both to the past and to the present, taking stock of the significant empirical and theoretical contributions that have been made and imagining a future research agenda, with new questions, data, and methods. In the conclusion, we also speak to the types of research and methods the next generation of scholars needs to take up to move this line of research forward. As editors, we hope each innovative chapter, and the volume as a whole, serves as a catalyst to move research and policy on same-sex unions and health forward in new and productive directions.

REFERENCES

Becker, Gary S. 1981. *A Treatise on the Family.* Cambridge, MA: Harvard University Press.
Buffie, William C. 2011. "Public Health Implications of Same-Sex Marriage." *American Journal of Public Health* 101 (6): 986–990.
Cao, Hongjian, Nan Zhou, Mark Fine, Yue Liang, Jiayao Li, and W. Roger Mills-Koonce. 2017. "Sexual Minority Stress and Same-Sex Relationship Well-Being: A Meta-analysis

of Research prior to the US Nationwide Legalization of Same-Sex Marriage." *Journal of Marriage and Family* 79 (5): 1258–1277.

Cherlin, Andrew J. 2013. "Health, Marriage, and Same-Sex Partnerships." *Journal of Health and Social Behavior* 54 (1): 64–66.

Denney, Justin T., Bridget K. Gorman, and Cristina B. Barrera. 2013. "Families, Resources, and Adult Health: Where Do Sexual Minorities Fit?" *Journal of Health and Social Behavior* 54 (1): 46–63.

Felter, Claire, and Danielle Renwick. 2017. "Same-Sex Marriage: Global Comparisons." Council on Foreign Relations. Retrieved from https://www.cfr.org/backgrounder/same-sex-marriage-global-comparisons.

Frost, David M., Allen J. LeBlanc, Brian de Vries, Eli Alston-Stepnitz, Rob Stephenson, and Cory Woodyatt. 2017. "Couple-Level Minority Stress: An Examination of Same-Sex Couples' Unique Experiences." *Journal of Health and Social Behavior* 58 (4): 455–472.

Gates, Gary J. 2012. "Same-Sex Couples in Census 2010: Race and Ethnicity." UCLA: Williams Institute. Retrieved from https://escholarship.org/uc/item/66521994.

Gonzales, Gilbert, and Carrie Henning-Smith. 2015. "Disparities in Health and Disability among Older Adults in Same-Sex Cohabiting Relationships." *Journal of Aging and Health* 27 (3): 432–453.

Hatzenbuehler, Mark L., Anna Bellatorre, Yeonjin Lee, Brian K. Finch, Peter Muennig, and Kevin Fiscella. 2014. "Structural Stigma and All-Cause Mortality in Sexual Minority Populations." *Social Science & Medicine* 103: 33–41.

Herek, Gregory M. 2006. "Legal Recognition of Same-Sex Relationships in the United States: A Social Science Perspective." *American Psychologist* 61 (6): 607.

Institute of Medicine. 2011. *The Health of Lesbian, Gay, Bisexual, and Transgender People: Building a Foundation for Better Understanding.* Washington, DC: National Academies Press.

Liu, Hui, Corinne Reczek, and Dustin Brown. 2013. "Same-Sex Cohabitors and Health: The Role of Race-Ethnicity, Gender, and Socioeconomic Status." *Journal of Health and Social Behavior* 54 (1): 25–45.

Liu, Hui, and Debra J. Umberson. 2008. "The Times They Are a Changin': Marital Status and Health Differentials from 1972 to 2003." *Journal of Health and Social Behavior* 49 (3): 239–253. https://doi.org/10.1177/002214650804900301.

Masci, David, Elizabeth Sciupac, and Michael Lipka. 2017. "Gay Marriage around the World." Pew Research Center. Retrieved from http://www.pewforum.org/2017/08/08/gay-marriage-around-the-world-2013/.

Merin, Yuval. 2010. *Equality for Same-Sex Couples: The Legal Recognition of Gay Partnerships in Europe and the United States.* Chicago: University of Chicago Press.

Meyer, Ilan H. 1995. "Minority Stress and Mental Health in Gay Men." *Journal of Health and Social Behavior* 36 (1): 38–56.

Musick, Kelly, Jennie E. Brand, and Dwight Davis. 2012. "Variation in the Relationship between Education and Marriage: Marriage Market Mismatch?" *Journal of Marriage and Family* 74 (1): 53–69.

Reczek, Corinne, Hui Liu, and Dustin Brown. 2014. "Cigarette Smoking in Same-Sex and Different-Sex Unions: The Role of Socioeconomic and Psychological Factors." *Population Research and Policy Review* 33 (4): 527–551.

Reczek, Corinne, Hui Liu, and Russell Spiker. 2014. "A Population-Based Study of Alcohol Use in Same-Sex and Different-Sex Unions." *Journal of Marriage and Family* 76 (3): 557–572.

Reczek, Corinne, and Debra Umberson. 2012. "Gender, Health Behavior, and Intimate Relationships: Lesbian, Gay, and Straight Contexts." *Social Science & Medicine* 74 (11): 1783–1790.

Umberson, Debra, and Jennifer Karas Montez. 2010. "Social Relationships and Health: A Flashpoint for Health Policy." *Journal of Health and Social Behavior* 51 (1): S54–S66. https://doi.org/10.1177/0022146510383501.

Umberson, Debra, Mieke Beth Thomeer, and Kristi Williams. 2013. "Family Status and Mental Health: Recent Advances and Future Directions." In *Handbook of the Sociology of Mental Health*, edited by Carol S. Aneshensel, Jo Phelan and Alex Bierman, 405–431. Dordrecht: Springer.

Waite, Linda J., and Maggie Gallagher. 2000. *The Case for Marriage: Why Married People Are Happier, Healthier, and Better Off Financially.* New York: Doubleday.

Wight, Richard G., Allen J. LeBlanc, and M. V. Lee Badgett. 2013. "Same-Sex Legal Marriage and Psychological Well-Being: Findings from the California Health Interview Survey." *American Journal of Public Health* 103 (2): 339–346.

PART ONE

Mental Health

1

Serious Mental Illness in Same-Sex and Different-Sex Unions

DUSTIN BROWN

CORINNE RECZEK

HUI LIU

Sexual minorities have a higher lifetime risk of mental health problems than their heterosexual counterparts (Herek and Garnets 2007; Institute of Medicine [IOM] 2011; Plöderl and Tremblay 2015). Minority stress theory posits that the heightened social stigma sexual minorities encounter over their life course causes them to experience more stress than their heterosexual counterparts (Meyer 1995, 2003), and exposure to chronic stressors undermines psychological well-being (Thoits 2010). One key source of stress may be reduced access to legal marriage, as same-sex marriage was only legalized federally in 2015. Although public acceptance of sexual minorities and support for same-sex unions have increased recently in United States, acceptance is not universal and same-sex relationships remain highly stigmatized (Baunach 2012; Twenge, Sherman, and Wells 2016). Thus, social opprobrium and legal discrimination may reinforce social stigma and decrease access to psychologically protective resources.

Recent research provides evidence for this possibility. A nationally representative study conducted before the landmark decision by the U.S. Supreme Court in *Obergefell v. Hodges*, which ruled that same-sex and different-sex marriages are entitled to equal protection under federal law, showed that sexual minorities residing in states with laws barring same-sex marriage had higher rates of psychiatric morbidity than sexual minorities residing in states without these laws (Hatzenbuehler, Keyes, and Hasin 2009). Another nationally representative study (Wienke and Hill 2009) pooled multiple years of General Social Survey (GSS) data to examine associations between marital status, sexual orientation, and happiness. The results suggested that heterosexual cohabiters and persons in same-sex relationships are less happy than heterosexual married persons (Wienke and Hill 2009). Interestingly, persons in same-sex relationships were slightly less happy than heterosexual cohabiters, but differences in happiness levels between the two groups generally were small. However, prior research has yet to examine whether serious mental illness (SMI) differs across union status among same-sex and different-sex couples, limiting our understanding of how the intersection of union status and sexual orientation matters for mental health. SMI is an understudied but important outcome because it provides unique insight into the most severe effects of sexual minority stigma and discrimination.

Union Status and Mental Health

A lack of access to, and social stigma around, same-sex marriage, may contribute to poor mental health among individuals in same-sex unions. Although relatively few studies address this possibility, prior research consistently finds that different-sex married persons report better mental health than unmarried persons (Carr and Springer 2010; Waite and Gallagher 2001). Previous studies also show that different-sex cohabiters report lower levels of psychological distress than previously married persons do and higher levels of psychological distress than different-sex married persons do (Brown 2000; Marcussen 2005; Waite and Gallagher 2001). It is likely that different-sex marriage and, to a lesser extent, different-sex cohabitation promote psychological well-being at least partly because they are associated with increased economic and psychosocial resources that directly and indirectly reduce psychological distress through either protection or selection processes (Waite and Gallagher 2001).

Union status disparities in mental health are well documented in heterosexual populations, through the mechanisms of greater social and financial resources as well as selection, but most extant research overlooks same-sex unions. Thus, whether same-sex cohabiters experience a mental health disadvantage relative to different-sex married and different-sex cohabiting counterparts is unknown. Theoretically, it is reasonable to assume that marriage and cohabitation confer relatively similar mental health advantages to persons in same-sex and different-sex unions. Prior research comparing self-rated health, smoking patterns, and alcohol use between same-sex cohabiting unions and different-sex unions indicates that same-sex cohabiters and different-sex cohabiters generally are similar in terms of health (Liu, Reczek, and Brown 2013; Reczek, Liu, and Brown 2014; Reczek, Liu, and Spiker 2014). These studies also show that same-sex and different-sex cohabiters fare worse on these health outcomes relative to different-sex married persons. These similarities between same-sex and different-sex unions are somewhat expected because both groups generally seem to have similar relationship dynamics (Peplau and Fingerhut 2007). At the same time, differences in relationship stability may contribute to mental health disparities between cohabiters and married persons. Previous research shows that heightened relationship instability, broadly construed, is a major reason that different-sex cohabiters report worse mental health than their different-sex married counterparts (Brown 2000; Marcussen 2005). Recent research suggests that while different-sex married unions are more stable than same-sex or different-sex cohabiting unions, same-sex and different-sex cohabiting unions have similar levels of stability (Manning, Brown, and Stykes 2016). Taken together, these studies suggest that same-sex and different-sex cohabiters will report similar levels of mental illness and that both cohabiting groups will report higher levels of mental illness in comparison to different-sex married persons.

Socioeconomic Status and Mental Health

Socioeconomic disparities in mental health are pronounced in the United States. Prior research consistently shows that socioeconomic advantage protects against deleterious mental health (Mirowsky and Ross 2003) and differences in socioeconomic resources are a key reason that different-sex married persons have a mental health advantage relative to different-sex cohabiters and other unmarried groups (Waite and Gallagher 2001). Cohabitation is similar to marriage in many respects, but cohabiters typically are less socioeconomically advantaged than married persons (Waite and Gallagher 2001). However, there is also evidence that same-sex cohabiters have some socioeconomic advantages relative to different-sex cohabiters or even the different-sex married (Liu, Reczek, and Brown 2013). Thus, cohabitation and/or marriage may be especially important for sexual minority mental health because they help reduce economic hardship.

The Current Study

The current study pools multiple years of nationally representative data from the U.S. National Health Interview Surveys (NHIS) to examine disparities in SMI between same-sex cohabiters, different-sex cohabiters, different-sex married, divorced, widowed, and never married persons (sexual identity not specified). We expect that persons in same-sex unions (marriage or cohabitation) will have a higher likelihood of SMI than different-sex married persons. We also expect that persons in different-sex unions and, to a lesser extent, persons in same-sex unions will have a lower likelihood of SMI when compared with divorced, widowed, and never married persons. Moreover, to the extent that minority stress adversely affects sexual minority mental health, it is also conceivable that same-sex cohabiters will have a higher likelihood of SMI in comparison to different-sex married persons and potentially even different-sex cohabiters. Finally, we expect that socioeconomic status (SES) will account for some of the association between union status and SMI. Controlling for socioeconomic resources will reduce disparities in serious mental illness between different-sex married persons and the other union status groups. Empirical evidence comparing mental health outcomes among persons in same-sex and different-sex unions is relatively sparse, but prior research on other health outcomes suggests that both cohabiting groups will have a higher risk of SMI relative to different-sex married persons and that same-sex and different-sex cohabiters may have a similar risk of SMI.

Methods

Data

We analyze data from the 1997–2016 National Health Interview Surveys (NHIS) downloaded from the International Public Use Microdata Series (IPUMS) Health Surveys website (Blewett et al. 2018). The NHIS is a cross-sectional survey of U.S. households conducted annually by the National Center for Health Statistics (NCHS). The survey is conducted in-person and is nationally representative of the U.S. civilian noninstitutionalized population. A core questionnaire is administered to all adult household members, but the items used to create our serious mental illness measure come from a supplementary questionnaire administered to one randomly selected adult within each household (i.e., adult sample respondents). We exclude interviews conducted between 2004 (quarter 1) and 2007 (quarter 2) due to a data processing error that misidentifies some different-sex married respondents as same-sex married (National Center for Health Statistics 2015b).

We listwise delete observations with missing data. Item missing rates are low for the dependent variable (2.12%) and most key covariates including union status (2.00%), race-ethnicity (.03%), nativity status (.10%), age (no missing), gender (no missing), educational attainment (.75%), and employment status (.11%). A relatively large proportion of sample adult respondents have missing income-to-poverty data (14.20%). Our analyses do not incorporate multiply imputed income-to-poverty data created by NCHS because sensitivity tests (available on request) revealed that incorporating these data does not alter our substantive results. Analyses are weighted and complex variances are computed using survey commands in Stata. Following the recommendation on the IPUMS Health Surveys website, we divide the NHIS sample weights by the number of survey years analyzed. (i.e., 16.5 because we exclude surveys conducted between quarter 1, 2004 and quarter 2, 2007). Our final sample contains 429,447 respondents (190,990 men and 238,457 women).

Measures

The dependent variable is serious mental illness (SMI) measured via the Kessler Six-Item Psychological Distress Scale (K6) (Kessler et al. 2003). The K6 was developed to monitor the prevalence of probable *Diagnostic and Statistical Manual of Mental Disorders*, 4th Edition (*DSM-IV*) diagnosable mood and anxiety disorders in population-based surveys, and research shows that it is a valid and reliable measure of nonspecific psychological distress in the general population

(Kessler et al. 2003). The items on the K6 ask respondents to indicate how often they felt "so sad that nothing could cheer you up," "nervous," "restless or fidgety," "hopeless," "worthless," and/or that "everything was an effort" in the last thirty days. Possible responses include "none of the time" (0), "a little of the time" (1), "some of the time" (2), "most of the time" (3), or "all of the time" (4). These six items are summed into a scale (range: 0–24). Validation research with clinical samples has established that persons with summed K6 scores ≥13 likely meet the clinical criteria for a mood or anxiety disorder diagnosis (Kessler et al. 2003). Various scoring rules have been proposed for the K6, but we follow a common approach and dichotomize the summed scale to indicate the probable absence (0 = 0–12) versus presence (1 = 13–24) of serious mental illness (SMI).

Our main independent variable is current union status, which has six mutually exclusive categories representing different-sex married (reference group), different-sex cohabiters, same-sex cohabiters (includes married), divorced (includes separated), widowed, and never married. Respondents in same-sex and different-sex co-residential unions (marriage or cohabitation) are identified via the NHIS household and family rosters, which list the relationship of all household/family members to an interviewer-designated household/family reference person. IPUMS Health Survey analysts used information from these rosters and other variables to link spouse or partner records within families (Gorsuch and Williams 2017). We cross-classify married/cohabitating respondents' own gender with that of their spouse or partner to distinguish same-sex and different-sex unions (marriage and cohabitation). We combine same-sex cohabiters and same-sex married persons into one group (i.e., "same-sex cohabiters") because few sample respondents are same-sex married ($n = 376$). Results with and without same-sex married persons are the same (not shown). Our union status variable excludes married (1.6%) and cohabiting (.01%) respondents with missing spouse or partner union status or gender.

Socioeconomic controls include educational attainment, labor force participation, and poverty status. We recode self-reported education into four categories that roughly correspond to less than a high school education, high school graduate (includes GED or equivalent), some college education (no bachelor's degree), and college graduate (bachelor's degree or higher, reference group). Labor force participation (self-reported employment status in the previous week) has three categories indicating whether a respondent is employed (reference group), unemployed, or not in the labor force. Income-to-poverty ratios were calculated by NCHS using self-reported information on family income, family size, and the number of children present under age eighteen. Respondents with income-to-poverty ratios ≤1.00 are considered at or below the federal poverty threshold, and income-to-poverty ratios >1.00 reflect increasing affluence. Our poverty status variable contains three broad categories: "poor" (.00–.99), "near poor" (1.00–1.99), and "not poor" (2.00–5.00+, reference).

Sociodemographic controls are all self-reported and include age, race-ethnicity, nativity status, and gender. Age in years is categorized into three groups: 18–44, 45–59 (reference), and 60–85+. The association between age and SMI is nonlinear, and sensitivity tests (not shown) indicated that our age specification captures these nonlinearities reasonably well. Race-ethnicity has the following mutually exclusive categories: non-Hispanic white (reference), non-Hispanic black, Hispanic (any race), and non-Hispanic other race-ethnic group. Nativity status (0 = U.S. born, 1 = foreign born) and gender (0 = men, 1 = women) are measured dichotomously.

Analyses

We estimate three nested models for the total population, men, and women, respectively. Model 1 regresses SMI on union status and age. Model 2 regresses SMI on union status, race-ethnicity, nativity status, gender, and age. Model 3 regresses SMI on union status, educational attainment, labor force participation, poverty status, race-ethnicity, nativity status, gender, and age. Gender-specific models when paired with formal statistical tests (partial F-tests) allow us to examine whether the expected association between union status and SMI varies by gender. As noted earlier, different-sex married persons are the reference group in our regression models because doing this makes it easier to reconcile our findings with previous research on union status and mental health.

Results

Descriptive Statistics

The descriptive results discussed in the following text are for the total sample unless otherwise noted. The prevalence of SMI is low in the sample overall (3.3%), but SMI prevalence is significantly higher among women (3.9%) than men (2.6%). Most respondents are different-sex married (55.4%), and relatively few are different-sex cohabiters (6.3%) or same-sex cohabiters/married (.6%). However, substantial proportions of sample respondents are never married (21.0%), divorced (11.2%), or widowed (5.6%). Most respondents either have some college education (30.6%) or graduated college (27.8%), have family incomes two or more times the poverty threshold (70.4%), and are employed (64.5%). Sample respondents have a mean age of 45.3 and are mostly non-Hispanic white (70.3%), native-born (84.5%), and female (51.4%).

Regression Models

Table 1.1 displays estimated odds ratios from binary logistic regression models regressing SMI on union status and control variables. Results are displayed for the total population (columns 1–3), men (columns 4–6), and women (columns 7–9). To conserve space, we focus on results for the total sample unless

TABLE 1.1
Odds Ratios of Serious Mental Illness (SMI) by Union Status for the Total Population, Men, and Women, NHIS 1997–2016[a]

	Total (N=429,447)			Men (N=190,990)			Women (N=238,457)		
	Model 1	Model 2	Model 3	Model 1	Model 2	Model 3	Model 1	Model 2	Model 3
Union status									
Married, different-sex (ref)									
Cohabiting, different-sex	1.84***	1.81***	1.40***	1.65***	1.61***	1.11	1.99***†	1.97***†	1.59***
Cohabiting, same-sex[b]	1.85***	1.82***	2.27***	2.14***	2.11***	2.30***	1.65**	1.63**	2.08***
Divorced	2.83***	2.72***	2.06***	2.69***	2.66***	1.75***	2.79***	2.76***	2.16***†
Widowed	2.33***	2.10***	1.29***	2.11***	2.09***	1.23*	2.17***	2.17***	1.34***
Never married	1.62***	1.63***	1.10**	1.68***	1.65***	0.84**	1.63***	1.62***	1.23***†
Education									
No high school			3.13***			2.65***			3.53***†
High school			2.24***			2.00***			2.44***†
Some college			1.96***			1.62***			2.23***†
College (ref.)									

(continued)

Table 1.1. Odds Ratios of Serious Mental Illness (SMI) by Union Status for the Total Population, Men, and Women, NHIS 1997–2016[a] (continued)

	Total (N=429,447)			Men (N=190,990)			Women (N=238,457)		
	Model 1	Model 2	Model 3	Model 1	Model 2	Model 3	Model 1	Model 2	Model 3
Income-to-poverty ratio									
Poor (0.00–0.99)			2.49***			2.32***			2.51***
Near poor (1.00–1.99)			1.85***			1.85***			1.81***
Not poor (≥2.00, ref.)									
Employment status									
Employed (ref.)									
Unemployed			2.99***			3.47***			2.79***†
Not in the labor force			3.31***			5.19***			2.63***†
Race-ethnicity									
Non-Hispanic white (ref.)									
Non-Hispanic black		.99	.70***		1.01	.68***		.98	.69***
Hispanic		1.31***	.85***		1.24***	.85**		1.36***	.85***
Non-Hispanic other		.92	.88*		.97	.86		.89	.87
Nativity status									
U.S. born (ref.)									
Foreign born		.81***	.74***		.75***	.77***		.85***	.74***

	Col1	Col2	Col3	Col4	Col5	Col6	Col7	Col8
Gender								
Male (ref.)								
Female	1.43***		1.22***					
Age group								
18–44	.68***	.67***	.67***	.64***	.77***	.71***	.70***	.64***†
45–59 (ref.)								
60–85+	.60***	.60***	.33***	.62***	.27***	.58***	.59***	.35***†
Intercept	.03***	.03***	.01***	.03***	.01***	.04***	.04***	.01***

Notes:[a] Psychological distress is measured via the Kessler 6 scale (K6). The six items on the scale are summed (Range: 0–24) and dichotomized to indicate the likely presence (K6: 13–24 = 1) or absence (K6: 0–12 = 0) of serious mental illness (SMI). Respondents missing values on any K6 items or covariates are listwise deleted.

[b] The "cohabiters, same-sex" group includes married and cohabiting respondents. Divorced, widowed, and never-married respondents are unpartnered or unmarried. Married and cohabiting respondents with missing data on spouse or partner union status (<2% of 1997–2016 NHIS Sample Adults) are excluded. Interviews conducted between 2004 (quarter 1) and 2007 (quarter 2) are excluded due to a previously identified NCHS data processing error that misidentified some different-sex unions as same-sex unions.

[†] Odds ratios differ significantly by gender (p <.05). Models (not shown) include all main effects and all two-way interactions with gender.

* p <.05; ** p <.01; *** p <.001.

otherwise noted. Gender-combined and gender-specific results generally are very similar with one notable exception: the odds of SMI for different-sex cohabiters relative to different-sex married persons are significantly higher for women than men across all models.

Model 1 regresses SMI on union status and age. As expected, different-sex married persons have substantially lower age-adjusted odds of SMI than all other union status groups. Both different-sex cohabiters (odds ratio [OR] =1.84, $p<.001$) and same-sex cohabiters (OR =1.85, $p<.001$) have higher odds of SMI relative to different-sex married persons net of age. The age-adjusted odds of SMI for divorced (OR =2.83, $p<.001$) and widowed (OR =2.33, $p<.001$) respondents are more than two times higher than those for different-sex married persons. Never married persons have 62 percent higher odds of SMI than different-sex married persons net of age.

Model 2 regresses SMI on union status, race-ethnicity, nativity status, gender, and age. The results are almost identical to those from model 1. Different-sex married persons have lower odds of SIM than all other union status groups net of controls. Divorced persons (OR =2.72, $p<.001$) followed by widowed (OR =2.10, $p<.001$) persons have the highest odds of SMI relative to different-sex married persons across all union status groups, while never married (OR =1.63, $p<.001$) persons also have the higher odds of SMI relative to different-sex married persons net of controls. The odds of SMI relative to different-sex married persons are the same for same-sex (OR =1.82, $p<.001$) and different-sex (OR =1.81, $p<.001$) cohabiters net of age and sociodemographic controls.

Model 3 regresses SMI on union status, age, sociodemographic attributes, and SES. A comparison of results between models 2 and 3 suggests that for everyone except same-sex cohabiters, controlling for SES substantially reduces the odds of SMI relative to different-sex married persons. For example, the odds of SMI among different-sex cohabiters relative to different-sex married persons in the total sample decrease substantially between models 2 (OR =1.81, $p<.001$) and 3 (OR =1.40, $p<.001$) after SES is controlled. Observed changes in odds ratios relative to different-sex married persons between models 2 and 3 are similar for divorced, widowed, and never married persons. These results are consistent with the notion that SES mediates, or partially explains, differences in SMI among different-sex cohabiters, divorced, widowed, and never married persons. In contrast, SMI disparities between same-sex cohabiters and different-sex married persons widen between model 2 (OR =1.82, $p<.001$) and model 3 (OR =2.27, $p<.001$). These results imply that SES has a suppressor "effect" on disparities in SMI between same-sex cohabiters and same-sex married persons. Post-hoc tests (partial F-tests, not shown) comparing coefficients for union status between models 2 and 3 (total population) indicate that these changes are statistically significant.

Conclusions

Sexual minorities experience a higher lifetime risk of mental health problems relative to their heterosexual counterparts. Different-sex married persons and, to a lesser extent, cohabiters have a mental health advantage over previously married and never married persons who do not reside with a partner (Reczek, Liu, and Spiker 2017). These associations are well documented, but whether the mental health benefits that different-sex married persons and cohabiters receive also extend to persons in same-sex unions remains an open question. The extent to which the mental health of same-sex cohabiters is comparable to previously married and never married persons is also unclear. To address these gaps, we pooled multiple years of NHIS data to examine the association between union status and SMI for different-sex married, different-sex cohabiting, same-sex cohabiting, divorced, widowed, and never married persons.

Our analyses revealed that different-sex married persons have much lower odds of SMI than other union status groups. This finding was expected based on prior research on union status and mental health. Our results also showed that same-sex and different-sex cohabiters generally have similar odds of SMI when SES is not taken into account, which is consistent with previous research in the NHIS on other health outcomes that compare respondents in same-sex and different-sex unions (Liu, Reczek, and Brown 2013). Controlling for SES substantially reduced disparities in SMI between different-sex married persons and their different-sex cohabiting, widowed, divorced, and never married counterparts. Contrary to our expectations, the odds of SMI for same-sex cohabiters relative to different-sex married persons increased once SES was controlled. This may suggest that the higher SES in same-sex unions may suppress negative mental health outcomes; when controlling for SES, these negative health outcomes may become stronger. While we cannot test the factors that contribute to this finding, gender differences in the influence of SES on SMI may play a role. Formal comparisons of coefficients between models with and without SES measures (not shown) suggested that accounting for SES does not significantly change the odds of SMI among men in same-sex unions. However, accounting for SES significantly increases the odds of SMI among women in same-sex unions. Future research should examine these issues more closely.

Although this study provides valuable insights into union status disparities in SMI, it has several limitations. First, respondents in same-sex unions do not self-report their sexual orientation or identity. NHIS has collected self-reported sexual identity since 2013, but our analyses do not incorporate this information. Ancillary analyses (not shown) with the 2013–2016 NHIS indicated the proportion of same-sex married/cohabiting respondents identified via the household roster and self-reported sexual orientation is similar. Instead, we identify same-sex couples using the NHIS household roster and each spouse or partner's gender. This means our findings are not generalizable to sexual minorities who are not married or cohabiting. Slightly more than half of self-identified gay and lesbian respondents in the 2013–2016 NHIS were not married or cohabiting (ancillary analyses not shown). Measurement error may also exist if either spouse or partner's gender is miscoded, but this possibility is mitigated substantially in our analyses by excluding NHIS survey periods where an NCHS data processing error misidentified a large proportion of different-sex unions as same-sex unions (National Center for Health Statistics 2015). Second, the NHIS does not contain information on union stability or union duration. Marriages typically are more stable and last longer than cohabiting relationships (Manning, Brown, and Stykes 2016), and differences in union stability and relationship union duration contribute to mental health disparities between persons in different-sex married and different-sex cohabiting unions (Brown 2000; Marcussen 2005). Although different-sex and same-sex unions seem to have similar levels of union stability (Manning, Brown, and Sykes 2016), future research should examine the potential role that union stability and duration play in shaping mental health disparities between same-sex and different-sex cohabiters. Third, the analyses do not account for sociocontextual factors that may contribute to union status disparities in mental health. Marriage norms and attitudes toward sexual minorities in the United States vary considerably by geographic region and between urban and rural populations. The 1997–2016 public-use NHIS contains relatively little information about social context beyond Census region of residence, and our substantive conclusions did not change when region was included as a control (ancillary analyses not shown). Finally, our specification of psychological distress may be limited. Our categorization scheme is based on previous research with the K6 (Kessler et al. 2003), but future research should attempt to replicate our results with more nuanced specifications of psychological distress and other mental health outcomes.

Despite these limitations, this is one of the few large, nationally representative studies in the United States to examine disparities in serious mental illness between same-sex cohabiters, different-sex married persons, and different-sex cohabiters, and divorced, widowed, and never married persons. The analyses add to a growing body of research in the United States that uses nationally representative data to document health disparities between same-sex cohabiters and other union status groups. Our results imply that same-sex cohabiters and different-sex cohabiters are similar in that both groups are at higher risk of serious mental illness relative to different-sex married persons. The results also imply that differential access to socioeconomic resources contributes to mental health disparities between same-sex cohabiters and different-sex married persons. Overall, our findings are consistent with minority stress theory and provide additional evidence that the risk of psychological distress is high among U.S. sexual minorities.

REFERENCES

Baunach, Dawn Michelle. 2012. "Changing Same-Sex Marriage Attitudes in America from 1988 through 2010." *Public Opinion Quarterly* 76 (2): 364–378. https://doi.org/10.1093/poq/nfs022.

Blewett, Lynn A., Julia A. Rivera Drew, Risa Griffin, Miriam L. King, and Kari C. W. Williams. 2018. IPUMS Health Surveys: National Health Interview Survey, Version 6.3. Minneapolis, MN: IPUMS.

Brown, Susan L. 2000. "The Effect of Union Type on Psychological Well-Being: Depression among Cohabitors versus Marrieds." *Journal of Health and Social Behavior* 41 (3): 241–255.

Carr, Deborah, and Kristen W. Springer. 2010. "Advances in Families and Health Research in the 21st Century." *Journal of Marriage and Family* 72 (3): 743–761. https://doi.org/10.1111/j.1741-3737.2010.00728.x.

Gorsuch, Marina Mileo, and Kari Charlotte Wigness Williams. 2017. "Family Matters: Development of New Family Interrelationship Variables for US IPUMS Data Projects." *Journal of Economic and Social Measurement* 42 (2): 123–149.

Hatzenbuehler, Mark L., Katherine M. Keyes, and Deborah S. Hasin. 2009. "State-Level Policies and Psychiatric Morbidity in Lesbian, Gay, and Bisexual Populations." *American Journal of Public Health* 99 (12): 2275–2281. https://doi.org/10.2105/ajph.2008.153510.

Herek, Gregory M., and Linda D. Garnets. 2007. "Sexual Orientation and Mental Health." *Annual Review of Clinical Psychology* 3 (1): 353–375. https://doi.org/10.1146/annurev.clinpsy.3.022806.091510.

Institute of Medicine (IOM). 2011. *The Health of Lesbian, Gay, Bisexual, and Transgender People: Building a Foundation for Better Understanding*. Washington, DC.: National Academies Press.

Kessler, Ronald C., Peggy R. Barker, Lisa J. Colpe, Joan F. Epstein, Joseph C. Gfroerer, Eva Hiripi, Mary J. Howes, Sharon-Lise T. Normand, Ronald W. Manderscheid, Ellen E. Walters, and Alan M. Zaslavsky. 2003. "Screening for Serious Mental Illness in the General Population." *Archives of General Psychiatry* 60 (2): 184–189. https://doi.org/10.1001/archpsyc.60.2.184.

Liu, Hui, Corinne Reczek, and Dustin Brown. 2013. "Same-Sex Cohabitors and Health: The Role of Race-Ethnicity, Gender, and Socioeconomic Status." *Journal of Health and Social Behavior* 54 (1): 25–45. https://doi.org/10.1177/0022146512468280.

Manning, Wendy, Susan Brown, and Bart Stykes. 2016. "Same-Sex and Different-Sex Cohabiting Couple Relationship Stability." *Demography* 53 (4): 937–953. https://doi.org/10.1007/s13524-016-0490-x.

Marcussen, Kristen. 2005. "Explaining Differences in Mental Health between Married and Cohabiting Individuals." *Social Psychology Quarterly* 68 (3): 239–257. https://doi.org/10.1177/019027250506800304.

Meyer, Ilan H. 1995. "Minority Stress and Mental Health in Gay Men." *Journal of Health and Social Behavior* 36 (1): 38–56.

Meyer, Ilan H. 2003. "Prejudice, Social Stress, and Mental Health in Lesbian, Gay, and Bisexual Populations: Conceptual Issues and Research Evidence." *Psychological Bulletin* 129 (5): 674–697. https://doi.org/10.1037/0033-2909.129.5.674.

Mirowsky, John, and Catherine E. Ross. 2003. *Social Causes of Psychological Distress*. 2nd ed. New York: Aldine de Gruyter. Original edition, 1989.

National Center for Health Statistics. 2015. *Changes to Data Editing Procedures and the Impact on Identifying Same-Sex Married Couples: 2004–2007 National Health Interview Survey*

(National Health Interview Survey April 2015 Report). Hyattsville, MD: National Center for Health Statistics.

Peplau, Letitia Anne, and Adam W. Fingerhut. 2007. "The Close Relationships of Lesbians and Gay Men." *Annual Review of Psychology* 58 (1): 405–424. https://doi.org/10.1146/annurev.psych.58.110405.085701.

Plöderl, Martin, and Pierre Tremblay. 2015. "Mental Health of Sexual Minorities: A Systematic Review." *International Review of Psychiatry* 27 (5): 367–385. https://doi.org/10.3109/09540261.2015.1083949.

Reczek, Corinne, Hui Liu, and Dustin Brown. 2014. "Cigarette Smoking in Same-Sex and Different-Sex Unions: The Role of Socioeconomic and Psychological Factors." *Population Research and Policy Review* 33 (4): 527–551. https://doi.org/10.1007/s11113-013-9297-2.

Reczek, Corinne, Hui Liu, and Russell Spiker. 2014. "A Population-Based Study of Alcohol Use in Same-Sex and Different-Sex Unions." *Journal of Marriage and the Family* 76 (3): 557–572. https://doi.org/10.1111/jomf.12113.

Reczek, Corinne, Hui Liu, and Russell Spiker. 2017. "Self-Rated Health at the Intersection of Sexual Identity and Union Status." *Social Science Research* 63: 242–252.

Thoits, Peggy A. 2010. "Stress and Health: Major Findings and Policy Implications." *Journal of Health and Social Behavior* 51 (1 suppl.): S41–S53. https://doi.org/10.1177/0022146510383499.

Twenge, Jean M., Ryne A. Sherman, and Brooke E. Wells. 2016. "Changes in American Adults' Reported Same-Sex Sexual Experiences and Attitudes, 1973–2014." *Archives of Sexual Behavior* 45 (7): 1713–1730. https://doi.org/10.1007/s10508-016-0769-4.

Waite, Linda J., and Maggie Gallagher. 2001. *The Case for Marriage: Why Married People Are Happier, Healthier, and Better Off Financially.* New York: Broadway Books.

Wienke, Chris, and Gretchen J. Hill. 2009. "Does the 'Marriage Benefit' Extend to Partners in Gay and Lesbian Relationships?" *Journal of Family Issues* 30 (2): 259–289. https://doi.org/10.1177/0192513x08324382.

2

Well-Being during Time with a Partner among Men and Women in Same-Sex Unions

SARAH MARIE FLOOD

KATIE R. GENADEK

In 2013 there were an estimated 726,600 same-sex couples in the United States (U.S. Census Bureau 2013). Given the trend toward greater inclusion, as evidenced by state and federal legislation and growing popular acceptance, there is a heightened focus on generating knowledge about the health and well-being of same-sex couples (Institute of Medicine 2011; Powell 2017). Research shows that women in same-sex unions tend to report lower health than men in same-sex unions (Liu, Reczek, and Brown 2013; Reczek, Liu, and Spiker 2017) and have lower relationship stability (Andersson et al. 2006; Joyner, Manning, and Bogle 2017). Given that time with a spouse or partner (hereafter partner) is a key component of relationship quality and experienced well-being, we respond to the call for more research on same-sex couples by investigating individual well-being during time with a partner.

Recent evidence from the American Time Use Survey (ATUS) shows that women in same-sex unions spend substantially more time with a partner than men in same-sex unions, both in the aggregate and in specific types of activities performed with a spouse or partner (Genadek, Flood, and Garcia Roman 2017). Among different-sex married couples, experienced well-being is enhanced during time shared with a spouse, with individuals reporting greater happiness, meaning, and enjoyment when with a spouse versus not, as well as less stress (Flood and Genadek 2016; Sullivan 1996). However, whether this finding holds for same-sex couples has not been investigated. Furthermore, it is unknown whether the gap in shared time for men and women in same-sex couples is consequential for how time with a partner is experienced. Accordingly, we ask two research questions. First, is well-being enhanced during time with a partner for men and women in same-sex unions? Second, is the gap in time with a partner for men and women in same-sex unions indicative of a well-being gap?

Data from the ATUS offer a unique opportunity to investigate whether well-being is enhanced *when with a partner* and the extent to which gender differences in shared time translate into differences in well-being during time with a partner. Typical measures of individual or relationship well-being are global in nature, asking respondents to report, for example, on their life satisfaction (Diener et al. 1985), which is often influenced by recent experiences, aspirations, and current circumstances (Kahneman and Krueger 2006). Time-diary-based assessments of momentary well-being are more reliable (Kahneman et al. 2004) and more granular than global assessments of well-being. Momentary assessments of well-being are tied to particular contexts, in our case who else is present during an activity reported in a time diary, which allows us to examine experienced well-being during time with a partner versus not with a partner. We extend previous work on different-sex couples' well-being (Flood and Genadek 2016; Sullivan 1996) by focusing on same-sex couples' experienced well-being during time with a partner versus not with a partner.

Background

Families and couples are an example of Cooley's (1909) primary groups, which are fundamental groups in society characterized by face-to-face interaction and enduring relationships. Primary groups serve as a source of identity and support for members, both of which are built and maintained through ongoing social interaction. One way that couples build and sustain relationships is through spending time together, which may be especially true for same-sex couples who place more value on joint activities for maintaining relationships compared with different-sex couples (Haas and Stafford 2005).

Engaging with a spouse is beneficial for individual and relationship well-being for different-sex couples. Research shows that there are limited, if any, differences between same-sex and different-sex couples on global measures of relationship quality (Kurdek 2005, 2006; Peplau and Spalding 2000). Evidence that relationship quality is similar for same-sex and different-sex couples combined with the research showing that interaction with a partner is beneficial for both global (e.g., Amato et al. 2007; White 1983) and momentary (Flood and Genadek 2016; Sullivan 1996) assessments of well-being for different-sex couples suggests that men and women in same-sex couples will also benefit from shared time. We investigate this possibility with our first research question about whether men and women in same-sex couples experience enhanced momentary well-being when with a partner.

The literature on same-sex couples' shared time is sparse. A recent study by Genadek and colleagues (2017) finds that men in same-sex relationships spend much less time together than women in same-sex unions. The gap in daily shared time among men and women in same-sex couples is substantial. Women in same-sex couples who are nonparents spend about an hour more together per day, on average, than men in same-sex couples; this difference is about two hours for same-sex couples who are parents. This may be because women reap more benefits from being with a partner given the greater likelihood of women to value their connections with others. Or it may be that men in same-sex unions are more constrained in their time availability and therefore share less time with a partner.

Given research showing that couples who experience more marital support spend more time together and those who experience more marital strain spend less time together (Flood, Genadek, and Moen 2018), we might think about shared time as a proxy for relationship quality. To the extent that this is the case, greater amounts of shared time among women compared with men in same-sex unions (Genadek, Flood, and Garcia Roman 2017) may translate into greater well-being during time with a partner. This would be consistent with the double dose hypothesis (Kurdek 2001), which suggests that women in same-sex couples should benefit more from being partnered with another woman than men partnered with other men because women are socialized to place a higher value on relationships with others than are men.

Gendered emotion work and gender-as-relational approaches highlight important differences of doing gender in same-sex versus different-sex couples, especially regarding the emotional work of relationship maintenance (Umberson, Thomeer, and Lodge 2015). Women in same-sex couples report greater relationship cohesion and support, and men in same-sex couples report lower commitment and more autonomy (Ellis and Davis 2017; Kurdek 2001; Umberson, Thomeer, and Lodge 2015). Investigations of relationship satisfaction, however, show no differences between gay and lesbian couples (Graham and Barnow 2013; Julien et al. 2003), especially after controlling for differences in relationship support (Ellis and Davis 2017). Accordingly, differences in support (Ellis and Davis 2017) and boundaries (Umberson, Thomeer, and Lodge 2015) between men and women in same-sex couples suggest that a "more is better" description of shared time may be inaccurate. The quantity of shared time may not be an accurate reflection of how couples experience their shared time. This leads to our second research question, where we ask if men and women in same-sex unions experience similar well-being advantages during time with a partner.

Data

We use 2010, 2012, and 2013 ATUS well-being module data (Hofferth, Flood, and Sobek 2017) to examine the experienced momentary well-being of individuals in co-resident same-sex couples. The ATUS is a nationally representative time diary study of individuals of age fifteen or older in the United States; one individual per household is randomly selected to report that individual's activities over one twenty-four-hour period as part of the ATUS. Respondents report each of the activities they engaged in over a twenty-four-hour period from 4:00 A.M. of a specified day until 4:00 A.M. of the following day as well as where, when, and with whom activities were done. During three randomly selected activities, respondents are asked to report their momentary feelings. We focus on happiness, meaning, and stress. Data are collected all days of the week, and weekends are oversampled. We have time diary data from one member of each couple, but by using information on who was present during each activity in the time diary, we are able to identify when the couples are together (excluding personal care and sleep).

Sample Construction

We restrict the sample to respondents who have a same-sex partner living with them at the time of the ATUS interview and both of their ages are between twenty and sixty-nine. One hundred fifty-two individuals (82 women and 70 men) in co-resident same-sex relationships also provided well-being assessments. For a small subset of partners ($n = 6$), information about race and education is missing. To retain as many cases as possible, we impute race and educational status for the partners using multiple imputation with the partner's characteristics and the respondent's characteristics.

Our analysis is based on the activities during which individuals in same-sex unions reported momentary assessments of well-being ($n = 450$). Almost the entire sample reported well-being for three activities (96.71%), while four respondents reported well-being for two activities and one respondent had only one activity report.

Measures

Our key dependent variables are momentary happiness, meaning, and stress. Respondents were asked to rank how they felt on each emotion on a scale of 0 to 6. For example, for the happiness measure, respondents answered "From 0–6, where a 0 means you were not happy at all and a 6 means you were very happy, how happy did you feel during this time?"

Activity-level controls account for differences in the context in which respondents report momentary assessments of well-being. Our key independent variable is the *presence of a partner* during the activity. We also differentiate *types of activities*: housework, meals, leisure, travel, and all other activities (reference) and control for the *duration of the activity*, that is, how many minutes it lasted.

Individual-level demographic and socioeconomic controls are as follows. *Race* is a couple-level variable indicating if both members of the couple are white, if one is white and the other is nonwhite, or if both are nonwhite. The *education* variable includes three categories: both members have at least a college degree, one member has at least a college degree while the other does not, or neither member of the couple has a college degree. Similarly, *employment status* indicates if both members are employed, if one member is employed, or if neither of the partners is employed. The *parental status* variable identifies couples with own children (including biological, step, and adopted children) under the age of eighteen in the household. The *income* variable is categorical and is based on household income. We have five categories for income: less than $25,000; $25,000–$74,999; $75,000–$149,999; $150,000+, and missing. The *region* variable includes the four major regions of the country. Finally, we create indicators for whether the diary day was on a *weekend*. Given the controls in our models for the day the diary was reported, age and sex of the respondent, and the broad region where the respondent lives as well as ATUS weights not being calibrated to ensure representativeness of the sample based on being in a same-sex couple, we present unweighted means and estimates.

Methods

First, we describe our sample and their shared time use. We then describe the average reports of happiness, stress, and meaningfulness for same-sex couples for activities spent with and without a partner. Third, we leverage the multiple well-being reports per respondent to estimate activity-level random effects models and fixed effects models. The random effects model allows for the clustering of well-being responses by individuals while estimating the relationship between being with a partner during an activity (versus not) and their subjective well-being during that activity, net of controls. The individual fixed effect model is a within-person analysis that contrasts well-being during time spent with and without a partner for individuals who reported at least one activity with their partner and one activity without their partner. Because this is a within-person analysis rather than a between-person analysis, we have greater confidence in the causal impacts of the presence of a partner on experienced well-being. However, despite the appeal of the within-person fixed effect model, the estimates from the model are based on only respondents with variation in reports of momentary well-being (the dependent variable). Thus, we present both random effects and fixed effect estimates because they have slightly different features that are useful for our analysis of a small sample.

Results

Sample Characteristics

The majority of the same-sex couples in our sample are both white (89% of female same-sex couples and 81% of male same-sex couples). For 39 percent of the men, both partners have a college degree, while this is the case for 44 percent of the women. Nearly 70 percent of all of the same-sex couples are dual earners, but male same-sex couples have higher average incomes than the female same-sex couples in our sample. Finally, only 12 percent of the men have children in the household (or nine couples) versus 38 percent of the women. Compared with national estimates of same-sex couples (U.S. Census Bureau 2013), our sample is similar in racial composition but is more highly educated and more likely to be in dual-earner arrangements. The women are more likely to have co-resident children compared with national estimates.

Women in same-sex couples spend much more time with a partner than men in same-sex couples (for estimates of shared time, see Genadek et al. 2017). As in our previous work (Genadek et al. 2017), the differences we observe between the amount of time men and women in same-sex relationships spend together are substantial. In this sample, women in same-sex unions spend nearly two hours more together per day than the men. Men spend more of their time with a partner alone with the partner, while women are more likely to have someone else present when they are with the partner, partially explained by the greater likelihood of women to have co-resident children.

Several activity-level characteristics are relevant for our analysis of momentary well-being. Of the 450 activities we analyze, 40 percent were done with a partner present. Most common were eating (20.9%) and leisure (19.8%) followed by housework and travel (both 19.2%). These activities are spread throughout the diary day, with most occurring between 5 P.M. and 9 P.M. (34.6%) and 9 A.M. and 12 P.M. (30.2%).

Well-Being Analysis

The results from our random and fixed effect analyses by gender are presented in table 2.1. The activity-level random effects model controls for type of activity, duration of the activity, and person-level and diary-day characteristics described previously. The first column of coefficients shows the effect of being with a partner versus not for happiness, stress, and meaning while accounting for the activity-level and person-level characteristics. Coefficients for the fixed effect analyses are in the second column for each outcome. These within-person analyses fully account for the individual's characteristics, and we control for the varying characteristics, including the activity during which affect was measured as well as the duration of the activity.

For our first research question, we investigate whether men and women in same-sex couples experience enhanced well-being when with a partner. Our bivariate results suggest that men and women in same-sex relationships are better off when they are with a partner in terms of happiness and meaning, and women report lower stress, too. Our multivariate results are more conservative, however. Our second research question asks whether the shared time gap we observe between men and women is also evident in well-being reports of shared time. Without direct tests of gender differences, our results suggest that this may not be the case. We describe unadjusted average well-being by dependent

TABLE 2.1

Multivariate Models Showing the Relationship between Being with a Partner and Momentary Well-Being for Men and Women in Same-Sex Couples

Panel A. Men

	Happy		Stress		Meaning	
	M1 (RE)	M2 (FE)	M1 (RE)	M2 (FE)	M1 (RE)	M2 (FE)
With spouse/ partner	.50⁺ (.28)	.67* (.31)	−.13 (.29)	−.13 (.33)	.39 (.31)	.38 (.35)
Constant	3.03** (1.08)	3.96*** (.33)	3.06** (1.09)	1.91*** (.36)	3.94** (1.28)	3.75*** (.37)
N activities	207	207	207	207	207	207
N people	70	70	70	70	70	70

Panel B. Women

	Happy		Stress		Meaning	
	M1 (RE)	M2 (FE)	M1 (RE)	M2 (FE)	M1 (RE)	M2 (FE)
With spouse/ partner	.03 (.20)	.06 (.23)	−.51* (.23)	−.69** (.26)	.22 (.26)	.45 (.32)
Constant	3.31*** (.67)	3.74*** (.30)	3.91*** (.87)	2.47*** (.34)	2.71** (.89)	3.30*** (.41)
N activities	243	243	243	243	243	243
N people	82	82	82	82	82	82

Note: Fixed effects (FE) models control for duration of the activity (in minutes) and activity type. Random effects (RE) models also control for the presence of a co-resident child under age eighteen; couple-level race, education, and employment; respondent age, family income, day of week, and region.

⁺$p < .10$; * $p < .05$; ** $p < .01$; *** $p < .001$.

variable for men and women in tandem with the multivariate results for each outcome (table 2.1).

Regarding happiness, on the 0 to 6 scale, same-sex men report average happiness of 3.9 for activities without a partner present and 4.3 during activities when partners are present. Models 1 and 2 predicting happiness for men show that sharing time with a partner is associated with increased happiness. The strongest relationship is in the fixed effects model, where men in same-sex couples who report being with a partner have happiness scores that are .67 units higher when with a partner than not, which is large in magnitude considering happiness is measured on a seven-point scale. Women in same-sex relationships report slightly higher average happiness when with a partner (4.6) than when not with a partner (4.4). In our random effect and fixed effect models, women's happiness is not significantly higher when with a partner compared with not.

Stress levels are quite low for all respondents whether a partner was present during the activity or not. Men in same-sex relationships report more stress on average when with a partner (2.1) than when they are not with a partner (1.8), but this difference is not significant in the random and fixed effect models. However, for women in same-sex couples, being with a partner is associated with lower momentary stress. On average, women's self-reported stress is 2.2 when they are not with their partner and 1.6 when they are with a partner. The random effects model shows that when with a partner, women in same-sex couples report at least half a point less stress on the seven-point scale. Likewise, the fixed effect model shows a boost in well-being when with a partner as indicated by the .69-point reduction in stress when with a partner.

We find that meaningfulness is higher when individuals are with a partner versus not when comparing means for both men and women (4.1 compared with 3.3 for men and 4.0 compared with 3.4 for women, respectively). In the multivariate analyses, however, we see no significant relationship between being with a partner and experiencing greater meaning for either men or women in same-sex couples.

Conclusions

While there is a growing literature on well-being in same-sex relationships (e.g., Chen and van Ours 2017; for a review see Cao et al. 2017), this is the first analysis to our knowledge linking momentary well-being and shared time for same-sex couples. Time diary data provide a lens for understanding the everyday experiences of same-sex couples (see Genadek, Flood, and Garcia Roman 2017), and when coupled with momentary assessments of well-being, we get a glimpse into how experienced well-being is tied to time with a partner. This is particularly important as the number of same-sex couples in the United States grows in a context of limited, but increasing, acceptance (Cao et al. 2017).

Based on research on different-sex couples—which has linked time with a spouse to global indicators of relationship well-being (e.g., Amato et al. 2007; White 1983) and momentary indicators of individual well-being (e.g., Flood and Genadek 2016; Sullivan 1996)—our first aim was to examine whether men and women in same-sex couples also experienced enhanced well-being during time with a partner. We find evidence that being with a partner enhances some dimensions of momentary well-being, though in different ways for men and women. Men are happier when with their partners than not, but their reports of stress and meaningfulness are no different with a partner or not. Women experience less stress when they are with a partner versus not, though they do not report higher happiness or meaning when they are with a partner. There is not a consistent boost in well-being across these outcomes for same-sex couples as was found for different-sex couples. On the one hand, our results are generally in the same direction as the results found for different-sex couples, and findings that are not statistically significant may be due to relatively small sample sizes. On the other hand, the differences between same- and different-sex couples should be tested with an interaction in a multivariate framework, which is beyond the scope of this paper.

Our second aim in this study was to examine whether gender differences in same-sex couples' shared time were indicative of gender gaps in well-being. We showed that in our sample men in same-sex couples spend much less time together than women in same-sex couples, which is consistent with a larger sample of ATUS respondents (Genadek, Flood, and Garcia Roman 2017). This raises the question of why. Cooley (1909) argued that interaction is a key element of primary groups but did not provide detail on how much interaction couples should have. Our findings are consistent with theory and research about the gendered nature of emotion work; specifically, the sheer quantity of time may not reflect the quality of the relationship. Men and women may need different amounts of support and interaction from their relationships. In same-sex relationships, gendered expectations about shared time may be more similar between partners and reflected in men's and women's substantially different reports of shared time. These results provide evidence of a complex, gendered relationship between shared time and well-being, which warrants further exploration.

The primary limitation of this study is the small sample size. While sample sizes might be large in contrast to other studies of same-sex couples, they are small compared with previous research studying variation in momentary affect even after leveraging up to three reports of well-being and focusing on activities rather than people as the unit of analysis. Furthermore, the types of activities for which respondents report experienced well-being are quite detailed, and we only have up to three reports of experienced well-being per person. About half of men (46%) and one-quarter of women (26%) were not with a partner during any of the activities for which they provided well-being reports. While our results suggest differences in experienced well-being during time with a partner, larger sample sizes would increase statistical power and precision of our estimates.

An additional limitation includes using only one member's report of time with a partner and well-being. This is potentially problematic given discrepancies between survey-based responses to questions about the division of household labor and direct observation of same-sex couples' daily lives (Carrington 1999). Fortunately, diary-based measures of time use are found to be less subject to social desirability bias than survey-based measures (e.g., Hofferth 2006). Furthermore, while it is possible that our results would have been different if we had time diaries from the other member of the couple, previous research shows that couples report similar shared time when both participate in diaries (Freedman et al. 2012). It is also possible that both partners are not in complete agreement about their experience of shared activities. Given the design of the ATUS and inclusion of only one individual per household in the sample, investigation of such disconnects between partner reports of both shared time and well-being are beyond the scope of this investigation.

Even with these limitations, our results highlight the multidimensionality of well-being and gender differences in the benefits of being with a partner versus not for same-sex couples. The well-being enhancements of being with a partner largely come in the form of reduced stress for women and increased happiness for men. These results complement the extant research on same-sex couples, which focuses on more global, or evaluative, measures of well-being such as relationship satisfaction, cohesion, and stress. Our findings provide a more nuanced perspective on the everyday lived experiences of same-sex couples, which are arguably the building blocks of the evaluative measures generally examined in social science research.

REFERENCES

Amato, Paul R., Alan Booth, David R. Johnson, and Stacy J. Rogers. 2007. *Alone Together: How Marriage in America Is Changing.* Cambridge, MA: Harvard University Press.

Andersson, Gunnar, Turid Noack, Ane Seierstad, and Harold Weedon-Fekjaer. 2006. "The Demographics of Same-Sex Marriages in Norway and Sweden." *Demography* 43 (1): 79–98.

Cao, Hongjian, Nan Zhou, Mark Fine, Yue Liang, Jiayao Li and W. Roger Mills-Koonce. 2017. "Sexual Minority Stress and Same-Sex Relationship Well-Being: A Meta-analysis of Research Prior to the U.S. Nationwide Legalization of Same-Sex Marriage." *Journal of Marriage and Family* 79 (5): 1258–1277. https://doi.org/10.1111/jomf.12415.

Carrington, Christopher. 1999. *No Place like Home. Relationships and Family Life among Lesbians and Gay Men.* Chicago: University of Chicago Press.

Chen, Shuai, and Jan C. van Ours. 2017. "Subjective Well-Being and Partnership Dynamics: Are Same-Sex Relationships Different?" *IZA Working Paper Series* no. 11043.

Cooley, Charles Horton. 1909. *Social Organization: A Study of the Larger Mind.* New York: Charles Scribner's Sons.

Diener, Ed, Robert A. Emmons, Randy J. Larsen, and Sharon Griffin. 1985. "The Satisfaction with Life Scale." *Journal of Personality Assessment* 49 (1): 71–75. https://doi.org/10.1207/s15327752jpa4901_13.

Ellis, Lillian, and Mark Davis. 2017. "Intimate Partner Support: A Comparison of Gay, Lesbian, and Heterosexual Relationships." *Personal Relationships* 24 (2): 350–369. https://doi.org/10.1111/pere.12186.

Flood, Sarah M., and Katie R. Genadek. 2016. "Time for Each Other: Work and Family Constraints among Couples." *Journal of Marriage and Family* 78 (1): 142–164. https://doi.org/10.1111/jomf.12255.

Flood, Sarah M., Katie R. Genadek, and Phyllis Moen. 2018. "Does Marital Quality Predict Togetherness? Couples' Shared Time and Happiness during Encore Adulthood." *Minnesota Population Center Working Paper Series* #2018-1. https://pop.umn.edu/research/working-papers.

Freedman, Vicki A., Frank Stafford, Norbert Schwarz, Frederick Conrad, and Jennifer Cornman. 2012. "Disability, Participation, and Subjective Wellbeing among Older Couples." *Social Science & Medicine* 74 (4): 588–596. https://doi.org/10.1016/j.socscimed.2011.10.018.

Genadek, Katie R., Sarah M. Flood, and Joan Garcia Roman. 2017. "Same-Sex Couples' Shared Time in the United States." Paper presented at the 2017 meetings of the Population Association of America, Chicago, IL.

Graham, James M., and Zoe B. Barnow. 2013. "Stress and Social Support in Gay, Lesbian, and Heterosexual Couples: Direct Effects and Buffering Models." *Journal of Family Psychology* 27 (4): 569–578. https://doi.org/10.1037/a0033420.

Haas, Stephen M., and Laura Stafford. 2005. "Maintenance Behaviors in Same-Sex and Marital Relationships: A Matched Sample Comparison." *Journal of Family Communication*, 5 (1): 43–60.

Hofferth, Sandra L. 2006. "Response Bias in a Popular Indicator of Reading to Children." *Sociological Methodology* 36 (1): 301–315. https://doi.org/10.1111/j.1467-9531.2006.00182.x.

Hofferth, Sandra L., Sarah M. Flood, and Matthew Sobek. 2017. American Time Use Survey Data Extract Builder: Version 2.6 [data set]. College Park: University of Maryland and Minneapolis: University of Minnesota. https://doi.org/10.18128/D060.V2.6.

Institute of Medicine (IOM). 2011. "The Health of Lesbian, Gay, Bisexual, and Transgender People." Washington, DC: National Academies Press.

Joyner, Kara, Wendy Manning, and Ryan Bogle. 2017. "Gender and the Stability of Same-Sex and Different-Sex Relationships among Young Adults." *Demography* 54 (6): 2351–2374.

Julien, Danielle, Elise Chartrand, Marie-Claude Simard, Donald Bouthillier, and Jean Bégin. 2003. "Conflict, Social Support, and Relationship Quality: An Observational Study of Heterosexual, Gay Male and Lesbian Couples' Communication." *Journal of Family Psychology* 17 (3): 419–428. https://doi.org/10.1037/0893-3200.17.3.419.

Kahneman, Daniel, and Alan B. Krueger. 2006. "Developments in the Measurement of Subjective Well-Being." *Journal of Economic Perspectives* 20 (1): 3–24. https://doi.org/10.1257/089533006776526030.

Kahneman, Daniel, Alan B. Krueger, David A. Schkade, Norbdert Schwarz, and Arthur A. Stone. 2004. "A Survey Method for Characterizing Daily Life Experiences: The Day Reconstruction Method." *Science* 306 (5702): 1776–1780. https://doi.org/10.1126/science.1103572.

Kurdek, Lawrence A. 2001. "Differences between Heterosexual-Nonparent Couples and Gay, Lesbian, and Heterosexual-Parent Couples." *Journal of Family Issues* 22 (6): 727–754. https://doi.org/10.1177/019251301022006004.

Kurdek, Lawrence A. 2005. "What Do We Know about Gay and Lesbian Couples?" *Current Directions in Psychological Science* 14 (5): 251–254.

Kurdek, Lawrence A. 2006. "Differences between Partners from Heterosexual, Gay, and Lesbian Cohabiting Couples." *Journal of Marriage and Family* 68 (2): 509–528.

Liu, Hui, Corinne Reczek, and Dustin Brown. 2013. "Same-Sex Cohabitors and Health: The Role of Race-Ethnicity, Gender, and Socioeconomic Status." *Journal of Health and Social Behavior* 54 (1): 25–45. https://doi.org/10.1177/0022146512468280.

Peplau, LetitiaAnne, and Leah R. Spalding. 2000. "The Close Relationships of Lesbians, Gay Men, and Bisexuals." In *Close Relationships: A Sourcebook*, edited by C. Hendrick and S. S. Hendrick, 111–123. Thousand Oaks, CA: Sage. https://doi.org/10.4135/97814522 20437.n9.

Powell, Brian. 2017. "Changing Counts, Counting Change: Toward a More Inclusive Definition of Family." *Journal of the Indiana Academy of the Social Sciences* 17 (1): 1–15.

Reczek, Corinne, Hui Liu, and Russell Spiker. 2017. "Self-Rated Health at the Intersection of Sexual Identity and Union Status." *Social Science Research* 63: 242–252.

Sullivan, Oriel. 1996. "Time Co-ordination, the Domestic Division of Labour and Affective Relations: Time Use and the Enjoyment of Activities within Couples." *Sociology* 30 (1): 79–100. https://doi.org/10.1177/0038038596030001006.

Umberson, Debra, Mieke Beth Thomeer, and Amy C. Lodge. 2015. "Intimacy and Emotion Work in Lesbian, Gay, and Heterosexual Relationships." *Journal of Marriage and Family* 77 (22): 542–556.

U.S. Census Bureau. 2013. "Characteristics of Same-Sex Couple Households." Accessed June 25, 2013, from https://www2.census.gov/programs-surveys/demo/tables/same-sex/time-series/ssc-house-characteristics/ssex-tables-2013.xlsx.

White, Lynn K. 1983. "Determinants of Spousal Interaction: Marital Structure or Marital Happiness." *Journal of Marriage and the Family* 45 (3): 511–519.

3

Consequences of Unequal Legal Recognition

Same-Sex Couples' Experiences of Stress Prior to *Obergefell v. Hodges*

ELI ALSTON-STEPNITZ

DAVID M. FROST

ALLEN J. LEBLANC

Over the last two decades, same-sex marriage has been a prominent topic in political, legal, and public debates. Research has focused on the association between the legal recognition of same-sex relationships and the mental health of sexual minority populations (Badgett 2009; Herdt and Kertzner 2006; King and Bartlett 2006; Kurdek 2004; Patterson 2000; Peplau and Fingerhut 2007). The findings of this research have highlighted the negative associations between governmental bans on same-sex marriage and sexual minority mental health (Hatzenbuehler et al. 2010; Riggle, Rostosky, and Horne 2010), as well as the positive associations between access to same-sex marriage and mental health among sexual minority populations (Gonzales and Blewett 2014; LeBlanc, Frost, and Bowen 2018; Wight et al. 2012; Wight, LeBlanc, and Badgett 2013).

Expanding on this research, LeBlanc, Frost, and Wight (2015) theorized that minority stressors (e.g., discrimination, expectations of rejection, concealment, and internalized stigma) are not only experienced by sexual minority individuals but also shared by people in same-sex relationships. Regarding the latter, they have offered the concept of "couple-level minority stress," which—by introducing this novel domain of minority stress—facilitates more holistic understandings of minority stress in the lives of sexual minority persons not only as individuals but also as partners in stigmatized relationships. It extends stress scholarship more generally by simultaneously considering both identity-based (sexual minority) and role-based (partner) stress domains. It also takes into consideration existing explanations of stress proliferation (Pearlin and Bierman 2013)—referring to how stress begets more stress—involving multiple domains of social stress, including both general and minority stressors, individual and couple-level stressors, and past, ongoing, and anticipated stressors (Thomeer et al. 2018).

Despite the Supreme Court's 2015 ruling legalizing same-sex marriage across the United States (*Obergefell v. Hodges*), it is important to remember that same-sex couples have long faced opposition to achieving their basic relational pursuits, and that they will continue to do so. The social, political, and legal controversies surrounding same-sex marriage in the United States are deeply rooted, and as such their effects endure over time, and they vary across social settings and geographic locations (Frost and Fingerhut 2016).

In this chapter, we draw on data from a large-scale study of same-sex couples in the Greater Atlanta (ATL) and San Francisco Bay (SF) areas to focus on how people in same-sex relationships articulated the challenges they faced prior to the U.S. Supreme Court ruling in *Obergefell v. Hodges* (2015), which legalized same-sex marriage at the federal level. We focus in particular on how these individuals—in their own voices, and in their shared narratives with their partners—illustrate the unique stressors they faced at this critical juncture in the history of civil rights for sexual minority populations.

Background

In order to fully understand same-sex couples' lived experiences prior to *Obergefell*, we must first understand the unique sociopolitical histories of same-sex marriage in Georgia and California. In Georgia, aside from a domestic partnership registry for city employees who were in same-sex relationships, same-sex couples had no legal recognition. In 2004, voters approved Georgia Constitutional Amendment 1, a referendum which made it unconstitutional for the state to recognize or perform same-sex marriages or civil unions. In 2015, upon the outcome of *Obergefell*, Georgia, along with fourteen other states, filed a brief with the U.S. Supreme Court appealing the ruling, arguing that it violated the state's Fourteenth Amendment right to determine the "meaning and shape" of marriage. The Court rejected the appeal.

Same-sex marriages were first recognized by the state of California in early 2004 when the City and County of San Francisco issued marriage licenses to approximately 4,000 same-sex couples residing in and outside California. By August of 2004, the Supreme Court of California ruled that these marriages were void, and same-sex marriage was banned, only to later overturn this ban with the 2008 ruling *In re Marriage Cases*. Later that year, as part of the presidential election, the passage of Proposition 8 prohibited same-sex marriage across the state once again, leaving the marriages of the roughly 20,000 couples who had married during the window before Proposition 8 in an uncertain state. By 2010, Proposition 8 was ruled to be unconstitutional by the Ninth Circuit Court in California. In December of 2012, the U.S. Supreme Court agreed to hear challenges to the ban of Proposition 8 (*Hollingsworth v. Perry*), and on June 26, 2013, the same day the U.S. Supreme Court overturned the Defense of Marriage Act (DOMA) which had prohibited married same-sex couples from collecting federal benefits (*U.S. v. Windsor*), the Court upheld Judge Walker's ruling, legalizing same-sex marriage in California.

Methods

The data on which this chapter is based are from a large-scale study of minority stress and mental health of same-sex couples (Frost et al. 2017; LeBlanc, Frost, and Wight 2015). The sample consisted of 120 same-sex couples equally distributed across two study sites (the Greater Atlanta and San Francisco Bay areas), sex (male and female), and relationship duration (at least six months but less than three years, at least three years but less than seven years, and seven or more years). Except for ten participating couples (five in each study site), interviews were conducted prior to the 2013 Supreme Court ruling that made same-sex marriage legal in California, and all were conducted prior to the 2015 Supreme Court ruling that made same-sex marriage legal across the country (*Obergefell v. Hodges*).

Eligibility criteria for participation in this study were that (1) both partners were at least twenty-one years old; (2) both individuals perceived of one another as their partner and of themselves as a "couple"; and (3) at some point in their shared history, they had been engaged in a sexual relationship. Eligible couples were interviewed in person at research offices.

Building on existing lifeline methodology, interviews were organized around the couples' joint construction of a "relationship timeline" (de Vries et al. 2017). Lifeline methods have been useful in the study of lived experience (Elder Jr. 1998; Gramling and Carr 2004). However, historically, lifeline methods and research have focused on individual experience, failing to account for the collective experiences of those in intimate relationships. Data elicited through methods focused on dyads are likely to reveal findings distinct from those drawn from methods focusing on individuals. As such, we allowed for the joint creation of relationship timelines—along which couples defined, labeled, and discussed key events or periods of time over the course of their relationships—to elicit narratives that focused explicitly on their shared experiences to better understand how stressors at the relationship level contribute to stress processes that influence couple well-being and individual partner health (de Vries et al. 2017; LeBlanc, Frost, and Wight 2015).

The qualitative dyadic data stemming from the couples' relationship timelines were systematically coded by a large coding team, leading to the identification of seventeen distinct couple-level minority stressors (Frost et al. 2017). Structural forms of discrimination were frequently discussed by couples and were coded as "consequences of unequal legal recognition of same-sex relationships." This code was defined by the research team as "the effects that uncertain and unequal legal recognition of same-sex relationships (in comparison to heterosexual relationships) has for the lived experiences of same-sex couples." Out of the 120 couples interviewed, more than half (*n*=75) of the couples spoke about their lived experiences related to unequal legal recognition. Using thematic analysis (Braun and Clarke 2013), a method for identifying, analyzing, and reporting on patterns within data, these interviews were further analyzed by the first author to obtain a more detailed and nuanced understanding of the lived experience of this particular form of couple-level minority stress. Themes presented in the following text were discussed, revised, and refined by the three authors.

Findings

Findings focused around three themes. Couples discussed *challenges regarding the legitimacy of same-sex relationships*, which they described as something they felt internally, as well as something they saw as externally reinforced. Couples also discussed *emotional and material costs of being in same-sex relationships*, which included references to missing out on the automatic protections that come from marriage and having to undertake efforts—including emotional and actual labor—in pursuit of protections. Finally, couples articulated *challenges relating to how they anticipated the future together.*

"Make-Believe Marriage": Challenges regarding the Legitimacy of Same-Sex Relationships

Regardless of whether participants had engaged in symbolic ceremonies or resisted them, participants reported that the lack of access to legal marriage affected their attitudes and feelings about the legitimacy of their relationships. Despite a difference in access to legal protections for same-sex couples in California and Georgia, male and female couples of all relationship durations discussed feeling as if their partnerships were less-than—in some way—when compared with legal marriage.

In the Greater Atlanta metropolitan area, where at the time of the interviews couples were barred from any legal recognition, including registered domestic partnership, participants often framed marriage or weddings as "playing pretend." Sandra and LaToya (ages 43 and 36; ATL), two African American women who had been together thirteen years, explained the conflict that arose when LaToya expressed her reticence to get married:

LATOYA: I have ill feelings about the fact that—to say I'm married, and not have the legal rights to that title. So to me, anything other than that is pretend. It's make-believe, you're just pretending to be married. You're not really married. So, to me . . . it's not validated by having a ceremony. . . . I felt like we didn't need that make-believe title on our relationship. . . . When I said that to her . . . shit hit the fan. . . . She was really hurt by it. I mean, she was really hurt. And I felt really bad but . . . I just had ill feelings about how our country treats gays as far as giving us the legal rights that you would give anyone else. . . . In my opinion, the state, the government, didn't recognize it, and I just wasn't going to fall victim of being in a make-believe marriage.

Harry and Scott (ages 49 and 46; ATL), two non-Hispanic white men who had been together twenty-five years, echoed the sentiments expressed by LaToya in the explanation of their uncertainty about getting married:

SCOTT: We've gone back and forth because I was very adamant that I did not want to get married because it's not recognized federally and it's meaningless. And we love each other, and I can't have this fake piece of paper—until we get benefits, what's the point?

In the San Francisco Bay area, despite having access to some government protections via registered domestic partnership status, participants also reported feeling that their relationships were not as legitimate as those of their heterosexual, married counterparts. Couples often felt conflicted about their domestic partnership, on one hand finding it meaningful enough to do it, but still characterizing it as "fake," "not real," or "not the same" as marriage. Further, some couples living in the San Francisco Bay area characterized having domestic partnership as a constant reminder of their "other" status. Judy and Karmen (ages 37 and 35; SF), an interracial female couple who had been together five years, explained how it felt to have domestic partnership but not marriage:

KARMEN: I think it does affect us quite a bit and—and it affects our relationship. Domestic partnership has some of that but it's not—it's not the same.

JUDY: Yeah, the domestic partnership it's like it was nice but it's like a—it's almost like a sad consolation prize so even though it's—it's meaningful to me in terms of that's the best I can get . . . [but] as soon as it becomes legal to get married I'm not gonna feel bad about even tossing out that [domestic partnership] certificate. In the meantime, though, I want to frame it practically you know but who does that? No one's gonna display their domestic partnership certificate.

In addition, because some same-sex couples' marriages were not voided in California, while others were, some couples in the San Francisco Bay area sample felt a particular sense of "other"ness even in regard to other same-sex couples.

Gayle and Joan (ages 34 and 31; SF), two non-Hispanic white women who had been together eight years, reflected on their feelings of loss around missing the "legal window" to marry before Proposition 8 was passed:

GAYLE: I remember—oh, okay. So, Prop 8 happened in 2008. Um, and we were like, "There's no way the State of California will ban gay marriage. We don't— we don't have to rush in to anything." But, then Prop 8 happened. And, we were like, oh god, we should probably—we need to do this. So, we decided to get our domestic partnership. We printed out our forms, filled them out, took them to the UPS Store, and got them notarized. It was a happy occasion. A little bit ridiculous.

JOAN: I was—I was a little sad, too. Because, we had missed our window of opportunity the previous year. And, it—I mean, you know. If anything can highlight the separate but equal status of a Registered Domestic Partnership, it's going to a notary in a UPS Store, versus going to City Hall to get an actual marriage license.

Couples explained that it was not only their internalized feelings about their relationships but the feelings expressed by their friends and families that furthered their feelings of illegitimacy. Continuing to discuss their feelings about their domestic partnership after Proposition 8 repealed their access to marriage, Gayle and Joan reported feeling unseen by family, friends, and co-workers:

JOAN: I think, because we did it that way rather than have some sort of ceremony, um, other people don't recognize our relationship. Or, think of our relationship the same way we do. I mean—I refer to Gayle as my wife. I think of us as married. We're as married as we can possibly be in this state today. But, other people don't see us that way. Because, they didn't see us, you know, walking down the aisle in white and exchanging vows.

Even when couples had decided to engage in some sort of ceremony, they were often met with skepticism. Angela and Julia (ages 28 and 30; SF), two non-Hispanic white women who had been together four years, described the stress they felt while planning their wedding:

ANGELA: Aside from planning the actual wedding, [the stress] was, like, telling our families, you know, we're getting married. We're having a wedding. And, dealing with all of them, you know, saying to us, "You know, why do you want to bother having a wedding? You know, it's not a legal marriage. It's not real." Why are you wasting money, basically?

The couple went on to explain that they felt their families' skepticism was not just about them being a same-sex couple; rather, it largely had to do with the fact that their wedding would not be legal.

ANGELA: I mean, I was really defensive. And hurt by it. Because, you know, people just drop everything to go and be with my brother when he was getting married to his girlfriend from high school, when they were twenty years old, and she was pregnant. . . . And, even though people didn't really believe in their relationship, they supported the wedding because that's what you do. You know? And, they—they just think, like, we're silly. You know, we're just playing a game. Like we're playing house.

JULIA: Right. And, even "Why are you getting married?" Not even because of the whole, you know, gay thing. It's because it's not legal, either. So, it's like, [to them] why are we just going to put on a show, too?

Sergio and Jack (ages 35 and 45; SF), an interracial couple who had been together six years, also felt that not being able to get married impacted their relationships with others:

SERGIO: I think that's one of the saddest things about gays not being able to get legally married in a lot of America is that you miss out on that whole community support, and the expectation of longevity. . . . I mean, aside from all the rights that come along with being married, and tax benefits.

Regardless of whether couples desired to be married, thought of themselves as married already, or did not desire to be married at all, they all reported feeling that because same-sex marriage was not legal, their relationships were not legitimate in comparison with legal, heterosexual marriage. Couples expressed feelings of shame and inadequacy that were reinforced both internally (e.g., feeling like they were playing pretend, being embarrassed or ashamed of their domestic partnership status) and externally (e.g., in interactions with friends, family, and co-workers that diminished the value of their relationships with their partners). Couples commonly reported not feeling as if their relationships were fully "seen," which happened in several ways. For example, some described how registering as domestic partners in a nongovernmental setting or outside of a religious setting, such as a neighborhood UPS Store, cannot compare with being legally married at City Hall or in a religious ceremony.

"Paying to Be Gay": Emotional and Material Costs of Being in Same-Sex Relationships

In addition to feeling that their relationships were not fully legitimized—as a result of unequal legal and social recognition—couples also talked at great length about how not having access to legal marriage resulted in a myriad of costs. Couples felt that seeking out alternatives to marriage, both domestic partnership in the case of California couples and power of attorney, wills, and other forms of protection in Georgia, required emotional and physical labor, and financial costs. These costs were not required of legally married couples. LaToya and Sandra, for instance, cited the need to pursue alternative legal protections as a bigger stressor on their relationship than the lack of equal legal recognition per se:

LATOYA: I don't care about the state [laughs]. I don't even care about waiting on the state. I would like to be able to legally marry her and live in whatever state or country I want to and not have to go to Canada to do it. Um— unfortunately, we don't live in that right now, so—we took the wills and powers of attorney to protect ourselves, to protect our things that we're working hard to create together, to make sure we both have a say-so, um, in the unfortunate event that something should happen to the other person. But with or without papers, God knows that I—I have loved this woman more than I've loved anybody else.

Relatedly, many couples discussed not wanting to be legally responsible for each other's debts without access to the benefits afforded married couples. To illustrate, Harry and Scott felt that it was more protective not to pursue an alternative set of legal ties in the absence of access to legal marriage:

SCOTT: The rational, practical side of me is like I don't want to tie this legally if we can't get all the benefits. I mean, if god-forbid one of us got really sick or something, we could you know, make the other person look poor so they can get government assistance. Play all these games like, if the system is going to screw us, in terms of not giving us benefits and all this stuff then I want to use that to screw the system back. I don't want us to be responsible legally for each other's debts if we're not getting [protections] you know.

Another challenge emerged from the reality that some couples struggled to balance an indifference—or even an opposition—to the idea of legal marriage with their very real need for the socioeconomic benefits that accompany legal marriage. Heather and Maggie (ages 32 and 28; SF), two non-Hispanic white women who had been together for three years, spoke about this as follows:

HEATHER: And I think I personally waffle back and forth between, well, who cares what the state says? Who cares what the government says? We're get- ting married. It doesn't really matter. And then being really pissed off like we have to file for domestic partnership. We have to do all this crazy tax stuff, and you know we can't buy a house together easily. When we have kids one of us is going to have to wait a year and then adopt. You know? It's just all that sort of stuff. Like, I get really resentful when it comes to that sort of stuff, and I guess there's like a rights issue in there too. Part of me is just like, I don't really care what they—like, you know, everyone is like, "Well, I want people to think that our marriage is as legit." I'm like, "I don't really care if they think it's legit or not. I just want the same rights." Like, I just want—I don't want to have to pay more because I'm—that stuff makes me angry. I'm like, you can't change people's ignorance, but having to pay more to be gay makes me angry.

International couples in the study were also negatively impacted by lack of access to socioeconomic benefits that stem from legal marriage. Margaux and Diane (ages 31 and 40; SF), two non-Hispanic white women who had been together three years when they participated, spoke about the stress from not being able to use marriage as a pathway to citizenship for Margaux:

MARGAUX: That's—that is a constant, like an everyday source of stress for me 'cause my visa keeps expiring every year so I have to renew and that's conditioned by me doing a good job at work and so you can never leave your career. It's not like "I don't like this job anymore" where I can apply to this other place; I can't. Um, and I need to move from an exchange visa to a permanent visa—for a green card and so I have—have this pressure on my shoulders every day.

Similarly, lacking access to legal marriage influenced how same-sex couples approached the prospects of having children. Margaux and Diane, for example, described how their inability to legally marry additionally affected their options for having children:

MARGAUX: That's also a conditioning like if we are deciding to have kids— there's no way we're gonna have kids with me having a nonpermanent visa and getting deported. And then what?

This was not only the case for international couples. Several couples felt the uncertainty of legal marriage and lack of protections for same-sex co-parents by extension precluded their ability to have a family. Kayla and Cat (both age 46; ATL), two non-Hispanic white women who had been together seventeen years, cited their feelings of loss around having a family:

KAYLA: I do think that um that being gay shut down the adoption area for us because it—it's very cost prohibitive to adopt overseas um and I don't feel I'm equipped to deal with a special needs child, so you know. We really were interested, if anything, in a healthy [baby]—and that's just not a possibility in Georgia for a lesbian couple.

Once again, whether couples desired to be legally married or not, many reported being aware of a lack of material benefits afforded automatically through legal marriage. Same-sex couples recognized that before *Obergefell v. Hodges* (2015) they were required to do more emotionally, physically, and financially than were their heterosexual counterparts. As a result, some same-sex couples attempted to mitigate the potential harms of not having legal recognition by acquiring the legal protections they could attain (e.g., wills and power of attorney). In contrast, others resisted such alternative legal protections out of fear that doing so might create future challenges that are presently unforeseeable, stemming from the extra effort they might have made in the absence of having legal marriage as an option.

"It Depends": Challenges regarding Future Planning in Same-Sex Relationships

Couples' narratives also demonstrated how dealing with couple-level minority stressors relating to unequal legal recognition can lead to stress regarding how couples anticipate their futures together. When couples discussed what they anticipated in their shared future together, many expressed concerns about future challenges. Some stated that they had not had conversations about marriage or children because of the interrelated legal challenges associated with both. Jake and Hugo (ages 53 and 24; ATL), an interracial couple who had been together five years, explained they had never seriously considered important aspects of their future:

HUGO: I mean we've never really talked about those issues, like having children or having—or getting married or, you know, things that society is really going to look at you upon these issues, you know.

JAKE: It's something to think about. I mean—some people do ask, "Would you ever get married if it was legalized?" And I—and I wonder. Like I do think about it.

HUGO: Do you?

JAKE: It's like—is it? I don't know if it's something we would both be interested in doing. And would it ever be legalized in Georgia?

Other couples described how living with legal precarity regarding same-sex marriage left them feeling in limbo about other major life decisions. Rick and John (ages 73 and 74; ATL), two non-Hispanic white men who had been together thirty-seven years when they participated, described the uncertainty of where they would live in the future:

JOHN: I think a lot of this [the future] might depend on the marriage issue. We do want to get married.

RICK: [We're] considering relocation to a state where marriage would be legal.

John and Rick and several other couples in Greater Atlanta felt that the sociopolitical climate of Georgia barred the possibility that marriage would ever be an option:

RICK: What we had hoped [in our relationship], certainly, is to have been married. I mean, that's one thing that we could never do. And living in—it's frustrating living in Georgia because we know we might not even be here by the time Georgia ever passes anything. Which I doubt they ever will.

Having children was discussed again, this time regarding the uncertainty around whether marriage was made legal. Sam and Hector (ages 23 and 43; SF), an interracial couple that had been together two years, described their uncertainty about having children together because of the legal uncertainty of same-sex marriage:

HECTOR: Do you want to say 2014 on, exploring parenting options? We should stay tuned on the legal marriage.

SAM: Oh, yeah. That would be a huge one. Can't have no kids before I'm married.

HECTOR: That's a big question mark because we decided that we wouldn't do it unless it's legal, so there's a lot of—

SAM: Federally legal.

HECTOR: Yeah, federally legal. So, a lot of uncertainty there.

Jill and Kim (ages 35 and 31; ATL), two non-Hispanic white women who had been together five years, discussed the uncertainty of having children because they would not be allowed to adopt children together as a lesbian couple in Georgia. They described how they felt they were not in control of the entire process, and were not sure what would happen despite both wanting to have children:

JILL: The part that I get frustrated with about the adoption process is that we have to go through it twice. Like, we had to do a second home study because you cannot—lesbian couples cannot adopt together. One—she will be adopting. And then, after her adoption, the adoption go-to for her, I will do a second parent adoption.

KIM: And it depends on which county we live in.

JILL: And which judge we get.

KIM: Because it depends on the county and the judge if they will allow a same-sex couple to have equal parenting rights.

Running throughout the couples' narratives about future planning and next steps for their relationship was a common feeling of lack of agency. Different couples coped with the lack of agency differently. Couples like Hugo and Jake found avoiding conversations about the future more comfortable than confronting the reality that their future could be impacted by legal decisions. Other couples, like Jill and Kim, discussed future plans and desires, but made decisions to not pursue any desires (e.g., having children) which meant making themselves more vulnerable than they already felt in their current positions. And finally, couples like Rick and John surrendered, deciding to let legal decisions ultimately decide their fate (e.g., relocating).

Conclusions

Using data from a large-scale study investigating the nature of couple-level minority stress experienced by same-sex couples, this paper highlights the lived experiences of same-sex couples, prior to the legalization of same-sex marriage with *Obergefell v. Hodges* (2015). It illuminates the relational context of minority stress and identifies unique hardships faced by same-sex couples during this important historical moment. Our findings indicate that legal access to marriage contributes not only to the legitimacy of the relationship in the eyes of the law but to society at large. In addition, this legitimization brings with it important material and social benefits. As an emerging body of empirical research has begun to suggest, it may also be associated with health-related benefits (Gonzales and Blewett 2014; LeBlanc, Frost, and Bowen 2018; Wight, LeBlanc, and Badgett 2013).

Although this study includes same-sex couples living in two distinct geographical locations, it does not support a rigorous examination of how couples' experiences of minority stress relating to unequal legal recognition prior to the ruling in *Obergefell v. Hodges* (2015) may have varied by location. Although these data did suggest that SF couples appeared more confident that same-sex marriage would be legalized in California, while ATL couples expressed greater skepticism that this would ever happen in Georgia, findings from the larger study do not suggest significant differences between the two study sites in terms of the prevalence of couple-level minority stressors more generally (Frost et al. 2017).

Nonetheless, the Greater Atlanta and the San Francisco Bay areas are unique from one another, as they represent different regions of the country, with populations that are sociodemographically distinct. Future research is needed to more thoroughly examine how variations in place—as determined by geography, population, history, and culture—may well play a role in couple-level minority stress experience (e.g., differences in the prevalence of such stressors as well as variations in their substance) related to unequal relationship recognition. At present, very little is known about this topic.

In closing, this research demonstrates the need for deeper interrogation into the lived experiences of same-sex couples and couple-level minority stress, as our findings suggest that the consequences of unequal legal recognition of same-sex couples prior to *Obergefell* (2015) will not be fully remedied by the relatively recent access to legal same-sex marriage. Indeed, new research has started to illustrate the multidimensionality of couple-level minority stressors, some relating to issues of unequal legal recognition and others relating to stressful circumstances faced by same-sex couples in other life domains (e.g., familial relationships) (Frost et al. 2017).

ACKNOWLEDGEMENTS

This work was supported by National Institutes of Health Grant 1R01HD070357 (Allen J. LeBlanc, Principal Investigator). We also acknowledge research team members in both the Greater Atlanta and San Francisco Bay areas who conducted the lifeline interviews on which this study is based.

REFERENCES

Badgett, M. V. Lee. 2009. *When Gay People Get Married: What Happens When Societies Legalize Same-Sex Marriage.* New York: NYU Press.

Braun, Virginia, and Victoria Clarke. 2013. *Successful Qualitative Research: A Practical Guide for Beginners.* London: Sage.

de Vries, Brian, Allen J. LeBlanc, David M. Frost, Eli Alston-Stepnitz, Rob Stephenson, and Cory R. Woodyatt. 2017. "The Relationship Timeline: A Method for the Study of Shared Lived Experiences in Relational Contexts." *Advances in Life Course Research* 32: 55–64.

Elder, Glen H., Jr. 1998. "The Life Course as Developmental Theory." *Child Development* 69 (1): 1–12.

Frost, David M., and Adam W. Fingerhut. 2016. "Daily Exposure to Negative Campaign Messages Decreases Same-Sex Couples' Psychological and Relational Well-Being." *Group Processes & Intergroup Relations* 19 (4): 477–492.

Frost, David M., Allen J. LeBlanc, Brian de Vries, Eli Alston-Stepnitz, Rob Stephenson, and Cory Woodyatt. 2017. "Couple-Level Minority Stress: An Examination of Same-Sex Couples' Unique Experiences." *Journal of Health and Social Behavior* 58 (4): 455–472.

Gonzales, Gilbert, and Lynn A. Blewett. 2014. "National and State-Specific Health Insurance Disparities for Adults in Same-Sex Relationships." *American Journal of Public Health* 104 (2): e95–e104.

Gramling, Lou F., and Rebecca L. Carr. 2004. "Lifelines: A Life History Methodology." *Nursing Research* 53 (3): 207–210.

Hatzenbuehler, Mark L., Katie A. McLaughlin, Katherine M. Keyes, and Deborah S. Hasin. 2010. "The Impact of Institutional Discrimination on Psychiatric Disorders in Lesbian, Gay, and Bisexual Populations: A Prospective Study." *American Journal of Public Health* 100 (3): 452–459.

Herdt, Gilbert, and Robert Kertzner. 2006. "I Do, but I Can't: The Impact of Marriage Denial on the Mental Health and Sexual Citizenship of Lesbians and Gay Men in the United States." *Sexuality Research and Social Policy Journal of NSRC* 3 (1): 33–49.

Hollingsworth v. Perry, 133 S. Ct. 2652, 570 U.S. 693, 186 L. Ed. 2d 768. 2013.

In re Marriage Cases, 183 P.3d 384, 76 Cal. Rptr. 3d 683, 43 Cal. 4th 757. 2008.

King, Michael, and Annie Bartlett. 2006. "What Same Sex Civil Partnerships May Mean for Health." *Journal of Epidemiology & Community Health* 60 (3) :188–191.

Kurdek, Lawrence A. 2004. "Are Gay and Lesbian Cohabiting Couples Really Different from Heterosexual Married Couples?" *Journal of Marriage and Family* 66 (4): 880–900.

LeBlanc, Allen J., David M. Frost, and Kayla Bowen. 2018. "Legal Marriage, Unequal Recognition, and Mental Health among Same-Sex Couples." *Journal of Marriage and Family* 80 (2): 397–408.

LeBlanc, Allen J., David M. Frost, and Richard G. Wight. 2015. "Minority Stress and Stress Proliferation among Same-Sex and Other Marginalized Couples." *Journal of Marriage and Family* 77 (1): 40–59.

Obergefell v. Hodges, 135 S. Ct. 2071, 576 U.S., 191 L. Ed. 2d 953 (2015).

Patterson, Charlotte J. 2000. "Family Relationships of Lesbians and Gay Men." *Journal of Marriage and Family* 62 (4): 1052–1069.

Pearlin, Leonard I., and Alex Bierman. 2013. "Current Issues and Future Directions in Research into the Stress Process." In *Handbook of the Sociology of Mental Health*, 325–340. Dordrecht: Springer.

Peplau, Letitia Anne, and Adam W. Fingerhut. 2007. "The Close Relationships of Lesbians and Gay Men." *Annual Review of Psychology* 58: 405–424.

Riggle, Ellen D. B., Sharon S. Rostosky, and Sharon G. Horne. 2010. "Psychological Distress, Well-Being, and Legal Recognition in Same-Sex Couple Relationships." *Journal of Family Psychology* 24 (1): 82.

Thomeer, Mieke Beth, Allen J. LeBlanc, David M. Frost, and Kayla Bowen. 2018. "Anticipatory Minority Stressors among Same-sex Couples: A Relationship Timeline Approach." *Social Psychology Quarterly* 81 (2): 126–148.

US v. Windsor, 133 S. Ct. 2675, 570 U.S. 12, 186 L. Ed. 2d 808 (2013).

Wight, Richard G., Allen J. LeBlanc, Brian De Vries, and Roger Detels. 2012. "Stress and Mental Health among Midlife and Older Gay-Identified Men." *American Journal of Public Health* 102 (3): 503–510.

Wight, Richard G., Allen J. LeBlanc, and M. V. Lee Badgett. 2013. "Same-Sex Legal Marriage and Psychological Well-Being: Findings from the California Health Interview Survey." *American Journal of Public Health* 103 (2): 339–346.

4

Postpartum Depression and Anxiety in Male-Partnered and Female-Partnered Sexual Minority Women

A Longitudinal Study

ABBIE E. GOLDBERG
JULIANNA Z. SMITH
LORI E. ROSS

Postpartum depression (PPD) is a significant public health issue for women and their families, with 13 to 19 percent of new mothers meeting criteria for PPD (O'Hara and McCabe 2013). The first six months postdelivery is an especially high-risk time for depression (O'Hara and McCabe 2013). Postpartum anxiety is less frequently studied, but an estimated 8.5 percent of mothers experience at least one postpartum anxiety disorder (Goodman, Watson, and Stubbs 2016).

Research on PPD has focused almost exclusively on heterosexual women (O'Hara and McCabe 2013), reflecting heterosexist frameworks that conflate heterosexuality with parenthood, thus perpetuating the invisibility of sexual minority mothers' experiences and contributing to health care disparities between heterosexual and sexual minority women (SMW; Trettin, Moses-Kolko, and Wisner 2006). With few exceptions (Goldberg and Smith 2011; Ross et al. 2007), research has not explored the role of sexual orientation in postpartum well-being.

The few studies that have studied perinatal mental health in SMW found higher depression in early parenthood compared with a previously published heterosexual sample (Ross et al. 2007) and increases in anxiety across the transition to parenthood at levels higher than published norms for heterosexual women (Goldberg and Smith 2008, 2011). These disparities echo the findings of studies that show elevated rates of depression and anxiety among SMW at other stages of the life cycle, and point to the role of sexual orientation–based stigma and stress in such disparities (Goldberg, Gartrell, and Gates 2014).

Significantly, these studies of perinatal mental health in SMW focus on visible sexual minority women (VSMW)—women partnered with other women. Another group of SMW that may be at greater risk are women who, based on their male-partnered status, are likely to be "read" as heterosexual by society—and counted as "heterosexual" by researchers who study male-female couples—but who, based on their self-expressed sexual identity (e.g., bisexual) or recent sexual histories (i.e., that involve women) are sexual minorities. These women, whom we refer to as "invisible" SMW (ISMW), or male-partnered SMW, were at elevated risk for PPD compared with visible SMW (VSMW; i.e., female-partnered women) and heterosexual women, in a pilot study of depression in the immediate postpartum (Flanders et al. 2016). Furthermore, other work suggests bisexual mothers are especially vulnerable to feelings of invisibility (e.g., their identity is not seen or recognized) and lack of social support or a sense of community, possibly placing them at elevated risk for mental health issues (Ross et al. 2012).

The current longitudinal, multisite (United States and Canada) study treats ISMW (i.e., male-partnered women with recent sexual histories that include women), VSMW, and heterosexual (or non-sexual minority women; NSMW) as distinct groups. It examines whether ISMW and VSMW exhibit more depressive and/ or anxious symptoms than NSMW (a) prenatally, and, after accounting for prenatal symptoms, (b) three months postpartum and (c) six months postpartum. It examines the extent to which differences in mental health can be accounted for by established prenatal predictors of postpartum depression/anxiety. It also examines the implications of "lumping" ISMW with VSMW (as sexual minorities), or NSMW (as male-partnered)—and of treating ISMW as a distinct group.

Sexual Minority Women: Not a Monolithic Group

Minority stress theory (Meyer 1995) highlights external stressors (e.g., discrimination) and internalized stressors (e.g., binegativity; negative ideas about bisexual people) that sexual minorities may encounter related to their sexual minority status. In turn, due to the stress of living in a heterosexist society, sexual minorities are theorized to show poorer mental health than heterosexual individuals. Within the larger population of sexual minorities, it is possible that same-gender partnered individuals (i.e., visible sexual minorities [VSM]) are exposed to more discrimination, increasing their risk for mental health difficulties—especially during the transition to parenthood due to the combined stresses of sexual minority and new parenthood statuses (Trettin et al. 2006). In addition, there may be other subgroups of SMW who are at elevated risk for mental health difficulties.

Indeed, although SMW are diverse in terms of identity, sexual history, and partner gender, research has rarely differentiated among subgroups, thus obscuring potential differences in risk for mental health problems across groups based on partner gender in particular. That studies rarely distinguish between male- and female-partnered SMW is problematic, as SMW experience different social contexts that impact their well-being (e.g., male-partnered SMW may experience invisibility in dominant heterosexual and LGBTQ communities). Some exceptions to this trend are notable, and actually suggest that ISMW may be at greater risk for mental health issues than VSMW—for example, due to the invisibility and lack of community they face. In a rare study that differentiated between male- and female-partnered bisexual women in examining mental health disparities, Dyar, Feinstein, and London (2014) found that bisexual women with different-gender partners had higher depression than bisexual women with same-gender partners, a difference that was explained by the greater levels of binegative exclusion reported by the former group.

Failure to examine the experiences of ISMW, especially during the perinatal period, is problematic. Male-partnered SMW likely make up a large proportion of SMW, and, specifically, childbearing SMW (Moegelin, Nilsson, and Helström 2010). Bisexual identities are more common than lesbian identities, and bisexual women are more likely to have children than lesbians (59% vs. 31%; Goldberg et al. 2014).

Established Predictors of Postpartum Depression and Anxiety

In addition to examining group differences in mental health, we assess the role of established predictors of mental health across the transition to parenthood, given the paucity of research to examine predictors of perinatal mental health in SMW. These predictors constitute demographic, reproductive, and psychosocial factors (e.g., related to stress and support). Regarding demographics, lower education and income is linked to prenatal and postnatal depression and anxiety (Martini et al. 2015). Regarding reproductive and pregnancy factors, unintended pregnancy is associated with higher anxious and depressive symptoms, and pregnancy complications and health issues (e.g., urinary tract infections) are also linked to PPD (Biaggi et al. 2016). The role of parity is unclear: some studies show women having their first child (primiparous women) to be at greater risk than those who are already mothers (multiparous women), and others find multiparous women to be at greater risk (Biaggi et al. 2016). Regarding psychosocial factors, experiencing a higher number of stressful life events in the past year or during pregnancy has been linked to higher risk of depressive and anxious symptoms, prenatally and postnatally (Biaggi et al. 2016). Low social support is a well-documented risk factor for PPD (Edwards et al. 2012), and has been linked to postpartum anxiety (Martini et al. 2015). Finally, although many studies of postpartum well-being fail to take prenatal symptoms into account, prenatal mental health problems represent a strong risk factor for postnatal depression and anxiety (Biaggi et al. 2016).

Perinatal Mental Health among SMW

In addition to examining differences in depressive and anxious symptoms across the transition to parenthood, among VSMW, ISMW, and heterosexual (i.e., non–sexual minority) women (NSMW) and the role of known risk factors for PPD, we also examine a methodological question: how different classifications of women (e.g., grouping ISMW with NSMW or VSMW rather than treating them as a separate group) impact the findings. Researchers typically make decisions about groupings based on partner status, and male-partnered women are thus grouped as "heterosexual." Of interest was whether this—vs. grouping these women with their female-partnered counterparts, VSMW—might lead to different findings (e.g., the obscuring or emergence of group differences).

Drawing from minority stress theory (Meyer 1995) and work on VSMW (Goldberg and Smith 2008, 2011), we expect that, compared with NSMW, both ISMW and VSMW might report greater distress across the transition, given their shared vulnerability to sexual stigma in society, in that one's stigmatized identity need not be visible for individuals to be negatively affected by sexual stigma (Meyer 1995). Alternatively, ISMW may, because of their invisibility, experience low levels of community identification and support. Due to the need to consistently manage information about their ISM status, they may feel alienated from both LGBTQ and heterosexual communities, rendering them vulnerable to distress. Or, VSMW, who are partnered with women, may be more vulnerable to overt forms of societal stigma, placing them at greatest risk for distress (Meyer 1995).

In sum, it is important to study the mental health of VSMW and ISMW as separate groups with potentially differing experiences during the transition to parenthood—a time of elevated risk for distress (O'Hara and McCabe 2013). We examine depressive and anxious symptoms, given that these are distinct domains, with some women experiencing mood difficulties and others experiencing worry and fear (Lovibond and Lovibond 1995). We examine prenatal (T1) and postnatal (T2 [3 months postpartum] and T3 [6 months postpartum]) symptoms. Prenatal symptoms are strong predictors of postpartum symptoms (Martini et al. 2015); thus, we examine postpartum mental health controlling for prenatal mental health.

Research Questions

The following research questions framed the present study:

1. Are there group differences in prenatal and postpartum mental health?
2. Are there group differences in established predictors of prenatal and postpartum mental health?
3. What reproductive risk and psychosocial stressors are related to prenatal and postpartum mental health? Do they account for any group differences in postpartum mental health?
4. What are the implications of alternative groupings (e.g., VSMW+ISMW vs. SMW; ISMW+NSMW vs. male-partnered women; ISMW vs. everyone else) on the pattern of findings that emerges?

Method

Data are from eighty-eight women: twenty-nine VSMW (women partnered with women), twenty-eight ISMW (women partnered with men; sexual history involving women), and thirty-one NSMW (women partnered with men; no recent sexual history involving women), who were assessed prenatally, three months postpartum, and six months postpartum, in Toronto, Canada, and in Central and Western Massachusetts, United States.

Participants

A description of the sample appears in table 4.1. Women's average age was 32.35 years ($SE=4.76$). Twelve (13.2%) of eighty-eight women were of color (VSMW = 4, 13.2%; ISMW = 5, 16.7%; NSMW = 3, 9.7%). Average income was 7.02 ($SE=2.45$, $Mdn=7$, on a scale of 1–10) and average education was 4.26 ($SE=1.14$, $Mdn=4$ on a scale of 1–6). Analysis of variance (ANOVA) revealed that income varied by sexual category ($F=7.97$, $df=2$, $p<.001$), with ISMW reporting lower income than VSMW ($M_{Diff}=2.42$, $SE=.61$, $p<.001$) and, at the level of a trend, than NSMW ($M_{Diff}=1.31$, $SE=.60$, $p=.093$). Education also differed ($F=8.87$, $df=2$, $p<.001$), with VSMW reporting more education than ISMW ($M_{Diff}=1.15$, $SE=.28$, $p=.001$) and NSMW ($M_{Diff}=.77$, $SE=.27$, $p=.018$). There were no differences on the basis of country, race, or age.

Recruitment

Women were predominantly recruited through consecutive sampling from selected midwifery clinics and OB/GYNs during presentation for prenatal care. Sites were located in different geographic locations. Women attending a prenatal care visit at 25–32 weeks' gestation completed a brief questionnaire that included questions regarding (a) sexual orientation, (b) gender of sexual partners in the past five years, and (c) current partner status (partnered/not; partner gender). This prescreen enabled us to obtain a systematic sample of consecutive admissions wherein all SMW and a random selection of heterosexual women in our total population of pregnant women were invited to participate.

Women were considered SMW if they were partnered with women, identified as nonheterosexual, and/or reported having had at least one female sexual partner in the past five years. Within the SMW group, participants were categorized as VSMW or ISMW depending on the gender of their partner. NSMW were male-partnered and reported no female sexual partners in the past five years. To be eligible, women had to be partnered, be eighteen years of age or older, speak English fluently, and be pregnant.

Because numbers of participants currently partnered with women were initially low, this group only was supplemented through convenience sampling

TABLE 4.1

Descriptive Statistics for Sample and Regression Outcome, Predictor, and Control Variables

Variables	Entire sample (N=88) M (SD) or n (%)	Visible minority (VSM) (n=29) M (SD) or n (%)	Invisible minority (ISM) (n=28) M (SD) or n (%)	Nonminority (NSM) (n=31) M (SD) or n (%)
Sample descriptive statistics				
Race (of color vs. white)	12 (13.2%)	4 (13.3%)	5 (16.7%)	3 (9.7%)
T1 age	32.35 (4.76)	33.83 (3.89)	31.20 (4.99)	32.03 (5.06)
T1 income	7.02 (2.45)***[a,b]	8.20 (1.73)	5.77 (2.79)	7.10 (2.15)
T1 education	4.26 (1.14)***[a,c]	4.87 (0.86)	3.83 (1.29)	4.10 (1.01)
Regression variables *Outcomes*				
T1 depressive Sx (EPDS)	6.16 (3.77)*[d]	5.63 (3.60)	7.33 (3.85)	5.55 (3.71)
T2 depressive Sx (EPDS)	5.57 (3.84)	5.23 (3.26)	6.80 (4.54)	4.71 (3.42)
T3 depressive Sx (EPDS)	5.53 (4.23)*[d]	4.57 (3.16)	7.00 (4.52)	5.03 (4.59)
T1 anxious Sx (STAI)	33.79 (9.92)*[d]	30.63 (8.45)	37.13 (11.78)	33.48 (8.39)
T2 anxious Sx (STAI)	33.18 (10.84)*[d,e]	31.33 (9.28)	37.90 (11.53)	30.23 (9.88)
T3 anxious Sx (STAI)	34.21 (10.47)**[d]	31.97 (9.62)	37.80 (9.99)	32.90 (11.09)
Demographics				
Canadian (vs. U.S.)	31 (34.1%)	10 (33.3%)	11 (36.7%)	10 (32.3%)
T1 SES (PCA)	.00 (1.00)***[a,c]	.57 (.68)	−.50 (1.18)	−.06 (.80)
Reproductive health				
Primiparous (first child)	62 (68.1%)	23 (76.7%)	19 (63.3%)	20 (64.5%)
Reproductive risks	.60 (0.74)**[d,e]	.50 (.68)	.90 (.88)	.42 (.56)

(continued)

Table 4.1. Descriptive Statistics for Sample and Regression Outcome, Predictor, and Control Variables (continued)

Variables	Entire sample $(N=88)$ M (SD) or n (%)	Visible minority (VSM) $(n=29)$ M (SD) or n (%)	Invisible minority (ISM) $(n=28)$ M (SD) or n (%)	Nonminority (NSM) $(n=31)$ M (SD) or n (%)
Stressors				
Social support	85.11 (11.49)[+a]	88.20 (7.73)	81.53 (13.83)	85.45 (11.59)
Stressful life events	1.46 (2.73)[***d,e]	.93 (1.96)	2.833 (3.90)	.65 (1.08)

Note: Sx = symptoms; Hetero = heterosexual; SES = socioeconomic status; PCA = principal components analysis. Group differences were examined using ANOVAs with post hoc comparisons.

[a] VSM > ISM;[b] NMS(Nonminority) > ISM;[c] VSM > NMS;[d] ISM > VSM;[e] ISM > NSM.

[+] $p < .10$; [*] $p < .05$; [**] $p < .01$; [***] $p < .001$.

(e.g., we targeted perinatal health care centers and LGBTQ services). Comparison of female-partnered participants recruited through consecutive ($n = 14$) and convenience ($n = 17$) sampling revealed no significant differences in the two groups in terms of demographics.

Of the ninety-two eligible consecutively recruited participants who were successfully contacted, eighty-two (89%) consented. Three cases withdrew before completing the T1 questionnaires. Seventeen women were recruited via convenience sampling. The total sample included ninety-six women. Seven cases were dropped due to missing data on one or more variables, and one was dropped because many of her experiences were different (as her partner was a trans woman), for a final sample of $N = 88$.

Data Collection

Data were collected through an Internet survey. Upon providing verbal consent to participate, women were emailed a link to the questionnaire, which began with a consent form.

T1 occurred prenatally, T2 occurred eight to twelve weeks postpartum, and T3 occurred six months postpartum.

Outcome Measures

Depression (T1, T2, T3). The Edinburgh Postnatal Depression Scale (EPDS; Cox, Holden, and Sagovsky 1987) is a ten-item self-report screening tool for perinatal depression, yielding summed scores from 0 to 30, with higher scores indicating greater symptoms. Questions are about the past week, on a four-point response scale. Alphas ranged from .80 to .86.

Anxiety (T1, T2, T3). Anxiety was assessed using the state anxiety subscale (20 items) of the State-Trait Anxiety Inventory (STAI; Spielberger and Barratt 1972). Questions are asked in reference to the current moment. Responses (given on a 4-point scale) are summed, and higher scores indicate more symptoms. Alphas ranged from .93 to .94.

Predictor Measures

Primiparous versus Multiparous. Parity was coded such that 1=primiparous (first child) and 0=multiparous (has other children). Primiparous was not included as a reproductive risk factor, as preliminary analyses showed it to have a different relationship to the outcomes than the other reproductive factors assessed.

Reproductive Risk. A sum of reproductive risk factors for postpartum mental health was created based on women's reports of *unplanned pregnancy, prior miscarriage*, and *pregnancy complications*. Whether the pregnancy was planned was somewhat confounded with sexual category, as all VSMW had planned pregnancies.

Sexual Category. Sexual category was coded using three dummy variables: ISM, for which 1=ISMW (male-partnered; sexual minority identity and/or sexual history with women in the past 5 years) and 0=other; VSMW, for which 1=VSM (female-partnered) and 0=other; NSMW, for which 1=NSMW (male-partnered, heterosexual identified; no sexual history with women in the past 5 years) and 0=other.

Social Support (T1). Social support was assessed at T1 using the Medical Outcomes Study (MOS) Social Support Scale, which consists of nineteen items and is answered on a five-point scale (Sherbourne and Stewart 1991). The scale was summed across all items; higher scores indicate more support. As the distribution of responses was highly, negatively skewed, it was transformed by cubing it (and dividing by 100,000). The alpha was .96.

Stressful Life Events (T1). We assessed whether, and how many times, during the past year, participants experienced a list of twelve life event categories that are typically considered stressful (i.e., to have marked or moderate long-term threat; e.g., death of a first-degree relative), using a widely used measure (Brugha et al. 1985). We use the sum of events. A high score indicates more stressful events; sample scores ranged from 0 to 15. As responses were positively skewed (many participants reported no such events), we used the square root.

Control Variables

Country. Country was coded such that United States = 0 and Canada = 1.

Socioeconomic Status (SES). SES was a composite of *family income* and *education*, based on a principal components analysis.

Data Analysis

Group differences in summed EPDS and STAI scores at three months and at six months postpartum were examined among the three groups (ISMW, VSMW, NSMW) using ANOVA. Group differences in known prenatal risk factors for post-partum depression or anxiety (SES, reproductive risk, psychosocial stressors, prenatal symptoms) were examined using ANOVAs for continuous variables and chi-square tests for categorical variables.

A series of nested regression models were used to examine what factors predicted depressive and anxious symptoms. In step I, sexual minority status (ISMW, VSMW) and control variables (country, SES, and T1 symptoms for the T2 and T3 outcomes) were entered as predictors. In step 2, known predictors of perinatal mental health were added (first child, reproductive risks, psychosocial stressors). Separate models were fit with NSMW replacing ISMW, to change the default category and enable comparisons between ISMW and VSMW.

In order to examine group differences when distinct groups were grouped together (e.g., all male-partnered women), we fit models similar to the first step above with just a single sexual minority status variable (VSMW, NSMW, or ISMW) and the controls country, SES, and T1 symptoms (for T2 and T3). Significance was considered to be $p < .05$; trends are reported at $p < .10$.

Results

Descriptive statistics for predictors and outcomes are presented across the sample and by sexual category in table 4.1.

RQ 1: Differences in Depressive and Anxious Symptoms

Looking at differences across all three sexual categories (VSMW, ISMW, NSMW), one-way ANOVAs showed differences in mean levels of depressive symptoms at T1 ($F = 3.54$, $df = 2$, $p = .033$). Post hoc analyses showed ISMW reported more symptoms than VSMW ($M_{diff} = 2.29$, $SE = .93$, $p = .047$). There were no differences according to sexual category in levels of depressive symptoms at T2. There were differences at T3 ($F = 3.28$, $df = 2$, $p = .042$): ISMW reported more symptoms than VSMW at the level of a trend ($M_{diff} = 2.68$, $SE = 1.11$, $p = .054$).

ANOVAs showed differences in anxious symptoms according to sexual category at T1 ($F = 3.27$, $df = 2$, $p = .043$): ISMW reported more symptoms than VSMW ($M_{diff} = 8.42$, $SE = 2.36$, $p = .002$). T2 anxious symptoms also differed according to sexual category ($F=6.39$, $df=2$, $p=.003$): ISMW reported higher symptoms than VSMW ($M_{diff}=7.18$, $SE=2.77$, $p=.034$) and NSMW ($M_{diff}=8.43$, $SE=2.72$, $p=.008$). T3 also showed differences in anxious symptoms ($F=5.47$, $df=2$, $p=.006$), with ISMW's symptoms higher than VSMW's at the level of a trend ($M_{diff}=6.53$, $SE=2.74$, $p=.058$).

RQ 2: Differences in Time 1 Predictors of Postpartum Mental Health

According to ANOVAs, SES differed by sexual category ($F=10.92$, $df=2$, $p<.001$), with VSMW having higher SES than ISMW ($M_{diff}=1.12$, $SE=.24$, $p<.001$) and NSMW ($M_{diff}=.63$, $SE=.24$, $p=.026$). There were no differences in the control variable, country. Reproductive risk factors differed according to sexual category ($F=4.96$, $df=2$, $p=.009$): ISMW had more risks than VSMW ($M_{diff}=.48$, $SE=.19$, $p=.039$) and NSMW ($M_{diff}=.54$, $SE=.19$, $p=.014$).

In terms of psychosocial stressors, social support differed by sexual category at the level of a trend ($F=2.94$, $df=2$, $p=.058$), with VSMW reporting higher support than ISMW at the level of a trend ($M_{diff}=1.31$, $SE=.55$, $p=.061$). There were significant group differences in number of stressful events ($F=7.22$, $df=2$, $p=.001$), with ISMW reporting more stressful events than VSMW ($M_{diff}=.69$, $SE=.23$, $p=.011$) and NSMW ($M_{diff}=.79$, $SE=.22$, $p=.002$).

RQ 3: Regression Analyses

Depressive and anxious symptoms were examined in two steps. In step I, sexual minority status (ISMW, VSMW) and control variables (country, SES, T1 symptoms for T2 and T3) were entered as predictors. In step 2, known predictors of perinatal mental health were added (primiparous, reproductive risks, psychosocial stressors).

In predicting T1 depressive symptoms, in step I (with sexual minority status and controls) only SES was significant, with higher SES related to lower symptoms (table 4.2). In step 2, there were differences at the level of trend for country, with Canadians reporting higher symptoms, after taking into account the other variables in the model. SES was no longer significant. Reproductive risks and stressful life events were positively related to T1 symptoms, and social support was negatively related to T1 symptoms.

Looking at T2 postpartum depressive symptoms, in step I, SES was positively related to symptoms at the level of a trend, and T1 depressive symptoms were positively related to T2 symptoms. In step 2, only T1 symptoms were significantly associated with T2 depressive symptoms.

For T3, in step I, T1 symptoms were positively related to T3 symptoms. In step 2, T1 symptoms remained significant, and social support was negatively associated with T3 depressive symptoms, at the level of a trend.

In predicting perinatal anxious symptoms, the same approach was used. When T1 anxious symptoms were the outcome, step I showed no significant predictors. Step 2 showed social support to be negatively related to T1 anxious symptoms.

For T2 anxious symptoms, step 1 showed ISMW and T1 symptoms to be positively related to T2 anxious symptoms. In step 2, ISMW remained positively related to T2 symptoms, at the level of a trend, and T1 symptoms remained significant.

For T3 anxious symptoms, step 1 showed T1 symptoms to be positively related to T3 symptoms. In step 2, T1 symptoms remained significant, social support was negatively related to T3 symptoms, and stressful events were positively related to T3 symptoms, at the level of a trend.

To examine differences between ISMW and VSMW, the default variable was changed from NSMW to ISMW. This revealed no significant differences between ISMW and VSMW once controls were entered into the model, except at T1 (step 1), where VSMW had lower anxious symptoms ($\beta = -6.63$, $SE = 2.65$, $t = 2.50$, $p = .014$); no other predictors were significant. There were no significant differences in step 2, once the other predictors were added to the model; however, social support was negatively associated with T1 anxious symptoms ($\beta = -1.71$, $SE = .46$, $t = 3.73$, $p < .001$).

RQ 4: Implications of Different Groupings on Assessing Differences in Depressive and Anxious Symptoms

We reexamined the differences between groups when certain groups were combined, with control variables included in the model. When comparing male-partnered women (NSMW + ISMW) to VSMW, the only significant differences were for T1 anxious symptoms: VSMW reported lower symptoms at the level of a trend ($\beta = -4.37$, $SE = 2.22$, $t = 1.97$, $p = .053$), while SES was negatively related to T1 anxiety at the level of a trend ($\beta = -2.02$, $SE = 1.06$, $t = 1.91$, $p = .060$). Looking at NSMW versus SMW (ISMW + VSMW combined) showed no significant differences for depressive symptoms, but NSMW had lower T2 anxious symptoms ($\beta = -4.74$, $SE = 1.88$, $t = 2.52$, $p = .014$), with country, SES, and T1 symptoms in the model. T1 symptoms were positively related to T2 symptoms ($\beta = .74$, $SE = .10$, $t = 7.31$, $p < .001$).

When ISMW were compared with all others, they reported higher T1 anxious symptoms ($\beta = 4.77$, $SE = 2.21$, $t = 2.16$, $p = .034$), while SES was negatively related to symptoms at the level of a trend ($\beta = -2.01$, $SE = 1.04$, $t = 1.93$, $p = .057$). ISMW also reported higher T2 anxious symptoms ($\beta = 4.45$, $SE = 2.18$, $t = 2.04$, $p = .044$), after taking into account the controls. T1 symptoms were positively related to T2 symptoms ($\beta = .69$, $SE = .11$, $t = 6.61$, $p < .001$).

Discussion

This exploratory study is the first to examine, longitudinally, depression and anxiety among male- and female-partnered SMW. It builds on a small literature

TABLE 4.2

Regression Models Predicting Depressive and Anxious Symptoms (N = 88)

| | *Depressive symptoms* | | | | | |
| | *Time 1* | | *Time 2* | | *Time 3* | |
Predictors	*SC + conts* β *(SE)*	*Full model* β *(SE)*	*SC + conts* β *(SE)*	*Full model* β *(SE)*	*SC + conts* β *(SE)*	*Full model* β *(SE)*
ISM	1.43 (.93)	−.56 (.88)	1.27 (.88)	.98 (.96)	.98 (.97)	.43 (1.05)
VSM	.24 (.93)	−.08 (.82)	.38 (.87)	.40 (.89)	−.50 (.95)	−.58 (.97)
Canadian	.82 (.79)	1.21 (.70)+	−1.17 (.75)	−1.05 (.78)	.61 (.82)	1.01 (.85)
SES	−.95 (.42)*	−.53 (.39)	.68 (.41)+	.50 (.43)	.32 (.45)	.29 (.47)
Primiparous	—	.57 (.74)	—	1.09 (.80)	—	1.09 (.88)
Repro Risk	—	1.04 (.48)*	—	.75 (.54)	—	.23 (.59)
T1 Soc Sup	—	−.62 (.16)***	—	−.22 (.19)	—	−.41 (.21)+
T1 Stressful Events	—	1.31 (.41)**	—	−.43 (.48)	—	.30 (.52)
T1 Dep	—	—	.63 (.10)***	.59 (.12)***	.67 (.11)***	.55 (.13)***
T1 Anx	—	—	—	—	—	—

Note: Dep = depressive symptoms; Anx = anxious symptoms; SC = stressful events and/or social support; SES = socioeconomic status; ISM = invisible sexual minority; VSM = visible sexual minority; conts = control variables.

+$p < .10$; *$p < .05$; **$p < .01$; ***$p < .001$.

on perinatal mental health among SMW (Goldberg and Smith 2008; Ross et al. 2007) and extends it to include the experiences of a largely neglected group: male-partnered, ISMW.

Insomuch as prenatal risk factors predict later mental health, it is important to comment on our descriptive data wherein we observed differences in these risk factors by group already in the prenatal period. Female-partnered, VSMW had higher SES than ISMW and NSMW, and male-partnered, ISMW had more reproductive and psychosocial risks, compared with VSMW and NSMW. ISMW's lower SES, and/or aspects of their sexual history, may help to explain these elevated risks. While the SES differences across groups may have resulted from sampling methods, they may also reflect the underlying reality that VSMW's pregnancies are almost always planned, and planning is generally associated with and facilitated by financial stability. In contrast, pregnant

			Anxious symptoms		
Time 1		Time 2		Time 3	
SC + conts	Full model	SC + conts	Full model	SC + conts	Full model
β (SE)	β (SE)	β (SE)	β (SE)	β (SE)	β (SE)
3.64 (2.38)	.81 (2.45)	5.75 (2.30)*	4.80 (2.50)+	2.49 (2.51)	.12 (2.60)
−2.99 (2.38)	−2.62 (2.29)	3.74 (2.29)	3.12 (2.46)	1.70 (2.51)	1.19 (2.44)
−.77 (2.04)	.51 (1.96)	−1.60 (1.94)	−1.23 (2.00)	1.64 (2.12)	2.90 (2.07)
−1.63 (1.08)	−1.75 (1.09)	.69 (1.05)	1.12 (1.13)	−1.04 (1.14)	−.69 (1.71)
—	1.62 (2.05)	—	1.60 (2.10)	—	.59 (2.18)
—	2.18 (1.34)	—	−.62 (1.39)	—	.03 (1.44)
—	−1.71 (.46)***	—	−.45 (.51)	—	−1.59 (.53)**
—	−.07 (1.16)	—	1.54 (1.18)	—	2.06 (1.23)+
—	—	—	—	—	—
—	—	.72 (.11)***	.68 (.12)***	.54 (.11)***	.40 (.12)**

ISMW may be more likely to have lower SES, which is supported by work showing that bisexual people tend to be of lower SES than other sexual orientation groups and, thus, are exposed to life stressors associated with fewer resources (Gorman et al. 2015).

Regarding support, prior work suggests that male-partnered SMW are at risk for nonsupport from LGBTQ communities, in part because they are seen as experiencing "heterosexual privilege" (Ross et al. 2012). Further, because of their male-partnered status, their sexual histories and/or identities are often rendered invisible, possibly inhibiting connection with others who share similar histories/identities, which may impact their well-being (Dyar et al. 2014). They may also feel alienated from parenting communities, which are largely heteronormative (Goldberg et al. 2014). Thus, their lower support may reflect their unique identities as ISMWs—although, as we did not look at sexual minority-specific or parent-specific forms of support, we cannot draw firm conclusions about reasons for and sources of nonsupport.

Compared with VSMW, ISMW reported more depressive symptoms prenatally and at a trend level at six months postpartum, and more anxious symptoms prenatally and postnatally—and at a trend six months postpartum. Yet in the regression models, once country, SES, and T1 symptoms (for T2 and T3) were taken into account, most differences disappeared. ISMW had higher anxious symptoms than VSMW at T1, even after taking into account country and SES—but this difference disappeared once other predictors were considered, with social support related to T1 symptoms. Immediately postpartum, ISMW had higher anxious symptoms than NSMW, after taking into account country, SES, and T1 symptoms—yet this finding remained significant, at the level of a trend, even after taking into account the other predictors, with none emerging as significant except T1 anxiety. Perhaps the effects of invisibility and isolation are most present soon after birth, when women are likely to be constrained socially and physically, and unlikely to have access to community resources or social groups that (a) are inclusive and tolerant of both their sexual identities and parenthood statuses and (b) provide postpartum-specific support (Manley, Goldberg, and Ross 2018). Alternatively, it is possible that this marginally significant finding emerged by chance.

Changing the sexual category groupings did impact the findings for anxiety, such that male-partnered women (NSMW+ISMW) had significantly higher prenatal anxious symptoms than VSMW at T1; and SMW (ISMW+VSMW) had significantly higher anxious symptoms at T2 when compared with NSMW. Significantly, when ISMW were compared with all other women, they had higher anxious symptoms at T1 and T2. These analyses shed insight into the importance of methodological decisions related to participant classification based on elements of sexual identity, relationship status, and sexual history (Gates and Badgett 2009), with different categorizations illuminating or obscuring patterns of potential risk for mental health problems. With multiple ways of classifying individuals according to more or less visible (or stigmatized) identities, each is associated with a somewhat different pattern of results. Our findings also show that SMW are not a monolithic group, and male-partnered SMW, who represent a large proportion of SMW, represent a unique group with key background, reproductive, psychosocial, and mental health risks that should be taken into account.

Predictors of depressive and anxious symptoms were similar, but not entirely the same, highlighting the need to assess these domains separately. Consistent with research on heterosexual mothers (Biaggi et al. 2016) and female-partnered SMW (Goldberg and Smith 2008), lower social support was related to prenatal and postpartum mental health—specifically, higher symptoms of depression and anxiety prenatally and six months postpartum. Stressful life events were associated with prenatal depression and six-month postpartum anxiety. There is evidence that the impact of stressful events—particularly those that involve threat—may be especially likely to lead to or manifest as the physical and psychological symptoms of anxiety, as opposed to depression, particularly during a challenging life transition such as becoming a parent (Epifanio et al. 2015). The relationship of these psychosocial stressors to prenatal depressive and anxious symptoms and the strong relationship between prenatal and postpartum symptoms suggest the importance of attending to prenatal mental health and psychosocial stressors.

Conclusions

This study has many limitations. Our sample is small. We did not examine sexual minority specific sources of support, stigma, or stress. Despite our use of a consecutive sampling approach, thus improving generalizability over the convenience samples that have typically been used in this type of work, our final sample was relatively homogenous and may not be representative of all SMW. This study's strengths include the exploration of perinatal mental health outcomes among SMW, assessment of mental health at multiple time points, inclusion of prenatal symptoms, and investigation of the methodological implications of diverse ways of classifying participants. In turn, this study makes several contributions. First, it illuminates mental health processes during a key life event that has been understudied in SMW, and which represents a period of enhanced risk. Second, it brings visibility to the experiences of a group that is rarely the focus of research attention. Third, it shows the research implications of different sexual and relational classification systems. Future work should build on this study to enhance our understanding of mental health among women, particularly mothers, of diverse sexual histories and relationship configurations.

REFERENCES

Biaggi, Alessandra, Susan Conroy, Susan Pawlby, and Carmine Pariante. 2016. "Identifying the Women at Risk of Antenatal Anxiety and Depression: A Systematic Review." *Journal of Affective Disorders* 191 (February): 62–77.

Brugha, Traolach, Paul Bebbington, Christopher Tennant, and Jane Hurry. 1985. "The List of Threatening Experiences: A Subset of 12 Life Event Categories with Considerable Long-Term Contextual Threat." *Psychological Medicine* 15, no. 1 (February): 189–194.

Cox, John, Jeni Holden, and Ruth Sagovsky. 1987. "Detection of Postnatal Depression: Development of the 10-Item Edinburgh Postnatal Depression Scale." *British Journal of Psychiatry* 150, no. 6 (June): 782–786.

Dyar, Christina, Brian A. Feinstein, and Bonita London. 2014. "Dimensions of Sexual Identity and Minority Stress among Bisexual Women: The Role of Partner Gender." *Psychology of Sexual Orientation and Gender Diversity* 1, no. 4 (December): 441–451.

Edwards, Renee, Matthew Thullen, Nucha Isarowong, Cheng-Shi Shiu, Linda Henson, and Sydney Hans. 2012. "Supportive Relationships and the Trajectory of Depressive Symptoms among Young, African American Mothers." *Journal of Family Psychology* 26, no. 4: 585–594.

Epifanio, Maria Stella, Vitalba Genna, Caterina De Luca, Mihcele Roccella, and Sabina La Grutta. 2015. "Paternal and Maternal Transition to Parenthood: The Risk of Postpartum Depression and Parenting Stress." *Pediatric Reports* 25, no. 2 (May): 58–72.

Flanders, Corey E., Margaret F. Gibson, Abbie E. Goldberg, and Lori E. Ross. 2016. "Postpartum Depression among Visible and Invisible Sexual Minority Women: A Pilot Study." *Archives of Women's Health* 19, no. 2: 299–305.

Gates, Gary, and M. V. Lee Badgett. 2009. *Best Practices for Asking Questions about Sexual. Orientation on Surveys.* Los Angeles, CA: Williams Institute.

Goldberg, Abbie E., Nanette K. Gartrell, and Gary J. Gates. 2014. *Research Report on LGB-Parent Families.* Los Angeles, CA: Williams Institute, UCLA School of Law.

Goldberg, Abbie E., and JuliAnna Z. Smith. 2008. "The Social Context of Lesbian Mothers' Anxiety during Early Parenthood." *Parenting: Science & Practice* 8, no. 3 (July): 213–239.

Goldberg, Abbie E., and JuliAnna Z. Smith. 2011. "Stigma, Social Context, and Mental Health: Lesbian and Gay Couples across the Transition to Adoptive Parenthood." *Journal of Counseling Psychology* 58 (1): 139–150.

Goodman, Janice H., Grace R. Watson, and Brendon Stubbs. 2016. "Anxiety Disorders in Postpartum Women: A Systematic Review and Meta-Analysis." *Journal of Affective Disorders* 203 (October): 292–331.

Gorman, Bridget K., Justin T. Denney, Hilary Dowdy, and Rose Anne Medeiros. 2015. "A New Piece of the Puzzle: Sexual Orientation, Gender, and Physical Health Status." *Demography* 52, no. 4 (August): 1357–1382.

Lovibond, Peter, and Sydney Lovibond. 1995. "The Structure of Negative Emotional States: Comparison of the Depression Anxiety Stress Scales (DASS) with the Beck Depression and Anxiety Inventories." *Behaviour Research and Therapy* 33, no. 3 (March): 335–343.

Manley, Melissa H., Abbie E. Goldberg, and Lori E. Ross. 2018. "Invisibility and Involvement: LGBTQ Community Connections among Plurisexual Women during Pregnancy and Postpartum." *Psychology of Sexual Orientation and Gender Diversity* 5 (2): 169–181.

Martini, Julia, Johanna Petzoldt, Franziska Einsle, Katja Beesdo-Baum, Michael Hofler, and Hans-Ulrich Wittchen. 2015. "Risk Factors and Course Patterns of Anxiety and Depressive Disorders during Pregnancy and after Delivery: A Prospective-Longitudinal Study." *Journal of Affective Disorders* 175 (April): 385–395.

Meyer, Ilan. 1995. "Minority Stress and Mental Health in Gay Men." *Journal of Health and Social Behaviour* 36, no. 1 (March): 38–56.

Moegelin, Lena, Bo Nilsson, and Lottie Helström. 2010. "Reproductive Health in Lesbian and Bisexual Women in Sweden." *Acta Obstetricia et Gynecologica Scandinavica* 89, no. 2 (February): 205–209.

O'Hara, Michael, and Jennifer McCabe. 2013. "Postpartum Depression: Current Status and Future Directions." *Annual Review of Clinical Psychology* 9 (March): 370–407.

Ross, Lori E., Amy Siegel, Cheryl Dobinson, Rachel Epstein, and Leah Steele. 2012. "'I Don't Want to Turn Totally Invisible': Mental Health, Stressors, and Supports among Bisexual Women during the Perinatal Period." *Journal of GLBT Family Studies* 8, no. 2 (March): 137–154.

Ross, Lori E., Steele, Leah, Chris Goldfinger, and Carol Strike. 2007. "Perinatal Depressive Symptomatology among Lesbian and Bisexual Women." *Archives of Women's Mental Health* 10, no. 2 (April): 53–59.

Sherbourne, Cathy, and Anita Stewart. 1991. "The MOS Social Support Survey." *Social Science & Medicine* 32 (6): 705–714.

Spielberger, Charles, and Ernest Barratt, eds. 1972. *Anxiety: Current Trends in Theory and Research*. New York: Academic Press.

Trettin, Shanthi, Eydie Moses-Kolko, and Katherine Wisner. 2006. "Lesbian Perinatal Depression and the Heterosexism That Affects Knowledge about This Minority Population." *Archives of Women's Mental Health* 9, no. 2 (March): 67–73.

PART TWO

Health Behaviors

5

Health and Health Behaviors among Same-Sex and Different-Sex Coupled Adults with and without Children

JUSTIN T. DENNEY
JARRON M. SAINT ONGE
BRIDGET K. GORMAN
PATRICK M. KRUEGER

The increasing diversity of household types has prompted recent investigations into the health of same-sex partnered adults (Denney, Gorman, and Barrera 2013; Liu, Reczek, and Brown 2013). Though extant literature documents the influence of partners and children for adult health and health behaviors (Carr and Springer 2010; Umberson 1987, 1992; Umberson, Crosnoe, and Reczek 2010), it is less clear how adult health is impacted by the presence of children across same- and different-sex unions. A historical lack of available data on same-sex coupled adults, particularly those that include children in the household, has made it difficult to include same-sex coupled adults in research efforts aimed at understanding household dynamics and health (Institute of Medicine 2011). In this chapter, we overcome important data limitations by compiling nine years of the National Health Interview Survey (NHIS) to examine and compare the health and health behaviors of different-sex and same-sex partnered men and women with and without children.

Background

We focus our examination on health statuses and behaviors that are major contributors to morbidity and mortality. Weight status, cigarette smoking, and alcohol consumption are widely established health factors that associate with acute and chronic morbidity and mortality. In particular, obesity, smoking cigarettes, and consuming large amounts of alcohol associate with long-term health deficits and are responsible for substantial disparities in length of life (U.S. DHHS 2013; CDC 2014).

For coupled adults, partners invest in one another's health and influence health behaviors by encouraging health-promoting behaviors and discouraging damaging behaviors related to smoking, obesity, and heavy drinking. Umberson (1987) suggested that family roles (e.g., partner or parent) encourage self-regulation, whereby adults deter negative health behaviors that might jeopardize partner investments. But behavioral investments are unequally linked to broader relationship factors such as marital status, duration of the intimate relationship, and available resources (Lau 2012; Meyler, Stimpson, and Peek 2007). For example, different-sex married adults have been shown to less often engage in health-compromising behaviors when compared with their cohabiting counterparts, in part due to advantages that come with marriage, including enhanced social support and socioeconomic resources (Carr and Springer 2010).

Research consistently documents higher-than-average population-level rates of smoking and problem substance use among sexual minorities when compared with heterosexuals (Dermody et al. 2014; Dilley et al. 2010; Tang et al. 2004). Recent work has found mixed evidence of more health-compromising behaviors among adults in same-sex unions compared with adults in different-sex marriages. For example, Reczek, Liu, and Brown (2014) find that the prevalence of both current smoking and heavy alcohol use is similar among same-sex and different-sex cohabitors and higher than among different-sex married adults. Research on weight status among coupled adults is less consistent, with few insights into how obesity is associated with same-sex unions. Pulling from research on body mass and sexual orientation not specific to partnered adults suggests heightened obesity among sexual minority women compared with heterosexual women (Bowen, Balsam, and Ender 2008). Gay men, however, have lower rates of obesity than heterosexual or bisexual men (Deputy and Boehmer 2010). How obesity varies for same-sex partnered men and women, compared with different-sex partnered adults, and considering whether children are present remains an almost entirely undeveloped area of research.

The presence of children is associated with health and behavioral patterns (Umberson 1987), indicating that studies on partners and health that ignore the presence or absence of children in the home are incomplete. Evidence on whether children associate with better or worse health for parents versus nonparents is mixed, perhaps because the social context of parenthood matters. This social context involves many of the established correlates of health disparities, including race, ethnicity, socioeconomic status (SES), and elements of family structure and, perhaps, the gender composition of the union. Indeed, some same-sex partner parenthood contexts may be more stressful and thus more likely to associate with poorer health than different-sex partner parenthood contexts.

Theoretically, the presence of children could associate with enhancements to health and well-being or health deficits through, for example, health-compromising behaviors. Through indirect social control processes (Reczek et al. 2014; Umberson 1992, 1987), parents internalize norms and expectations associated with the social role of parenting. This could be a health-promoting process, as parents feel obligated to provide a safe and stable environment where their children may thrive (Reczek et al. 2014). It is normative, therefore, for parents to be nonsmokers and to reduce heavy alcohol use. Some research supports this idea of parenting as role enhancement. Parents often successfully quit smoking and reduce their alcohol consumption to serve as positive role models and to help ensure the safety of their children (Bottorff et al. 2006; Fingerhut, Kleinman, and Kendrick 1990). Parents may also feel social pressure to maintain health-promoting behaviors and instill regular routines that benefit health, such as preparing and consuming nutritious meals at specific times (Umberson, Crosnoe, and Reczek 2010).

By contrast, the presence of children and the associated expectations that come with parenting may serve as a source of health-compromising role strain (Umberson and Gove 1989), particularly within unions facing more socioeconomic and emotional adversity. In some cases, the presence of children is associated with increased economic hardship and a decrease in emotional support within unions (Ross, Mirowsky, and Goldsteen 1990). This could result in less time or motivation to promote health as well as unhealthy coping strategies to deal with the economic and emotional stressors associated with parenting (Umberson, Crosnoe, and Reczek 2010).

We focus on the health and behaviors of adults by union type and the presence of children, separately for men and women. First, men and women have very different distributions of health. For example, men generally engage more often in negative behaviors such as smoking and drinking excessive amounts of alcohol, whereas women are slightly more likely to be obese (Umberson 1992). Second, among different-sex married adults, men benefit disproportionately from entering marriage in part due to risky premarital health behaviors (i.e., heavy alcohol use) and by frequent health care maintenance responsibilities (i.e., encouraging regular medical checkups) from women (Umberson 1992). Moreover, the presence of children in the home has been shown to have more of an impact on women's health behaviors due to heavily gendered family norms (Nomaguchi and Milkie 2003). It is possible that same-sex coupled adults take more of an egalitarian approach to household labor (Courtenay 2000, Kurdek 2006; Reczek and Umberson 2012), which could extend to caregiving for children.

Objectives

Our primary objective here is to highlight similarities and differences both *within* and *across* partnership types—same- and different-sex—with and without children. Within relationship types, does the presence of children associate with greater obesity, lower smoking, and lower heavy alcohol use for partnered adults?

Across relationship types with or without children, are there differences in the likelihoods of obesity, smoking, and heavy alcohol use for partnered adults?

Data and Method

Data

Our analysis is based on combined data from the 2008 to 2016 years of the National Center for Health Statistics' (NCHS) National Health Interview Survey (NHIS), a cross-sectional survey aimed at understanding the correlates of health in the United States. The Integrated Health Interview Series (IHIS), through the Minnesota Population Center (MPC), streamlines an otherwise arduous data consistency process and provides the data files used here (Blewett et al. 2016).

The NHIS is a household-level survey allowing examination between married and unmarried couple types. There were no indicators of sexual attraction or identity in the NHIS until 2013, so for the current study, partnerships are identified by matching the sex of respondent variable with the relationship to householder variable (see Denney, Gorman, and Barrera 2013; Liu, Reczek, and Brown 2013 for similar approaches). Married couple households are identified by one male and one female reporting married status. Same-sex couples are identified by two men or women reporting as married or as unmarried partners, and cohabiting different-sex couples as a man and a woman reporting as unmarried partners. We limit the analyses to years after 2008, given concerns with identifying same-sex couples in the NHIS prior to 2008 (NCHS 2015).

Independent Variables

The NHIS household rosters also provide information to assess whether children under the age of eighteen reside in the household. We use information on relationship type and the presence of children to create six family types: different-sex married with and without children (referred to as married with and without children from here forward), same-sex couple with and without children, and different-sex cohabiting couple with and without children (henceforth, cohabitors with and without children).

Compiling the 2008 to 2016 Sample Adult files (SAF; containing a randomly selected adult from each household) of the NHIS resulted in 118,436 partnered adults age eighteen and older. Notably, there are 586 same-sex coupled men without children, 31 same-sex coupled men with children, 528 same-sex coupled women without children, and 185 same-sex coupled women with children. A small proportion of same-sex coupled adults reported being married at the time of the survey, 9.9 percent for men and 11.2 percent for women. In the analyses that follow, we do not distinguish married from cohabiting same-sex coupled adults due to sample size limitations and our desire to examine parents and non-parents separately and separately by gender.

Dependent Variables

Only the SAFs of the NHIS contain items on weight status, cigarette smoking, and alcohol consumption, our outcomes of interest. We exclude less than 1.0 percent of adults from our study that fell into the underweight category of body mass index (BMI) because they may have underlying illness that influences other covariates. Remaining adults are categorized into healthy weight (BMI of 18.5 to 24.9), overweight (BMI ≥25.0 and ≤29.9), and obese (BMI ≥30.0). For smoking, adults are categorized into never smoker (have not smoked 100 cigarettes in lifetime), former smoker (have smoked 100 cigarettes in lifetime but do not currently smoke), and current smoker (have smoked 100 cigarettes in lifetime and currently smoke every day or some days). For alcohol consumption, we categorize adults into never drinker (fewer than 12 drinks in lifetime), former drinker (12 or more drinks in lifetime but no drinks in past year), light to moderate drinker (current drinker who consumes 2 or fewer drinks per day for men and 1 or fewer per day for women), and heavy drinker, defined as a current drinker who consumes more than two drinks per day for men and more than one drink per day for women (U.S. DHHS 2013).

Control Variables

We include a diverse set of control variables including age and age-squared; race and ethnicity (non-Hispanic white; non-Hispanic black; non-Hispanic other; and Hispanic); region of residence (Northeast; Midwest; South; West); year of survey; educational attainment (high school or less; some college; bachelor's degree or more); and household poverty status (<100% Federal Poverty Line [FPL]; 100%–200% FPL; >200% FPL).

Method

We estimate weighted and survey-adjusted multinomial logistic regression models on multiply imputed data for each of the three outcomes. The NHIS generally has low rates of missing data. The income-to-poverty measure used to generate household poverty was missing for over 15 percent of our sample, so we use multiple imputation techniques to estimate values for our regression analyses (Royston 2005). The baseline categories for the outcomes in these regressions are healthy weight, never smoker, and light to moderate drinker, respectively, and all the estimates are in reference to married adults without children. Consistent with our objectives, we test average marginal effects (AME) by computing adjusted average probabilities using all observed data for hypothetical populations across each of the family types to isolate the influence of the family type characteristic. We then conduct pairwise comparisons of the difference in adjusted probabilities (i.e., the average marginal effects) for group 1 (e.g., different-sex married with children) versus group 2 (e.g., same-sex couple with children).

Results

We provide results separately for men and women. Table 5.1 (men) and table 5.2 (women) provide predicted probabilities calculated from the fully adjusted multinomial regressions of weight status, smoking status, and alcohol consumption for adults in the different family types. The tables also provide significance tests of pairwise comparisons. Each family type is assigned a letter (i.e., same-sex couple without children is designated as "c"). Letters in the significance column for each family type indicate a statistically significant difference at the $p \leq .05$ level between living in that family type versus the other listed family type. In the interest of space, we primarily discuss results for obesity, current smoking, and heavy drinking in the following sections.

Obesity

The results for obesity in panel A of tables 5.1 and 5.2 show that the presence of children, compared with those same union types that do not have children, is associated with higher probabilities of obesity for men and women in same-sex and different-sex cohabiting couples, but not in different-sex married couples. With the exception of same-sex coupled men, the differences are small, and they reach statistical significance only for different-sex cohabiting women with (.29) and without (.25) children. For different-sex married men and women, the adjusted probability of obesity is the same whether children are present or not. The difference for same-sex coupled men with (.32) and without (.20) children is large but does not reach significance due, in part, to large standard errors given their relatively small sample size.

Looking within union types without children, panel A of table 5.1 shows that same-sex coupled men are less likely obese than either their different-sex married or cohabiting counterparts. For men with children, different-sex cohabiting men are less likely obese than married men. Panel A of table 5.2 shows that same-sex coupled women are more likely obese than their different-sex coupled counterparts, regardless of the presence of children. For different-sex coupled women, those who cohabit with children are less likely than married women without children to be obese. But the opposite is true when different-sex coupled women have children—cohabiting women are more likely obese than married women.

Current Cigarette Smoking

Panel B of tables 5.1 and 5.2 provides the results for smoking status. Focusing on the probabilities for current smoking, table 5.1 shows that the presence of children, compared with the absence of children, is only associated with a lower probability of smoking for married men. In table 5.2, the probability of current

TABLE 5.1

Adjusted Probabilities and Pairwise Comparisons from Multinomial Logistic Regressions on Weight, Smoking, and Drinking Status for Men

Panel A. Weight status

	Healthy weight		Overweight		Obese	
Without children		Sig.		Sig.		Sig.
Different-sex married (a)	.24	b, c	.45	b	.31	b, c, f
Same sex (b)	.41	a, c, d, f	.39	a, c, f	.20	a, c, d, f
Different-sex cohabiting (c)	.29	a, b, d, f	.45	b	.26	a, b, d
With children						
Different-sex married (d)	.23	b, c, f	.46	b	.31	b, c, f
Same sex (e)	.28		.40		.32	
Different-sex cohabiting (f)	.26	b, d, c	.46	b	.28	a, b, d

Panel B. Smoking status

	Never		Former		Current	
Without children		Sig.		Sig.		Sig.
Different-sex married (a)	.53	b, c, d, f	.30	c, d, f	.17	b, c, d, e, f
Same sex (b)	.42	a, d	.28		.30	a, d
Different-sex cohabiting (c)	.44	a, d	.28	a, f	.28	a, d
With children						
Different-sex married (d)	.56	a, b, c, f	.29	a, f	.15	a, b, c, e, f
Same sex (e)	.40		.27		.34	a, d
Different-sex cohabiting (f)	.46	a, d	.25	a, c, d	.29	a, d

(continued)

Table 5.1. Adjusted Probabilities and Pairwise Comparisons from Multinomial Logistic Regressions on Weight, Smoking, and Drinking Status for Men (continued)

	Never	Sig.	Former	Sig.	Light to moderate	Sig.	Heavy	Sig.
				Panel C. Drinking status				
Without children								
Different-sex married (a)	.11	b, c, d, f	.14	d	.69	d, f	.05	b, c, d, f
Same sex (b)	.08	a, d	.12		.71		.09	a, d
Different-sex cohabiting (c)	.06	a, d	.13	d	.70	d	.10	a, d, f
With children								
Different-sex married (d)	.12	a, b, c, f	.16	a, c	.68	a, c, f	.04	a, b, c, f
Same sex (e)	.07		.14		.68		.12	
Different-sex cohabiting (f)	.06	a, d	.14		.72	a,d	.08	a, c, d

Source: National Health Interview Survey Sample Adult Files, 2008–2016 (Blewett et al. 2016).

Note: All results control for age, race, educational attainment, household poverty, region of residence, and year of survey. Letters indicate a significant difference between household types at the $p < .05$ level.

smoking status is lower for women in all couple types with children, compared with those without children, although evidence for statistical significance is found only for married women.

Looking within union types without children, tables 5.1 and 5.2 show that same-sex coupled and different-sex cohabiting men and women are both more likely to be current smokers than their married counterparts. This same pattern also holds in relationships that include children, with the largest differences shown for same-sex coupled men compared with married men with probabilities of current smoking at .34 and .15, respectively.

Heavy Drinking

Panel C of tables 5.1 and 5.2 provides the adjusted probabilities for drinking status and shows the strongest evidence of the possible health benefits of the presence of children. With the exception of same-sex coupled men, men and women in all union types have statistically significantly lower probabilities of heavy alcohol consumption when children are present than when they are not. This finding is most evident among women. The adjusted probabilities for heavy drinking among women without children in different-sex married, same-sex coupled, and different-sex cohabiting relationships are .06, .11, and .12, respectively. When children are present, those probabilities are significantly lower at .03, .05, and .05, respectively. For same-sex coupled men, however, the probability of heavy drinking is relatively high and not statistically different if children are present (.12) or absent (.09).

Within couple types without children, both men and women in same-sex and different-sex cohabiting relationships are more likely to be heavy drinkers than their married counterparts. This same pattern generally holds in households with children, though not all comparisons reach statistical significance.

Conclusions

The preceding analysis presents a more nuanced examination of health and behavioral profiles of adults in unions than found in most past research. The results provide some support for the idea that parenting can potentially improve the health and behaviors of adults (Reczek et al. 2014), but this is specific to the type of union and the outcome of interest. We discovered important nuances in health status by estimating average marginal effects and making statistical comparisons across and within diverse family formations, something that has been called for in the literature on same-sex relationships (Umberson et al. 2015). We conclude by discussing the relevance of the findings in understanding family contexts and adult health.

Overall, we find considerable heterogeneity in well-being by specific outcome, union type, the presence or absence of children, and gender. Consider the results for men without children that both confirm and question the long-held marital health advantage (Carr and Springer 2010). After important adjustments, men partnered with men and men cohabiting with women are both *less* likely to be obese than men married to women. However, these same comparisons yield opposite results for current smoking status and heavy drinking—married men without children are less likely than their same-sex coupled and cohabiting counterparts to smoke cigarettes and drink heavily. These same results persist in households with children, indicating that, at least for current smoking and heavy drinking, married men fare better than men in other types of unions.

A similar pattern of smoking and drinking emerges for partnered women: married women are less likely than same-sex coupled and cohabiting women to currently smoke and drink heavily. But the advantage of marriage for health is

TABLE 5.2

Adjusted Predicted Probabilities and Pairwise Comparisons from Multinomial Logistic Regressions on Weight, Smoking, and Drinking Status for Women

Panel A. Weight status

	Healthy weight		*Overweight*		*Obese*	
Without children		Sig.		Sig.		Sig.
Different-sex married (a)	.42	b, c, e, f	.31		.27	b, c, e, f
Same sex (b)	.32	a, c, d, f	.29		.39	a, c, d, f
Different-sex cohabiting (c)	.46	a, b, d, e, f	.29	d, f	.25	a, b, d, e, f
With children						
Different-sex married (d)	.41	b, c, e, f	.32	c	.27	b, c, e, f
Same sex (e)	.30	a, c, d, f	.30		.40	a, c, d, f
Different-sex cohabiting (f)	.38	a, b, c, d, e	.32	c	.29	a, b, c, d, e

Panel B. Smoking status

	Never		*Former*		*Current*	
Without children		Sig.		Sig.		Sig.
Different-sex married (a)	.66	b, c, d, e, f	.21	b, e	.14	b, c, d, f
Same sex (b)	.52	a, d	.26	a, c, d, e	.22	a, c, d
Different-sex cohabiting (c)	.54	a, d, e	.20	b, e, f	.26	a, b, d, e
With children						
Different-sex married (d)	.69	a, b, c, e, f	.20	b, e, f	.11	a, b, c, e, f
Same sex (e)	.45	a, c, d	.37	a, b, c, d, f	.19	c, d
Different-sex cohabiting (f)	.53	a, d	.23	c, d, e	.24	a, d

(continued)

Table 5.2. Adjusted Predicted Probabilities and Pairwise Comparisons from Multinomial Logistic Regressions on Weight, Smoking, and Drinking Status for Women (continued)

	Never	Sig.	Former	Sig.	Light to moderate	Sig.	Heavy	Sig.
Without children		Sig.		Sig.		Sig.		Sig.
Different-sex married (a)	.22	b, c, d, e, f	.13	c, d	.59	b, c, d, f	.06	b, c, d
Same sex (b)	.11	a, d	.12		.66	a, d	.11	a, d, e, f
Different-sex cohabiting (c)	.11	a, d, f	.11	a, d, f	.66	a, d	.12	a, d, e, f
With children								
Different-sex married (d)	.25	a, b, c, e, f	.14	a, c	.58	a, b, c, f	.03	a, b, c, f
Same sex (e)	.13	a, d	.17		.65		.05	b, c
Different-sex cohabiting (f)	.14	a, c, d	.13	c	.67	a, d	.05	b, c, d

Panel C. Drinking status

Source: National Health Interview Survey Sample Adult Files, 2008–2016 (Blewett et al. 2016).

Note: All results control for age, race, educational attainment, household poverty, region of residence, and year of survey. Letters indicate a significant difference between household types at the $p < .05$ level.

questioned again for partnered women when considering weight status and the presence of children. Women married to men are more likely to be obese than women cohabiting with men when children are absent from the household. Same-sex partnered women, however, are more likely to be obese than either women married to men or women cohabiting with men. Indeed, the adjusted probability of obesity for same-sex partnered women with or without children remains higher at .40. This may highlight the unique contributions of sexual minority status (Meyer 2003) as a possible contributor to ill health. It could also be that women partnered with women more accurately report their weight, possibly because these women have a higher satisfaction with their current weight status than women partnered with men.

Previous research suggests that the presence of children in unions may lead to role strain from the social expectations and obligations of parenting as well as economic and social support stressors, leading, for example, to greater risk of obesity when children are present than when they are not (Umberson, Crosnoe, and Reczek 2010). For the most part, however, we find no differences or small increases in the likelihood of obesity by union types that include children, compared with those that do not. An exception may include men partnered with other men, where the differences were large but did not reach significance. For these men, the presence of children may add unique temporal stressors, reducing opportunities to exercise or increasing unhealthy eating habits, or through unique processes of stigma and discrimination toward these families (Meyer 2003; Powell et al. 2010).

Further, we find mixed support for indirect social control perspectives that suggest lower probabilities of health-compromising behaviors among partnered adults with children than among partnered adults without children. For example, cigarette smoking was lower for married men and women with children than for adults in those kinds of unions that did not include children. Children in these unions may inhibit adults from smoking in ways consistent with indirect social control and positive role-modeling perspectives. However, children had no clear associations with smoking for men and women in other relationship types. The clearest evidence of the presence of children promoting health is in the results for heavy alcohol use. In every union type except for same-sex partnered men, the presence of children is associated with a lower probability of heavy alcohol use compared with unions that did not include children. The results for same-sex partnered men on heavy alcohol use add to health-compromising behaviors for these men and, once again, suggest that future work needs to illuminate the family context, including the presence of children, and how family types are associated with same-sex partnered adult health (Umberson et al. 2015).

Overall, the NHIS data provide a large enough sample to investigate detailed differences by union type and presence of children, offering several strengths over previous research and highlighting several areas for future investigation. We were restricted, however, by a relatively small number of adults in some of the same-sex couple types and by an inability to further disaggregate by same-sex married and cohabiting couple types. As more years of NHIS data become available, separating same-sex married and cohabiting adults will afford an opportunity to assess whether marriage benefits health in similar or different ways for same-sex and different-sex married adults. The NHIS is also limited by a lack of family history information to fully consider how and when different family types were formed, a lack of information on relationship quality and duration, social support, and stigma, discrimination and minority stress that may contribute to disparities across groups. With regard to weight status, we examine only partnered adults, and it may be that these adults less often employ strategies to lose weight and by varying degrees depending on the type of relationship. Without data on weight history, we are unable to investigate these possibilities. Measurement issues also present special challenges in how, and even if, children in the home are recorded in a manner that would capture the parent/child relationship in same-sex couples, especially for children who are not the legal or biological kin of the adult in the survey (Baumle and Compton 2014).

In all, our results provide evidence that union type and the presence of children are important for understanding adult health. In their influential book *Counted Out*, Powell and colleagues (2010) describe an overall increase in public acceptance of same-sex families with children. Yet, even after the U.S. Supreme Court decision to eliminate the Defense of Marriage Act, and increasing public support for same-sex marriage, gaps in acceptance of same-sex families with children, and particularly those headed by men, remain. These differences likely contribute to health and behavior differences across groups and will evolve over time with diversifying social and legal environments for families.

ACKNOWLEDGMENTS

The first author acknowledges support from the Health Disparities Scholar Program with the National Institute on Minority Health Disparities (NIMHD), National Institutes of Health (NIH). The opinions and conclusions expressed herein are solely those of the authors and should not be construed as representing the opinions or policies of the NIMHD or NIH.

REFERENCES

Baumle, Amanda K., and D'Lane R. Compton. 2014. "Identity versus Identification: How LGBTQ Parents Identify Their Children on Census Surveys." *Journal of Marriage and Family* 76 (1): 94–104.

Blewett, Lynn A., Julia A. Rivera Drew, Risa Griffin, Miriam L. King, and Kari C. W. Williams. 2016. IPUMS Health Surveys: National Health Interview Survey, Version 6.2. Edited by University of Minnesota, Minneapolis, MN.

Bottorff, Joan L, John Oliffe, Cecilia Kalaw, Joanne Carey, and Lawrence Mroz. 2006. "Men's Constructions of Smoking in the Context of Women's Tobacco Reduction during Pregnancy and Postpartum." *Social Science and Medicine* 62 (12): 3096–3108.

Bowen, Deborah J., Kimberly F. Balsam, and Samantha R Ender. 2008. "A Review of Obesity Issues in Sexual Minority Women." *Obesity* 16 (2): 221–228.

Carr, Deborah, and Kristen W. Springer. 2010. "Advances in Families and Health Research in the 21st Century." *Journal of Marriage and Family* 72: 743–761.

Centers for Disease Control and Prevention (CDC). 2014. "Fact Sheets—Alcohol Use and Health." CDC. Accessed February 7, 2018. Retrieved from https://www.cdc.gov/alcohol/fact-sheets/alcohol-use.htm.

Courtenay, Will H. 2000. "Constructions of Masculinity and their Influence on Men's Well-being: A Theory of Gender and Health." *Social Science & Medicine* 50 (10): 1385–1401.

Denney, Justin T., Bridget K. Gorman, and Cristina B. Barrera. 2013. "Families, Resources, and Adult Health: Where Do Sexual Minorities Fit?" *Journal of Health and Social Behavior* 54 (1): 46–63.

Deputy, Nicholas P., and Ulrike Boehmer. 2010. "Determinants of Body Weight among Men of Different Sexual Orientation." *Preventative Medicine* 51 (2): 129–131.

Dermody, Sarah S., Michael P. Marshal, JeeWon Cheong, Chad Burton, Tonda Hughes, Frances Aranda, and Mark S. Friedman. 2014. "Longitudinal Disparities of Hazardous Drinking between Sexual Minority and Heterosexual Individuals from Adolescence to Young Adulthood." *Journal of Youth and Adolescence* 43 (1): 30–39.

Dilley, Julia A., Katrina W. Simmons, Michael J. Boysun, Barbara A. Pizacani, and Mike J. Stark. 2010. "Demonstrating the Importance and Feasibility of Including Sexual Orientation in Public Health Surveys: Health Disparities in the Pacific Northwest." *American Journal of Public Health* 100 (3): 460–467.

Fingerhut, Lois A., Joel C. Kleinman, and Juliette S. Kendrick. 1990. "Smoking before, during, and after Pregnancy." *American Journal of Public Health* 80 (5): 541–544.

Institute of Medicine (IOM). 2011. *The Health of Lesbian, Gay, Bisexual, and Transgender People: Building a Foundation for Better Understanding.* Washington, DC: National Institutes of Health.

Kurdek, Lawrence A. 2006. "Differences Between Partners from Heterosexual, Gay, and Lesbian Cohabiting Couples." *Journal of Marriage and Family* 68 (2): 509–528.

Lau, Charles Q. 2012. "The Stability of Same-Sex Cohabitation, Different-Sex Cohabitation, and Marriage." *Journal of Marriage and Family* 74: 973–988.

Liu, Hui, Corinne Reczek, and Dustin Brown. 2013. "Same-Sex Cohabitors and Health: The Role of Race/Ethnicity, Gender, and Socioeconomic Status." *Journal of Health and Social Behavior* 54 (1): 24–45.

Meyer, Ilan H. 2003. "Prejudice, Social Stress, and Mental Health in Lesbian, Gay, and Bisexual Populations: Conceptual Issues and Research Evidence." *Psychological Bulletin* 129 (5): 674–697.

Meyler, Deanna, Jim P. Stimpson, and Kristen M. Peek. 2007. "Health Concordance Within Couples: A Systematic Review." *Social Science & Medicine* 64 (11): 2297–2310.

National Center for Health Statistics (NCHS). 2015. *Changes to Data Editing Procedures and the Impact on Identifying Same-Sex Married Couples: 2004–2007 National Health Interview Survey* (National Health Interview Survey April 2015 Report). Hyattsville, MD: National Center for Health Statistics. Retrieved from https://www.cdc.gov/nchs/data/nhis/samesexedits.pdf.

Nomaguchi, Kei M., and Melissa A. Milkie. 2003. "Costs and Rewards of Children: The Effects of Becoming a Parent on Adults' Lives." *Journal of Marriage and Family* 65 (2): 356–374.

Powell, Brian, Catherine Bolzendahl, Claudia Geist, and Lala Carr Steelman. 2010. *Counted Out: Same-Sex Relations and Americans' Definitions of Family, Rose Series in Sociology.* New York: Russell Sage Foundation.

Reczek, Corinne, Hui Liu, and Dustin Brown. 2014. "Cigarette Smoking in Same-Sex and Different-Sex Unions: The Role of Socioeconomic and Psychological Factors." *Population Research and Policy Review* 33: 527–551.

Reczek, Corinne, Mieke Beth Thomeer, Amy C. Lodge, Debra Umberson, and Megan Underhill. 2014. "Diet and Exercise in Parenthood: A Social Control Perspective." *Journal of Marriage and Family* 76 (5): 1047–1062.

Reczek, C., and D. Umberson. 2012. "Gender, Health Behavior, and Intimate Relationships: Lesbian, Gay, and Straight Contexts." *Social Science & Medicine* 74 (1): 1783–1790.

Ross, Catherine E., John Mirowsky, and Karen Goldsteen. 1990. "The Impact of the Family on Health: Decade in Review." *Journal of Marriage and the Family* 52: 1059–1078.

Royston, Patrick. 2005. "Multiple Imputation of Missing Values: Update." *The Stata Journal* 5 (2): 188–201.

Tang, Hao, Greg L. Greenwood, David W. Cowling, Jon C. Lloyd, April G. Roeseler, and Dileep G. Bal. 2004. "Cigarette Smoking among Lesbians, Gays, and Bisexuals: How Serious a Problem? (United States)." *Cancer Causes and Control* 15 (8): 797–803.

Umberson, Debra. 1987. "Family Status and Health Behaviors: Social Control as a Dimension of Social Integration." *Journal of Health and Social Behavior* 28 (3): 306–319.

Umberson, Debra. 1992. "Gender, Marital Status, and the Social Control of Health Behavior." *Social Science & Medicine* 34: 907–917.

Umberson, Debra, Robert Crosnoe, and Corinne Reczek. 2010. "Social Relationships and Health Behaviors across the Life Course." *Annual Review of Sociology* 36: 139–157.

Umberson, Debra, and Walter R. Gove. 1989. "Parenthood and Psychological Well-Being Theory, Measurement, and Stage in the Family Life Course." *Journal of Family Issues* 10 (4): 440–462.

Umberson, Debra, Mieke Beth Thomeer, Rhiannon A. Kroeger, Amy C. Lodge, and Minle Xu. 2015. "Challenges and Opportunities for Research on Same-Sex Relationships." *Journal of Marriage and Family* 77 (1): 96–111.

U.S. Department of Health and Human Services (U.S. DHHS). 2013. *Healthy People 2020.* Available at www.healthypeople.gov. Washington, DC: Office of Disease Prevention and Health Promotion.

6

Couples' Conjoint Work Hours and Health Behaviors

Do Gender and Sexual Identity Matter?

WEN FAN

Despite widespread knowledge regarding the deleterious effects of smoking and insufficient sleep, a significant proportion of the U.S. population engages in these unhealthy behaviors (Schoenborn, Adams, and Peregoy 2013). To explain this puzzle, scholars have proposed a range of social factors that may constrain individuals' ability to lead a healthy life; long working hours is one such factor (Artazcoz et al. 2009). Indeed, internationally, Americans work longer hours compared with those in other industrialized countries, and given the growing number of U.S. workers who are stressed because of time pressures (Jacobs and Gerson 2004), it is critical to understand health behavioral consequences associated with work hours.

Existing research on the relationship between work hours and health behaviors, however, is limited in two ways. First, most investigations adopt a highly individualized approach—focusing on individual workers exclusively. Few studies have looked at couples' conjoint work hours (c.f., Fan et al. 2015; Kleiner and Pavalko 2014). Second, the current literature has either focused exclusively on different-sex couples or been inattentive to respondents' sexual identity, even as same-sex couples offer a theoretically interesting case to examine inquiries that are central to the sociology of health as well as research on work and family. A long-held tenet in sociology of the family, for example, is that the family is a battlefield of power with husbands typically gaining more than do their wives (Berk 1985). With two persons of the same sex, however, there is no default way to expect who does what; a different household arrangement and specialization may emerge, which may have implications for their health behaviors.

Drawing on couple data (different-sex and same-sex married or cohabiting couples) constructed from the 1997–2003 and 2008–2017 Integrated Health Interview Series (IHIS), this research addresses two questions. First, how do couples' conjoint work arrangements—in terms of employment status and work hours—shape their health behaviors (smoking and sleeping)? Second, do the relationships between couples' work arrangements and health behaviors vary by the intersection of gender and sexual identity? Building on the literature on family economics, sexual identity, intersectionality, and time use, this study makes two contributions. First, in light of the ever complex family dynamics, this is the first study that links work time and health behaviors in the context of different-sex and same-sex couples. Previous studies (e.g., Liu, Reczek, and Brown 2013; Reczek, Liu, and Brown 2014; Reczek and Umberson 2012) have laid a solid foundation by examining how self-reported health or health behaviors differ by sexual identity, but whether such variation extends to the relationship between couples' work time and health behaviors has not been investigated. My findings reveal the intersectionality of gender and sexual identity in shaping health-related behaviors. In particular, the findings point to the disadvantage of different-sex couples located in the wife-breadwinning arrangement as well as women (regardless of sexual identity) in couples where both partners work long hours. Second, from a practical point of view, understanding the work-place and family antecedents of health behaviors and their contingency on gen-der and sexual identity is a necessary first step to devise corresponding policies to promote healthy behaviors and to improve population health.

Work Time and Health Behaviors

I examine two health behaviors: smoking and sleep (sleep hours and sleep-related problems)—selected because of their close relationships with work time through a time-based or a stress-based mechanism. First, from a time availabil-ity point of view, the time constraint faced by everyone is fixed: There are only twenty-four hours a day. More hours spent on jobs means fewer hours left for family and personal life. This time constraint may affect sleep in particular given that sleeping requires focused time commitment that cannot be easily combined with work and family role obligations. A second mechanism is that deviation from a normative work-hour arrangement—positive or negative—is a potential stressor that may lead to sleep-related problems or induce coping behaviors such as smoking. For example, those who are marginally attached to the labor market—especially heterosexual men for whom the male-breadwinning ideol-ogy is the strongest—may resort to unhealthy coping strategies such as smoking to alleviate stress (Courtenay 2000). Likewise, long work hours can result in stress by creating time pressure.

Empirical evidence regarding the relationship between work hours and health behaviors is mixed (Artazcoz et al. 2009; Grzywacz and Marks 2001). One reason for the conflicting findings may have to do with their lack of attention to the larger context of couple time availability. Only a few studies have incorpo-rated spouses' work hours. One example is Kleiner and Pavalko (2014), who showed that, net of own work hours, compared with men whose wives work forty hours per week or part-time, men whose wives work moderately long hours (41–49) are less likely to exercise, but men whose wives work very long hours (50+) exercise at similar levels. Fan et al. (2015) examined the health behavioral effects of couples' conjoint work hours, finding that conventional breadwinning arrangements (i.e., husbands working longer hours than wives) constrain women's but facilitate men's exercise behaviors. These two studies are important improvements, but both were conducted in the context of different-sex couples. What pattern would emerge for same-sex couples is unclear, a gap this study begins to fill.

Couples' Conjoint Work Hours and Health Behaviors: Gender and Sexual Identity Differences

Following Moen and Sweet (2003) and Fan et al. (2015), I conceptualize work time as a couple-level construct by distinguishing four substantively meaningful groups: (1) respondent primary breadwinner (respondent long hours, spouse not working or working fewer hours), (2) spouse primary breadwinner (spouse long hours, respondent not working or working fewer hours), (3) moderate commitments (both lower hours), and (4) high commitments (both long hours). I expect the relationship between couples' work time arrangements and health behaviors to be moderated by the intersection of gender and sexual identity as they determine expectations around domestic and family care work, family behaviors such as having children, and occupations, among other factors. Therefore, the extent to which one could bargain out of the responsibilities associated with these expectations (the time availability mechanism), as well as to what extent low or long work hours are considered normative or experienced as stressful (the stress mechanism), will differ across the four gender/sexual-identity groups. Accordingly, my discussion and empirical analysis below will be presented separately for each of the four groups.

For straight men, it is considered normative to work longer hours than do their wives (Townsend 2002), given gendered expectations regarding breadwinning and homemaking roles. Wives' home production such as child care also frees straight men up to have more time availability to themselves. Therefore, straight men in couple dyads that conform to (neo-)traditional expectations—those who work long hours but have wives working fewer hours or not employed—are at lower risk of unhealthy behaviors. Conversely, straight men who violate (neo-)traditional expectations (working fewer hours than their wives) may compensate by resorting to health risk behaviors such as smoking to enact masculinity (Courtenay 2000).

Unlike their male counterparts, straight women usually have to juggle time demands from both the work and family domains (Mattingly and Bianchi 2003), which may translate into inadequate sleep time and heightened stress. This might be especially the case for breadwinning straight women, who theoretically could use their bargaining power to offload housework to their husbands but usually do not do so due to gender norms (Bittman et al. 2003). Indeed, husbands' share of housework remains low even in households where women spend more time than their husbands in paid work (Tichenor 2005). Therefore, I expect straight women who are at odds with conventional expectations (i.e., working long hours while their husbands do not) to have insufficient sleep time and to be more likely to smoke due to the strain resulting from their high obligations on both home and job fronts. Likewise, straight women located in dual high-commitment couples (i.e., both working long hours) may also engage in these unhealthy behaviors given the heightened stress resulting from conflicts between work and home.

For same-sex relationships, a "natural" starting point and social norms do not exist to guide the initial household division of labor. Compared with different-sex couples, gay men and lesbian women are arguably less constrained by the gendered expectation of breadwinning and homemaking roles. Time spent on housework and child care, for example, is more equal among same-sex couples than among their heterosexual counterparts (Bauer 2016). Reczek and Umberson (2012) also showed that whereas straight women performed the bulk of health behavior work, gay and lesbian respondents engaged in cooperative health behavior work, in which partners mutually influence one another's health behaviors. In addition, given that same-sex couples are less likely to have children than are different-sex couples, they may have more time available to themselves. Combined, in the absence of well-defined gender norms, I expect time availability to dominate, with men and women in same-sex couples who are the primary breadwinner or who are located in the high-commitments arrangement more likely to engage in unhealthy behaviors. This pattern might be accentuated for lesbians, who are likely pressured to compensate for the lost earnings a male partner would bring, given that men earn more than do women regardless of sexual identity.

Taken as a whole, my hypotheses are as follows (note that I use "moderate commitments" as the reference group, which tends to exhibit the healthiest behaviors; see Fan et al. 2015):

> *Hypothesis 1 (respondent primary breadwinner)*: The relationship between being a primary breadwinner and adverse health behaviors is strongest for straight women and weakest for straight men, with gay men and lesbians in between.
>
> *Hypothesis 2 (spouse primary breadwinner)*: The relationship between having a spouse who is the primary breadwinner and adverse health behaviors is strongest for straight men and weakest for straight women, with gay men and lesbians in between.

Hypothesis 3 (high commitments): The relationship between the high-commitments arrangement and adverse health behaviors is strongest for lesbians and straight women, compared with straight men or gay men.

Data, Measures, and Methods

Data

I draw on the 1997–2003 and 2008–2017 Integrated Health Interview Series (IHIS) to answer my research questions. The IHIS provides harmonized data and documentation based on the public-use files of the National Health Interview Survey (NHIS). Conducted continuously since 1957, the NHIS is a large-scale household survey. Each year, the NHIS collects data from a representative sample of the U.S. civilian noninstitutionalized population, with the annual response rate close to 90 percent for eligible households. From 1997, one adult in every household was randomly selected to receive the Sample Adult questionnaire for additional health-related questions including health behaviors.

My analytic sample includes pooled surveys spanning 1997–2003 and 2008–2017. I remove years 2004–2007 because of potential errors in identifying same-sex married couples during these survey years (National Center for Health Statistics 2015). Given my couple focus, I include only respondents who are married or cohabiting with a partner. I remove respondents who are not in the sample adult file, because information key to this study—health behaviors—was not collected. The sample is further restricted to individuals of prime working age (25 through 59) to avoid conflating not working and retirement. Finally, I remove couples in which neither spouse or partner has a paid job (about 4%), reasoning that this group may consist of highly selective individuals in terms of health or socioeconomic status.

To identify couples, I use the variable SPLOC constructed by the Minnesota Population Center indicating whether the respondent's spouse or partner lived in the same household and, if so, the person number of the spouse or partner within that household. Respondents were then coded as gays or lesbians if the reported sex was the same as that of their spouse or partner.

Measures

I examine three outcomes. Smoking is a dichotomous measure that takes the value of 1 if the respondent smoked cigarettes at the time of the survey and 0 otherwise. Lack of sleep is based on the question "On average, how many hours of sleep do you get in a 24-hour period?" Respondents are considered having insufficient sleep time if they reported less than seven hours of sleep (the recommended amount of sleep is 7–9 hours by the National Sleep Foundation). Excessive sleep time is also unhealthy, but given the small number of respondents who reported more than nine hours of sleep (2%), I do not further distinguish this group.

Sleep-related problems is the sum of three variables, which measure the number of times during the past week (ranging from 0 to 7) respondents had trouble falling asleep, had trouble staying asleep, and woke up feeling rested (reverse coded). Higher values indicate more sleep-related problems. Cronbach's alpha is .69.

My key explanatory variable is couple-level work arrangements, a categorical variable consisting of four substantively meaningful groups: (1) respondent primary breadwinner (respondent working and spouse not working, or both working but respondent ≥45 hours/week and spouse <45 hours/week), (2) spouse primary breadwinner (spouse working and respondent not working, or both working but respondent <45 hours/week and spouse ≥45 hours/week), (3) moderate commitments (both <45 hours/week), and (4) high commitments (both ≥45 hours/week). I chose 45 hours/week because it is a meaningful distinction between a normative number of full-time hours and long hours (for similar use, see Moen and Sweet 2003), and to ensure I have a sufficient number of respondents in each group.

All models control for age, age squared, race (non-Hispanic white, non-Hispanic black, Hispanic, and others), nativity, marital status (married vs. cohabiting), number of children (younger than 18, top coded at 4), presence of a preschool-aged child (younger than 6), and presence of older adults (65 or older). Socioeconomic status is adjusted for through education, income, and occupation. Both respondents' and their spouse's or partner's educational attainment is measured through a set of dichotomous variables: less than high school (reference), high school, some college, and college or more. To account for the roughly 18 percent of NHIS respondents who miss information on household income, the National Center for Health Statistics uses multiple imputation to create five versions of imputed income. These five versions, after log transformation to account for the skewed distribution, are combined along with other variables to form a single completed data set. Occupation is a forty-two-category variable created by Minnesota Population Center that is comparable across years. It is a modified version of the 1995 revised Standard Occupational Classification–based codes. I add a separate category to denote respondents who were unemployed or out of the labor force at the time of the survey. To capture work demands, I control for both respondent's and spouse's or partner's work hours. To address health selection, I adjust for both respondent's and spouse's or partner's self-reported health (a five-point measure from poor to excellent). I also control for survey-year fixed effects as well as a variable specifying which of the four census regions respondents resided in: Northeast (reference), North Central/Midwest, South, and West.

Methods

As described, the National Center for Health Statistics multiply imputed five versions of household income. These imputed data are combined, and I apply standard multiple imputation procedures to obtain relevant estimates. Missing values do not exceed 1 percent for any other variable used in this study. I therefore apply listwise deletion to deal with missingness on those variables. Binary logit regression models are used to predict smoking and lack of sleep; for sleep-related problems, a count variable, I use negative binomial regression models. All analyses are weighted to incorporate the sampling design of the survey.

Given my focus on differences by gender and sexual identity, models are presented first for the overall sample and then for each of the four groups: straight men, gay men, straight women, and lesbians. To determine whether the associations between couples' conjoint work time and health behaviors are significantly different across these four groups, I provide in table 6.1 pairwise comparison results based on interaction models (between work-time arrangements and gender/sexual-identity groups). These interaction models are not presented for the sake of space but are available upon request.

Results

When work-time arrangements are evaluated at the couple level, two descriptive findings are worth noting (results not shown). First, gender-based specialization is clearly evident among different-sex couples. Almost half of straight men (45%) are in couples where they work long hours (≥45) and their spouses or partners work fewer hours, compared with just 11 percent to 24 percent for the other groups. Correspondingly, straight women are concentrated in the "spouse breadwinner" category (47% vs. 12%–25% for the other groups). Second, same-sex couples are more likely to consist of both spouses or partners working similar hours. For example, the "high commitments" arrangement, where both spouses or partners work at least forty-five hours per week, is more prevalent among gay (16%) and lesbian (12%) couples than among different-sex couples (8%).

In table 6.1, I present estimates from binary logit models predicting smoking (models 1–5) and inadequate sleep time (models 6–10), as well as estimates from negative binomial models predicting sleep problems (models 11–15). Positive coefficients indicate higher and negative coefficients indicate lower odds of unhealthy behaviors (smoking, sleeping inadequately, and more sleep problems). All groups combined, respondents in the "moderate commitments" arrangement (both working less than forty-five hours per week) have the healthiest behaviors. Compared with respondents in this arrangement, those who put in long hours on the job, whereas their spouses or partners do not, are more likely to smoke (.06, $p < .05$, model 1), have inadequate sleep hours (.13, $p < .001$, model 6), and report more sleep problems (.08, $p < .001$, model 11). Similarly, respondents in couples where their spouses or partners work longer hours than themselves are more likely to sleep inadequate hours (.10, $p < .01$, model 6) and report sleep

TABLE 6.1

Estimates from Binary Logit and Negative Binomial Regression Models Predicting Unhealthy Behaviors, Overall and by Gender and Sexual Identity

Variables		Panel A. Smoking			
	Overall	Straight men	Gay men	Straight women	Lesbians
	Model 1	Model 2	Model 3	Model 4	Model 5
Couple's conjoint work hours (ref. = moderate commitments)					
Respondent breadwinner	.06*	.05[c]	.73*	.13*[a]	−.23
	(.03)	(.04)	(.37)	(.05)	(.44)
Spouse breadwinner	.05	.03	.15[d]	.12**	−.50[b]
	(.03)	(.06)	(.42)	(.04)	(.53)
High commitments	.06+	−.02[c]	−.09	.13*[a]	−.03
	(.04)	(.05)	(.53)	(.06)	(.51)
Observations	123,588	65,179	627	57,049	682

Variables		Panel B. Inadequate sleep hours			
	Overall	Straight men	Gay men	Straight women	Lesbians
	Model 6	Model 7	Model 8	Model 9	Model 10
Couple's conjoint work hours (ref. = moderate commitments)					
Respondent breadwinner	.13***	.11*[c]	−.68	.21***[a]	.99*
	(.03)	(.04)	(.45)	(.06)	(.49)
Spouse breadwinner	.10**	.17*	−.23	.10*	.24
	(.04)	(.07)	(.55)	(.05)	(.43)
High commitments	.13**	.14*	−1.29*[d]	.12*	.85+[b]
	(.04)	(.06)	(.57)	(.06)	(.50)
Observations	66,862	35,192	438	30,717	498

(continued)

Table 6.1. Estimates from Binary Logit and Negative Binomial Regression Models Predicting Unhealthy Behaviors, Overall and by Gender and Sexual Identity (continued)

| | | Panel C. Sleep-related problems | | | |
	Overall	Straight men	Gay men	Straight women	Lesbians
	Model 11	Model 12	Model 13	Model 14	Model 15
Couple's conjoint work hours (ref. = moderate commitments)					
Respondent breadwinner	.08***	.08**c	−.54*c	.09**a, b	.13
	(.02)	(.03)	(.23)	(.03)	(.21)
Spouse breadwinner	.09***	.17***c	−.08	.09***a	.06
	(.02)	(.04)	(.21)	(.03)	(.19)
High commitments	.11***	.09*	−.17	.14***	−.02
	(.02)	(.04)	(.24)	(.04)	(.26)
Observations	34,841	18,443	255	15,831	309

Source: 1997–2003 and 2008–2017 Integrated Health Interview Series.

Notes: 1. All models control for age, age squared, race-ethnicity, nativity, marital status, number of children living at home, presence of a preschool-aged child, presence of older adults, respondent's and spouse's or partner's educational attainment, household income (logged), occupation, respondent's work hours (linear and squared), spouse's or partner's work hours, respondent's and spouse's or partner's self-reported health, year dummies, and region. These estimates are not shown for simplicity.

2. I use interaction models to test for differences in the relationship between couples' conjoint work hours and health behaviors by the intersection of gender and sexual identity. Results are shown in superscripts:[a] ($p < .05$ compared with straight men),[b] ($p < .05$ compared with gay men),[c] ($p < .05$ compared with straight women),[d] ($p < .05$ compared with lesbians).

3. Sample sizes differ across outcomes because information on smoking was collected since 1997, information on sleep hours was collected since 2004, and information on sleep-related problems was collected since 2013.

*** $p < .001$, ** $p < .01$, * $p < .05$, + $p < .1$

problems (.09, $p < .001$, model 11). Lastly, respondents in couples where both work long hours are more likely to report lack of sleep (.13, $p < .01$, model 6) and have more sleep problems (.11, $p < .001$, model 11), compared with respondents in the "moderate commitments" arrangement.

The relationships between couples' conjoint work hours and health behaviors, however, differ by gender and sexual identity. Below, for each of the four gender/sexual-identity groups, I highlight key differences as compared with the overall sample and then discuss results from interaction models. For straight men, couples' conjoint work hours do not predict smoking (model 2) but are a strong predictor of sleep. In particular, unlike the pattern found for the overall sample, being a secondary breadwinner is associated with the highest odds of inadequate sleep time (.17, $p < .05$, model 7) and sleep problems (.17, $p < .001$, model 12). For gay men, compared with the "moderate commitments" arrangement, primary breadwinning is associated with higher odds of smoking (.73, $p < .05$, model 3) but also fewer sleep-related problems (-.54, $p < .05$, model 13). Additionally, contrary to the overall sample, for gay men the "high commitments" arrangement is associated with the lowest odds of inadequate sleep time (–1.29, $p < .05$, model 8).

For straight women, being a primary breadwinner is associated with the highest odds of smoking (.13, $p < .05$, model 4) and insufficient sleep hours (.21, $p < .001$, model 9); it also predicts more sleep-related problems (.09, $p < .01$, model 14). Similarly, straight women in couples where both work long hours are more likely to smoke (.13, $p < .05$, model 4), have inadequate sleep hours (.12, $p < .05$, model 9), and report more sleep-related problems (.14, $p < .001$, model 14). For lesbians, couples' conjoint work hours do not predict smoking or sleep-related problems, but being a primary breadwinner is associated with higher odds of insufficient sleep hours (.99, $p < .05$, model 10) compared with the "moderate commitments" arrangement.

Interaction models (results not shown but available upon request) reveal three key findings. First, the arrangement in which respondents put in at least forty-five hours whereas the spouse or partner works less than forty-five hours is more health damaging for straight women compared with straight men across all three outcomes. This "respondent breadwinning" arrangement is also associated with healthier behaviors for gay men than for straight men, for the outcome of sleep-related problems. Second, the "spouse breadwinning" arrangement is associated with unhealthy behaviors for men—straight and gay. It predicts significantly higher odds of smoking for gay men than for lesbians and significantly more sleep problems for straight men than for straight women. Third, women seem to suffer from the "high commitments" arrangement regardless of sexual identity. This arrangement is associated with significantly higher odds of smoking for straight women compared with straight men, as well as significantly higher odds of inadequate sleep time for lesbians than for gay men.

Conclusions

With same-sex marriage gaining legal recognition in the United States in 2015, more U.S. couples will consist of two individuals of the same sex. Empirical studies of this population, however, are falling behind. Drawing on nationally representative survey data over two decades, this study investigates how the relationships between couples' conjoint work hours and health behaviors are contingent on gender and sexual identity; by doing so, it deepens understanding regarding family economics, gender inequality, time use, and health. Below I summarize key findings and discuss their relevance to theory and practice.

As expected in hypotheses 1 and 2, different-sex couples suffer from deviation from the (neo-)traditional arrangement of husband breadwinning. Although for both straight men and straight women, the "respondent breadwinner" arrangement is associated with less healthy behaviors compared with the "moderate commitments" arrangement, this relationship is significantly stronger for straight women. Conversely, having a spouse who is the primary breadwinner is associated with more health-risky behaviors for straight men than for straight women. In other words, straight couples in the female-breadwinning arrangement exhibit the unhealthiest behaviors, indicating the power of traditional gender norms in shaping behaviors. Given the costs associated with smoking and lack of sleep, public policies and programs designed to promote population health should pay particular attention to this high-risk group.

The ideology of male breadwinning seems to extend to affect gay men as well. Indeed, gay men is the only group for which being a primary breadwinner is associated with significantly fewer (rather than more) sleep problems relative to the "moderate commitments" arrangement. Further, having a spouse or partner who is the primary breadwinner is associated with higher odds of smoking among gay men compared with lesbians. Combined, these findings echo a recent study showing that maintaining masculinity and power inequalities—presumably via being a provider—is salient to marriages with men, including unions consisting of two men (Pollitt, Robinson, and Umberson 2017). Gay men who are not the primary breadwinner, therefore, may feel their masculinity being threatened, due to both male homosexuality and inability to provide, which exerts stress and leads to smoking as a way to cope with stress or compensate for their threatened masculinity.

When it comes to the high-commitments arrangement, consistent with hypothesis 3, women—straight and lesbians—seem to be more vulnerable than are their male counterparts, although possibly for different reasons. Straight women who work long hours may feel increasing pressure to fit a healthy lifestyle into their busy schedule given that, unlike their straight male counterparts who can offload housework and child care to their spouse, gendered expectations constrain straight women's ability to shirk these responsibilities. For lesbians, given the particularly wide gender pay gap at the top of the earning distribution, those who work long hours may be pressured by the need to compensate for the lost earnings a male partner would bring. Data limitation precludes my ability to test for these speculations. Future research with more detailed measures or qualitative data could shed further light on these mechanisms.

Taken as a whole, this study has broader theoretical and policy implications. Theoretically speaking, the findings add supportive evidence to the "linked others" thesis of life course research, that is, the lives of individuals affect and are affected by the lives of others in salient relationships such as couples (Elder, Johnson, and Crosnoe 2003). By examining the context of gender and sexual identity, this study also sheds light on theories key to the understanding of how work hours relate to health behaviors. In particular, contrary to the expectation that health behaviors of same-sex unions will be shaped more by time adequacy, my findings point to the continuingly influential role of gender norms in shaping behaviors, as evidenced by the adverse health behaviors exhibited by gay men who do not live up to the male-breadwinning cultural ideal. From a practical viewpoint, the findings presented here show the externality of workplace interventions aiming to change worker's working hours. Specifically, to fully assess the effects of those interventions, one needs to take into account the cross-over effects on the significant others of workers as well as to consider possible differences by gender and sexual identity. At the societal level, given the health behavioral risk associated with female-breadwinning couples, efforts need to be devoted to break the link between gender and breadwinning.

There are several limitations of this study. First, sexual identity was inferred based on couples' sexes; if sex is miscoded for one member of a couple, the resulting measurement error may attenuate the differences reported here. This strategy, nevertheless, is widely used in previous literature on same-sex couples (Liu et al. 2013; Reczek et al. 2014), and given the still prevalent stigma associated with homosexuality, the extent to which a direct report would result in more accurate data is unclear. Second, despite the importance of work hours, smoking and sleep disturbance may also be affected by work schedules. For example, how night or irregular shifts—one's own, a spouse's, or a couple's conjoint—affect healthy behaviors, and how they differ by the intersectionality of gender and sexual identity are questions that future studies can examine.

Despite these limitations, this study is one of the first to examine health behaviors and their antecedents in the workplace and the family in the context of both different-sex and same-sex unions. With the growing number of same-sex couples, it becomes ever more important to understand the joint effects of working conditions and couple dynamics in order to improve population health.

REFERENCES

Artazcoz, Lucía, Imma Cortès, Vicenta Escriba-Agüir, Lorena Cascant, and Rodrigo Ville-gas. 2009. "Understanding the Relationship of Long Working Hours with Health Status and Health-Related Behaviours." *Journal of Epidemiology & Community Health* 63 (7): 521–527.

Bauer, Gerrit. 2016. "Gender Roles, Comparative Advantages and the Life Course: The Division of Domestic Labor in Same-Sex and Different-Sex Couples." *European Journal of Population* 32 (1): 99–128.

Berk, Sarah Fenstermaker. 1985. *The Gender Factory: The Apportionment of Work in American Households*. New York: Plenum.

Bittman, Michael, Paula England, Liana Sayer, Nancy Folbre, and George Matheson. 2003. "When Does Gender Trump Money? Bargaining and Time in Household Work." *American Journal of Sociology* 109 (1): 186–214.

Courtenay, Will H. 2000. "Constructions of Masculinity and Their Influence on Men's Well-Being: A Theory of Gender and Health." *Social Science & Medicine* 50 (10): 1385–1401.

Elder, Glen H., Monica Kirkpatrick Johnson, and Robert Crosnoe. 2003. "The Emergence and Development of Life Course Theory." In *Handbook of the Life Course*, edited by Jeylan Mortimer and Michael Shanahan, 3–19. Boston: Springer.

Fan, Wen, Jack Lam, Phyllis Moen, Erin Kelly, Rosalind King, and Susan McHale. 2015. "Constrained Choices? Linking Employees' and Spouses' Work Time to Health Behaviors." *Social Science & Medicine* 126: 99–109.

Grzywacz, Joseph G., and Nadine F. Marks. 2001. "Social Inequalities and Exercise during Adulthood: Toward an Ecological Perspective." *Journal of Health and Social Behavior* 42 (2): 202–220.

Jacobs, Jerry A., and Kathleen Gerson. 2004. *The Time Divide: Work, Family, and Gender Inequality*. Cambridge, MA: Harvard University Press.

Kleiner, Sibyl, and Eliza K. Pavalko. 2014. "Double Time: Is Health Affected by a Spouse's Time at Work?" *Social Forces* 92 (3): 983–1007.

Liu, Hui, Corinne Reczek, and Dustin Brown. 2013. "Same-Sex Cohabitors and Health: The Role of Race-Ethnicity, Gender, and Socioeconomic Status." *Journal of Health and Social Behavior* 54 (1): 25–45.

Mattingly, Marybeth J., and Suzanne M. Bianchi. 2003. "Gender Differences in the Quantity and Quality of Free Time: The U.S. Experience." *Social Forces* 81 (3): 999–1030.

Moen, Phyllis, and Stephen Sweet. 2003. "Time Clocks: Work-Hour Strategies." In *It's about Time: Couples and Careers*, edited by Phyllis Moen, 17–34. Ithaca, NY: Cornell University Press.

National Center for Health Statistics. 2015. *Changes to Data Editing Procedures and the Impact on Identifying Same-Sex Married Couples: 2004–2007 National Health Interview Survey*. Hyattsville, MD: National Center for Health Statistics. Retrieved from https://www.cdc.gov/nchs/data/nhis/samesexedits.pdf on August 14, 2019.

Pollitt, Amanda M., Brandon A. Robinson, and Debra Umberson. 2017. "Gender Conformity, Perceptions of Shared Power, and Marital Quality in Same- and Different-Sex · Marriages." *Gender & Society* 32 (1): 109–31.

Reczek, Corinne, Hui Liu, and Dustin Brown. 2014. "Cigarette Smoking in Same-Sex and Different-Sex Unions: The Role of Socioeconomic and Psychological Factors." *Population Research and Policy Review* 33 (4): 527–551.

Reczek, Corinne, and Debra Umberson. 2012. "Gender, Health Behavior, and Intimate Rela-
    tionships: Lesbian, Gay, and Straight Contexts." *Social Science & Medicine* 74 (11):
    1783–1790.
Schoenborn, C. A., P. F. Adams, and J. A. Peregoy. 2013. "Health Behaviors of Adults: United
    States, 2008–2010." Hyattsville, MD: National Center for Health Statistics. Retrieved
    from https://stacks.cdc.gov/view/cdc/21268 on August 14, 2019.
Tichenor, Veronica. 2005. "Maintaining Men's Dominance: Negotiating Identity and
    Power when She Earns More." *Sex Roles* 53 (3): 191–205.
Townsend, Nicholas. 2002. *Package Deal: Marriage, Work and Fatherhood in Men's Lives.* Phil-
    adelphia: Temple University Press.

7

Union Status and Overweight or Obesity among Sexual Minority Men and Women

ZELMA OYARVIDE TUTHILL

BRIDGET K. GORMAN

NAVYA R. KUMAR

Obesity prevalence has been increasing in the United States, with 40 percent of American adults classified as obese (Hales et al. 2017), and health care costs associated with obesity-related illnesses constituting 7.9 percent of total medical expenditures in 2015 (Biener, Cawley, and Meyerhoefer 2018). It is important to note that although there are corollaries between weight status and health outcomes, there is also research that higher body weight is not always linked with health (Wildman et al. 2008). However, for this study we focus on obesity and overweight status, since evidence suggests that both may be tied to a range of adverse health outcomes, including diabetes and coronary heart disease (Global BMI Mortality Collaboration 2016).

While studies have identified a variety of factors related to body weight, relationship status appears to be especially relevant (Umberson, Liu, and Powers 2009). Although marriage and high marital quality are often tied to better physical and psychological health, research has also shown that marriage is correlated with higher body mass index (BMI) for heterosexual couples (The and Gordon-Larsen 2009). Studies suggest that the link between marriage and unhealthy weight may be due to health concordance from spousal influences, such as a tendency to eat together as a shared activity, which increases food intake and contributes to higher BMI (Dinour et al. 2012).

A key limitation of existing scholarship is that sexual orientation is not considered when examining the relationship between union status and weight. In particular, few studies have examined whether the relationship between union status and weight operates similarly among sexual minorities compared with heterosexuals, even though a high proportion (40%) are married or cohabiting (Jeffery and Rick 2002). Recent studies suggest that the heterosexual pattern of weight gain and higher BMI among partnered adults is also evident in sexual minorities (Markey and Markey 2011). Studies that examine union and weight among sexual minorities suggest that partnered individuals have increased likelihood of reporting overweight and obesity (Liu et al. 2017). Yet, conclusions regarding the association between weight and union status among sexual minorities have been difficult to draw since many studies tend not to focus on partnered individuals, and when they do, aggregate samples into one sexual minority subgroup or focus on either lesbian women or gay men.

Also lacking is attention to differences across sexual minority identity, despite evidence of substantial variation in health-related risks across sexual minority groups (Institute of Medicine [IOM] 2011). Studies that examine the relationship between weight and sexual minority status by grouping lesbian/gay and bisexuals together find evidence that sexual minority women have higher prevalence of overweight and obesity relative to heterosexual women (Bowen, Balsam, and Edner 2008) and lower prevalence of overweight and obesity among sexual minority men relative to heterosexual men (Deputy and Boehmer 2010). However, studies that examine specific sexual minority groups find that lesbian women experience higher odds of obesity, while gay and bisexual men have lower odds of obesity relative to heterosexuals (IOM 2011).

Gender may also condition how union status associates with weight among sexual minority adults. Studies document that sexual minority men have a lower average BMI than heterosexual men (Deputy and Boehmer 2010), while lesbian women have a higher prevalence of overweight and obesity than heterosexual women and bisexual/alternative women (Bowen, Balsam, and Edner 2008). These gendered variations may influence the way sexual minorities in unions experience obesity and overweight, but studies testing this are sparse. Past research has shown a stronger relationship between marriage and health for men than for women, a pattern attributed to increased social connections, emotional support, and monitoring of health behavior provided by wives more than by husbands (Zhang, Liu, and Yu 2016). This implies that the relationship between union status and health may be lessened for gay and some bisexual and alternatively identified men. Yet, other work has shown that cohabiting gay men are similar to lesbians in the health work performed in intimate relationships (Reczek and Umberson 2012)—implying similarity in health status between sexual minority men and women.

That said, the positive correlation between marriage and weight observed among heterosexuals is distinctive, and while some work has shown that both men and women in relationships are more likely to be obese (The and Gordon-Larsen 2009), other work suggests a stronger association for women (Jeffery and Rick 2002). Scholars suggest that partnered women may be differentially impacted through a decline in desire to maintain a certain weight along with

decreased motivation to engage in physical activity for the purpose of attracting a mate (The and Gordon-Larsen 2009). To date, we found only one study
examining whether the relationship between union status and weight differed
by gender among sexual minorities (Liu et al. 2017), which found that adults in
unions are more likely to weigh more than those who are unpartnered and
that union status was more strongly related to the weight of sexual minority
women than to that of sexual minority men. Additionally, work by Markey and
Markey (2011) suggests that partnered sexual minority women experience
weight gains when they enter a union regardless of the gender of their partner.
While that work is informative, additional research is needed to examine
whether these relationships operate similarly across disparate sexual minority
groups.

A large body of research has detailed the variety of health-promoting
resources associated with marriage and intimate relationships, including economic resources, social control, and support (Carr and Springer 2010) that should
provide health benefits regardless of sexual orientation. Studies indicate that
demographic characteristics including nonwhite race, older age, and being U.S.
born may contribute to an increased likelihood of unhealthy weight among
sexual minorities (Boehmer and Bowen 2009). In terms of socioeconomic status, studies suggest that more educated and economically stable sexual minorities have a decreased likelihood of being an unhealthy weight (Deputy and
Boehmer 2010). This isn't surprising given the confounding effect of these factors
on rates of obesity among heterosexuals. Regarding aspects of social integration
and support, studies examining the effect of LGBTQ-related community integration and support on weight are rare. Although there is some evidence that
adults who are highly involved in lesbian/gay activities and report having more
sexual minority friends are less concerned with being overweight than those who
aren't (Bowen, Balsam, and Edner 2008), more evidence is needed in order to
identify how economic resources, relationships, and aspects of LGBTQ-related
community integration and support influence weight status among sexual
minority populations.

In order to address these gaps in the literature, we examine data from the
2010 Social Justice Sexual Project (SJSP) to examine how union status (legal
union, partnered, no partner) relates to overweight or obesity among sexual
minority adults. Specifically, we evaluate how union status intersects with gender of partner (men vs. women) to shape the odds of being overweight or obese,
separately for sexual minority men and women. We also test whether the relationship between union status and weight is dependent upon sexual identity
(gay/lesbian, bisexual, or alternative identity), and we examine these relationships before and after adjustment for factors that may shape the relationship
between union status and weight (i.e., demographic characteristics and aspects
of socioeconomic status and support/integration into the LGBTQ community).

Methods

Data

This chapter examines data from the 2010 Social Justice Sexuality Project (SJSP), a unique survey that contains a large sample of sexual minorities residing across the United States. Data were collected over a twelve-month period between January and December 2010, and the survey was tested through four rounds of piloting before administration of the final survey (Battle, Pastrana, and Daniels 2013). While the diversity of this data set is a strength, it is also a nonprobability sample (i.e., respondents were strategically recruited via venue-based sampling at nationwide LGBTQ events, snowball sampling through community partnerships with LGBTQ organizations, respondent-driven sampling, and the Internet). From the full sample of 4,953 respondents, we restricted our analytic sample to individuals of age eighteen and older (remaining $n=4,830$). We also removed persons who identified as heterosexual ($n=381$), didn't answer the sexual identity question ($n=23$), didn't report their weight or height ($n=101$), identified as transgender or non–gender conforming ($n=182$), or indicated "other" as their relationship status ($n=193$). Please note that transgender and non-gender conforming adults were excluded because we stratify our analysis by gender identity, and, regretfully, cell sizes were too small to support a multivariate analysis on this group. Since respondents were able to choose multiple relationship status categories, we removed those who were in more than one category ($n=72$) from the sample. Altogether, these restrictions resulted in a final analytic sample size of 3,878 sexual minority adults.

Statistical Analysis

Our dependent variable is a binary measure of overweight or obese weight status, generated using self-reported height and weight to calculate BMI (where 1=overweight or obese and 0=not overweight or obese). The categories of overweight and obese in this study are based on the Centers for Disease Control and Prevention (CDC) classifications, with overweight=BMI between 25.0 and 29.9 and obese=30.0 and above. The independent variable of interest, union status, reflects the current relationship status of respondents, including the gender of their partner. The SJSP questionnaire asked all respondents: "What is your current relationship status?," with the following response categories: (a) not partnered, (b) partnered with someone of the same sex, (c) partnered with someone of a different sex, (d) married to a same-sex partner, including civil union and/or domestic partnership, and (e) married to a different-sex partner, including civil union and/or domestic partnership. Please note that response categories of "partnered with . . ." could include those who are cohabiting but not in a legal union as well as respondents who are dating but not living together. This differs from "domestic partnership," which references persons who are in legally recognized domestic partnerships. In the remainder of the chapter, we refer to marital unions as legal unions in order to be inclusive of civil unions and domestic partnerships that are incorporated into this category.

For sexual identity, respondents were asked, "Which one label comes closest to how you describe your sexual identity?" The majority of respondents identified as either gay or lesbian. In addition, a substantial portion identified their sexual identity in nontraditional and more alternative ways (e.g., queer, same gender loving, in the life). Rather than exclude these individuals from the study, we include an additional "alternative" sexual identity category in our models.

We include demographic controls for age at interview, whether a child lives in the home (1=child in home, 0=no child in home), foreign-born status (1=foreign born, 0=not foreign born), and race-ethnicity (non-Hispanic white, non-Hispanic black, Latino, and other). Measures of socioeconomic status (SES) include education (high school or less, some college or associates, college graduate or higher), employment (1=employed full or part time, 0=unemployed or other), household income (less than $20,000, $20,000–$39,999, $40,000–$74,999, $75,000 and higher), and health insurance status (1=insurance, 0=uninsured).

We also include six measures of community integration and support, some of which are scales created by the SJSP research team (Battle, Pastrana, and Daniels 2013). First, we include a single item reflecting how important respondents' sexual orientation is to their identity (measured on a 6-point rating scale, where 1=not important at all and 6=extremely important). Second, respondents were asked, as an LGBTQ person, how supported they feel by their family (on a 7-point rating scale, where 0=does not know I'm LGBTQ, 1=not supported at all, and 6=completely supported). Third, respondents were asked how much their religious tradition or spiritual practice has been a negative or positive influence in coming to terms with their LGBTQ identity (measured on a 7-point rating scale, where 1=negative influence, 4=neither negative or positive, and 7=positive influence). Fourth, level of connection to the LGBTQ community was constructed from averaging three survey items (alpha=.71) that asked about the extent to which participants felt connected to their local LGBTQ community, felt that the problems of the LGBTQ community were also their problems, and felt a bond with the LGBTQ community (rating scale of 1 to 6, where 1=strongly disagree that they feel connected to the LGBTQ community, and 6=strongly agree).

Fifth, level of participation in LGBTQ groups, organizations, and activities was constructed from averaging six survey items (alpha=.75), where 0=never participated and 6=more than once a week. Respondents were asked: "Thinking about LGBT groups, organizations and activities in general, during the past 12 months how often have you (1) participated in political events, (2) participated in social or cultural events, (3) read newspapers or magazines, (4) used the Internet for chatrooms, social networking sites, blogs, etc., (5) received goods and/or services such as counseling, medical care, food, etc., and (6) donated money to an organization."

Sixth, level of outness in their social network was constructed from averaging six survey items (alpha = .86) that asked respondents to identify how many members of various communities they are "out" (including family members, friends, their religious community, co-workers, people in their neighborhoods, and people online), where 1 = none and 5 = all.

We utilized Stata 15 for all data management and analysis procedures. Item nonresponse was small (9.2%). We used multiple imputations to handle item nonresponse and avoid biasing the data. Following best practices, we included respondents with missing data in the imputation, but then excluded them from the analytic sample. In text we begin by describing findings from a descriptive analysis of our sample, stratified by gender, although those findings are not shown in tabular form. Following the descriptive analysis, we ran logistic regression models predicting the odds of overweight or obesity separately for men and women. In table 7.1 we present the odds ratios of overweight or obesity from the model-building process. The baseline model (model 1) includes only the sexual orientation and the union status x partner's gender variable; model 2 adds demographic controls; model 3 includes only socioeconomic status controls; model 4 shows controls only for indicators of community integration and support; and the full multivariate model (model 5) simultaneously adjusts for all control variables. The SJSP includes limited information on health behaviors, except for smoking status (which was excluded from table 7.1 since it was not a significant predictor of weight status in our sample).

Results

Sample Characteristics

Sample characteristics (not shown, but available upon request) showed that slightly more sexual minority men than women are overweight or obese (53.8% vs. 46.2%). In addition, regardless of the gender of their partner, a higher proportion of women are in relationships. While 9.9 percent of women are in a legal union with a same-sex partner, this drops to 4.7 percent of men. Similar differences are seen for respondents who report being in a legal union with a different-sex partner (2.7% of women and .7% of men), having a same-sex partner (46.1% of women and 34.1% of men), or having a different-sex partner (6.6% of women and 1.5% of men). As a result, a higher proportion of men (58.9%) are not currently partnered, compared with 34.6 percent of women.

Turning to demographic characteristics, well over half of the sample identifies as gay or lesbian. Twice as many women as men identify as bisexual (16.1% vs. 8.0%), although a sizable percentage of each gender (21.8% of women and 17.5% men) identify with an alternative label (e.g., queer, in the life, same gender

TABLE 7.1

Odds Ratios from Logistic Regression Models Predicting Overweight or Obesity among Women and Men

	Women					Men				
	Model 1	Model 2	Model 3	Model 4	Model 5	Model 1	Model 2	Model 3	Model 4	Model 5
Union status x partner										
Legal union, same-sex	—	—	—	—	—	—	—	—	—	—
Legal union, diff.-sex	.99	1.30	.95	1.08	1.29	.58	.18	.63	.44	.10
Same-sex partner	.61**	.84	.61*	.67*	.81	.66	.81	.70	.59	.79
Different-sex partner	.50*	1.08	.53*	.56*	1.04	.62	1.01	.72	.56	1.09
Not partnered	.61*	.75	.62*	.68	.74	.64	.82	.69	.57*	.83
Demographic										
Sexual orientation										
Gay/lesbian (ref.)	—	—	—	—	—	—	—	—	—	—
Bisexual	.62***	.67	.64**	.74	.74	1.06	1.16	1.12	.97	1.04
Alternative	.94	1.14	.97	.97	1.19	1.18	.89	1.16	1.11	.84
Age		1.04***			1.03***		1.04***			1.04***
Children in the home		1.08			1.00		.85			.96
Foreign born		.60			.60		1.21			1.09
Race-ethnicity										
White		—			—		—			—
Black		1.57*			1.60*		1.74**			1.53*
Latino		1.62			1.81		1.41			1.36
Other		.96			.97		1.30			1.19

Socioeconomic status

Education

	Model 1	Model 2	Model 3	Model 4	Model 5
High school or less	—	—	—		—
Some college/Associates	1.01	1.05	1.30		1.35
College graduate/higher	.95	.98	1.55**		1.33
Household income					
<$20,000	—	—	—		—
$20,000–39,999	.97	.92	1.08		1.01
$40,000–74,999	1.31	1.12	1.32*		1.36
$75,000+	.93	.75	1.16		1.36
Employed	1.40***	1.36*	1.10		1.06
Has health insurance	1.04	.92	1.35*		1.27
Integration and support					
Sexual identity importance		.98		1.05	1.00
Perceived family support		1.07*		1.09	1.01
Perceived religion support		1.06*		1.00	1.04
Connection to LGBTQ		1.01		.98	1.09
Participation in LGBTQ		1.05		1.03	1.12*
Outness		1.06		.82***	.79**

$N = 1,790$ for women and $2,088$ for men.

Notes: Model 1 = baseline, model 2 = demographics, model 3 = socioeconomic status, model 4 = integration and support, model 5 = full model.

$* p \leq .05; ** p \leq .01; *** p \leq .001.$

loving). On average, men in the sample are slightly older, while substantially more women report children living in their home (47.9% vs. 22.7% among men). We also see some differences in race-ethnicity, as a slightly higher percentage of women are white and a slightly higher percentage of men are black.

Socioeconomic status measures show modest differences between sexual minority men and women. More men are employed, and they report slightly higher rates of completed schooling (47.0% of women have at least a college degree, compared to 50.3% of men), while women are slightly overrepresented among the highest income group (23.1% report a household income of $75,000 or above, compared with 20.2% of men). Overall, however, the socioeconomic profiles of sexual minority men and women are quite similar.

For measures of community integration and support, we see substantial differences by gender. On average, sexual minority women report higher levels of sexual identity importance, perceived support from their religious community, and connection to the broader LGBTQ community than sexual minority men. However, sexual minority men report a higher level of participation in LGBTQ groups, and men and women report equivalent levels of perceived family support. The extent to which they are "out" to others is also significantly higher among sexual minority women than men.

Logistic Regression Models

Table 7.1 presents odds ratios from gender-stratified logistic regression models predicting overweight or obese status. In the columns on the left for women, the baseline model shows a significant association between union status and the odds of being overweight or obese. Relative to sexual minority women in a legal union with a same-sex partner, those not in a legal union (whether partnered with a woman or a man, or not partnered) have significantly lower odds of being overweight or obese. In addition, model 1 also shows that gender of partner does not significantly differentiate elevated weight status among sexual minority women in legal unions. Indeed, for women in a legal union, the odds ratio comparing those with a different-sex partner relative to a same-sex partner is .99, indicating nearly identical odds of elevated weight among these two groups of women. The baseline model 1 also shows that, relative to lesbians, bisexual women are significantly less likely to be overweight or obese, while the contrast between lesbian and alternatively identified women is not significant.

Models 2 through 4 sequentially test whether adjustment for controls (i.e., demographic, SES, and integration/support) reduces the association between union status and weight. All contrasts between union status and weight are nonsignificant after adjustment for demographic controls in model 2—particularly age at interview and racial-ethnic identity. Model 2 shows that the odds of overweight or obesity increase significantly with age, and that black women experience higher odds relative to white women. Supplemental analyses (not shown) revealed that sexual minority women who are in legal unions with a same-sex partner differ substantially from other women on these characteristics. They are substantially older (average age: 42.5 years) than all other women in our sample (who are between 7 and 14 years younger, depending on union status group). They are also half as likely to be foreign born than any other group, and they were the most likely to identify their race as white.

Looking at SES control measures for women in model 3, only one measure is significant: women who are employed have higher odds (OR = 1.40) of being overweight or obese than those who are not working. We also see that adjusting for SES had very little influence on the relationship between union status and weight. In model 4, controls are added for measures of social integration/support. Two are significant predictors of sexual minority women's weight, as perceived religion support and perceived family support were associated with elevated odds of being overweight or obese. Adjusting for integration/support had only a modest effect on the relationship between union status and weight. Only the contrast between women who were not partnered at interview was reduced to nonsignificance (relative to women in legal unions with a same-sex partner).

In model 5, the full multivariate model that adjusts for all control measures, the odds ratios for union status are nearly identical to those shown in model 2—indicating that demographic characteristics are indeed driving most of the differences in weight status seen between sexual minority women in different union statuses.

Turning to sexual minority men, logistic regression models in table 7.1 generally showed no significant association between union status and overweight or obesity, although odds ratios relative to men living in a legal union with a same-sex partner are lower for all other union status groups. Sexual orientation is also not significant in all models for men. In supplemental tests, we collapsed across gender of partner due to the small number of men in our sample in a partnership with a different-sex partner; those results are substantively similar to the findings presented in table 7.1.

Looking at control measures across models 2 through 5, we see that the odds of overweight or obesity are significantly higher among older men and those who identify as black (relative to white). While model 3 showed significant associations between multiple aspects of SES and overweight or obesity among men, all contrasts lose significance in the full model. And among the measures of integration/support in model 4, the strongest predictor of weight among men is outness. The more sexual minority men are out to members of their community, the lower their odds of being overweight or obese. Model 4 also indicates that adjusting for outness initially caused the odds ratio for unpartnered men to emerge as significant (with unpartnered men almost half as likely to be overweight or obese as men living in a legal union with a same-sex partner); however, this contrast between unpartnered men and those in same-sex legal unions lost significance once controls were added in the full model. Supplemental analyses revealed that as level of outness increases among sexual minority men, so does their propensity to have a same-sex partner. At the same time, with increasing outness men are less likely to report a different-sex partner, or that they have no partner at all.

Last, in results not shown, we tested the interaction between union status and sexual orientation and found no statistically significant relationship to weight status for either men or women.

Conclusions

Overweight and obesity are associated with premature death in the United States (Global BMI Mortality Collaboration 2016). A large number of studies have examined predictors of elevated weight among adults, including the role of union status. Many document a positive association between marriage and weight, with some finding similar patterns by gender (Dinour et al. 2012), and others finding evidence of a stronger association for women (Jeffery and Rick 2002). Yet of all these studies, almost none have considered how relationship status relates to weight status among sexual minority adults.

In response, our study examined how union status and gender of partner related to overweight or obesity among a sample of gay, lesbian, bisexual, and alternatively identified adults. Similar to scholarship examining marriage and health more generally, and weight specifically, we find more evidence that union status relates to weight among women than to men (Zhang, Liu, and Yu 2016). While the association between weight and union status is under-studied among sexual minorities, this finding is consistent with recent research documenting that longer relationship duration is associated with overweight and obesity among lesbian women in relationships (Mason and Lewis 2015), and other work showing that union status was more strongly related to the weight of sexual minority women than of sexual minority men (Liu et al. 2017).

Notably, regression modeling showed similarity in weight between women in legal unions with either a same-sex or different-sex partner. This indicates that the gender of one's partner is not responsible for shaping obesity risk among sexual minority women—being in a legal union is what correlates most strongly with a heavier weight, not the gender composition of the couple. While we are unable to test this explanation with our data, The and Gordon-Larsen (2009) suggest that decreased desire to maintain a certain weight or exercise due to diminished need to attract a mate are factors shaping elevated weight among women in partnerships. Similar to heterosexual women who marry, we see the highest odds of overweight or obesity among sexual minority women in legal unions regardless of the gender of their partner.

Regression models for women also showed that adjusting for demographic covariates explained overweight or obesity differences between sexual minority women in legal unions and sexual minority women who were partnered and not partnered. Indeed, our findings demonstrated that differences in weight across union status groups among women were driven by compositional differences related to age and racial identity. These factors confound the association between union status and weight among sexual minority women, indicating that the heightened odds of a heavier weight seen among women in legal unions are driven more by the dynamics of who enters into those unions (where supplemental testing revealed an overrepresentation of white women who are older among those in legal unions with a same-sex partner).

For men, union status was not significantly related to weight status. Instead, our findings highlight the strong relationship between outness and weight. The more out that men are to members of various communities in their life (e.g., family, friends, co-workers, etc.), the lower their odds of being overweight or obese. Studies show that compared with heterosexual men, gay men report more concerns about their weight, desire a thinner body shape, and appear more susceptible to media images and social pressures promoting thinness (Cohane and Pope 2001). In contrast, lesbian women report lower body dissatisfaction and a larger ideal body size than heterosexual women (Alvy 2013).

Also notable from our findings is the limited evidence that specific sexual identity differentiated the odds of being overweight or obese among this sample of sexual minority adults. Bisexual women had lower odds of overweight or obesity, but this difference became nonsignificant after adjustment for controls. For men, sexual orientation was never a significant predictor of weight status. Additionally, interaction tests between union status and sexual orientation were not significant, for either men or women. So, despite differences in their weight overall, we find similarity across sexual minority subgroups in how weight relates to union status.

While our study makes a needed contribution to the literature on union status and weight among sexual minorities, readers should keep in mind that the sample of respondents included in the SJSP was drawn using nonprobability methods, so our findings may be biased to an unknown extent. Yet as a recent assessment by the Institute of Medicine concluded, limited research has examined how sexual orientation may be associated with a variety of health outcomes, including overweight and obesity (IOM 2011). Scholars have also noted that the structural aspects of unions, including whether the union is composed of same-sex or different-sex couples, are potentially relevant in shaping connections to health and well-being (Carr and Springer 2010).

Our findings highlight similarity with scholarship on relationships and health among heterosexuals, as we found that legal unions are associated with heavier weight among sexual minorities, especially among women. And while we don't contrast patterns relative to heterosexuals, our findings show similarity in the odds of overweight or obesity between sexual minority women and men who report either a same-sex or a different-sex partner. Overall, these findings align with the prediction made by Cherlin (2013): the meanings attached to relationships appear similar for same- and different-sex partners, and so the health effects of occupying these relationship statuses should also be similar. Although more comparative research between heterosexual and sexual minority adults is warranted, it seems that when it comes to weight status, what matters more is being in a union rather than an individual's sexual orientation or the gender of the individual's partner.

REFERENCES

Alvy, Lisa M. 2013. "Do Lesbian Women Have a Better Body Image? Comparisons with Heterosexual Women and Model of Lesbian-Specific Factors." *Body Image* 10 (4): 524–534.

Battle, Juan, Antonio Jay Pastrana, and Jessie Daniels. 2013. *Social Justice Sexuality Project: 2010 National Survey, including Puerto Rico.* Produced and distributed by the Interuniversity Consortium for Political and Social Research, ICPSR 34363.

Biener, Adam, John Cawley, and Chad Meyerhoefer. 2018. "The Impact of Obesity on Medical Care Costs and Labor Market Outcomes in the US." *Clinical Chemistry* 64 (1): 108–117.

Boehmer, Ulrike, and Deborah J. Bowen. 2009. "Examining Factors Linked to Overweight and Obesity in Women of Different Sexual Orientations." *Preventative Medicine* 48 (4): 357–361.

Bowen, Deborah, Kimberly Balsam, and Samantha Edner. 2008. "A Review of Obesity Issues in Sexual Minority Women." *Obesity* 16 (2): 221–228.

Carr, Deborah, and Kristen W. Springer. 2010. "Advances in Families and Health Research in the 21st Century." *Journal of Marriage and Family* 72 (3): 743–761.

Cherlin, Andrew J. 2013. "Health, Marriage and Same-Sex Relationships." *Journal of Health and Social Behavior* 54 (1): 64–66.

Cohane, G. H., and H. G. Pope. 2001. "Body Image in Boys: A Review of the Literature." *International Journal of Eating Disorders* 29 (4): 373–379.

Deputy, Nicholas, and Ulrike Boehmer. 2010. "Determinants of Body Weight among Men of Different Sexual Orientation." *Preventative Medicine* 51 (2): 129–131.

Dinour, Lauren, May May Leung, Gina Tripicchio, Sahar Khan, and Ming-Chin Yeh. 2012. "The Association between Marital Transitions, Body Mass Index, and Weight: A Review of the Literature." *Journal of Obesity* 2012 (294974): 1–16.

Global BMI Mortality Collaboration. 2016. "Body-Mass Index and All-Cause Mortality: Individual-Participant-Data Meta-Analysis of 239 Prospective Studies in Four Continents." *The Lancet* 388 (10046): 776–786.

Hales, Craig, Margaret Carroll, Cheryl Fryar, and Cynthia Ogden. 2017. "Prevalence of Obesity among Adults and Youth: United States, 2015–2016." *National Center for Health Statistics* 288: 1–8.

Institute of Medicine (IOM). 2011. *The Health of Lesbian, Gay, Bisexual and Transgender People: Building a Foundation for a Better Future.* Washington, DC: National Academic Press.

Jeffery, Robert W., and Allison M. Rick. 2002. "Cross-Sectional and Longitudinal Associations between Body Mass Index and Marriage-Related Factors." *Obesity Research* 10 (8): 809–815.

Liu, Hui, Corinne Reczek, Samuel C. H. Mindes, and Shannon Shen. 2017. "The Health Disparities of Same Sex Cohabitors at the Intersection of Race-Ethnicity and Gender." *Sociological Perspectives* 60 (3): 620–639.

Markey, Charlotte, and Patrick Markey. 2011. "Leaving Room for Complexity in Attempts to Understand Associations between Romantic Relationships and Health: Commentary on Wanic and Kulik." *Sex Roles* 65, no. 5 (September 2011): 313–319. https://doi.org/10 .1007/s11199-011-9986-4.

Mason, Tyler, and Robin Lewis. 2015. "Minority Stress and Binge Eating among Lesbian and Bisexual Women." *Journal of Homosexuality* 62 (7): 971–992.

Reczek, Corinne, and Debra Umberson. 2012. "Gender, Health Behavior, and Intimate Relationships: Lesbian, Gay, and Straight Contexts." *Social Science & Medicine* 74 (11): 1783–1790.

The, Natalie S., and Penny Gordon-Larsen. 2009. "Entry into Romantic Partnership Is Associated with Obesity." *Obesity* 17 (7): 1441–1447.

Umberson, Debra, Hui Liu, and Daniel Powers. 2009. "Marital Status, Marital Transitions, and Body Weight." *Journal of Health and Social Behavior* 50 (3): 327–343.

Wildman, Rachel, Paul Muntner, Kristi Reynolds, Aileen McGinn, Swapnil Rajpathak, Judith Wylie-Rosett, and MaryFran Sowers. 2008. "The Obese without Cardiometabolic Risk Factor Clustering and the Normal Weight with Cardiometabolic Risk Factor Clustering: Prevalence and Correlates of 2 Phenotypes among the US Population (NHANES 1999–2004)." *Archives of Internal Medicine* 168 (15): 1617–1624.

Zhang, Zhenmei, Hui Liu, and Yan-Liang Yu. 2016. "Marital Biography and Health in Mid and Late Life." In *Couple Relationships in Mid and Late Life: Current Perspectives*, edited by Jamila Bookwala, 199–218. Washington, DC: American Psychological Association.

8

Same-Sex Contact and Alternative Medicine Usage among Older Adults

LACEY J. RITTER

KOJI UENO

In the last two decades, alternative medicine—or unconventional interventions such as acupuncture, chiropractic practices, herbal medicine, and massage (Clark 2000, 447)—has become much more popular in the United States. In 2007, 35 percent of Americans reported using alternative medicine, and they spend the total amount of $33.9 billion on related purchases every year (Smith et al. 2010). Users of alternative medicine are more likely to be women and older (Smith et al. 2010), and whites, Native Americans, and Alaskan Natives are more likely to use it than other racial groups (Barnes, Bloom, and Nahin 2008). Many people seek alternative medicine because of limitations of the conventional medicine including ineffectiveness, serious side effects, and institutional philosophy that does not fit the patient's belief (Banu, Varela, and Fernandes 2011; Clark 2000).

People also are drawn to alternative medicine because of its low costs and long history. Although many alternative practices outdate Western medicine, these practices are now being integrated into medical school curricula and even covered in health insurance plans (Clark 2000). Proponents of alternative medicine point out that nonpharmaceutical alternatives including plant extracts, natural dietary supplements, and nutritional changes reduce pain and discomfort at lower costs with more accessible rates (Banu, Varela, and Fernandes 2011). Other alternative practices, such as acupuncture, have been around throughout much of human history and have shown positive results for both medical and dental ailments alike (Vaidya et al. 2013).

Previous studies have looked into older adult users of alternative medicine to determine how widely it is used, who uses it, and why. One study reported that among people between ages sixty-five and seventy-four, 43 percent reported using alternative medicine, and that they were more educated and affluent than nonusers (McMahan and Lutz 2004). Among various types of alternative medicine, older adults tend to use spiritual practices, exercise movement and/or therapy, herbal therapy, chiropractic treatment, massage therapy, and acupuncture (McMahan and Lutz 2004, 100). Alternative medicine may be particularly beneficial for older adults because many of them have pains and other chronic conditions, which Western medicine is not always effective at treating (McMahan and Lutz 2004).

In this study, we analyze sexual orientation differences in alternative medicine usage among older adult populations. Specifically, we hypothesize that older adults who report same-sex contact (SSC) in their lifetime will have higher rates of alternative medicine usage than older adults who report no SSC in their lifetime. Using Wave I (2005) data from the National Social Life, Health, and Aging Project (NSHAP), our analysis will test whether sexual contact as a measure of sexual orientation is associated with alternative medicine usage in the past twelve months for older adults. Answering the question is important for two reasons. The first reason is that sexual orientation differences in alternative medicine use, if found, may indicate sexual minorities and heterosexuals' different experiences with the traditional Western medical care, and poor experiences would discourage people from using the care and turn to alternative medicine. In that case, the sexual orientation in alternative medicine use may reflect sexual minorities' constrained choices in health care. The second reason is that alternative medicine is less regulated than Western medicine, and sexual minorities' higher use would indicate that their health care is monitored to lesser degree than that of heterosexuals.

Background

Sexual Minorities' and Heterosexuals' Alternative Medicine Usage

Although the existing literature on sexual minorities' alternative medicine usage is scarce, past studies found that sexual minorities are more likely to use alternative medicine than heterosexual individuals. For example, London and colleagues (2003) reported that gay and lesbian patients with HIV/AIDS are more likely to use alternative medicine therapists than heterosexual patients. Among sexual minority patients, lesbians have higher rates of lifetime alternative medicine usage even when controlling for age, education, race, and health status (Matthews et al. 2005), and they have greater odds of having ever used alternative medicine and having used it in the past twelve months (Smith et al. 2010). Social locations also matter; white, highly educated people living in large cities who experienced discrimination in health care settings were the most likely to use alternative medicine within the sexual minority population (Smith et al. 2010).

Explanations for Sexual Minorities' Higher Frequency of Alternative Medicine Use

The literature suggests several reasons why sexual minorities may utilize alternative medicine more frequently than heterosexuals. One reason is that sexual minorities may be more likely to face discrimination by Western, mainstream health care professionals, which may lead sexual minorities to seek alternative options (Fenkl 2012; Fredriksen-Goldsen and Muraco 2010). One source of discrimination is a lack of understanding of sexual minority health in the medical community (Brotman, Ryan, and Cormier 2003; Orel 2014). In particular, sexual minority older adults experience a double marginalization for their age and sexual orientation, which functions as a sort of "cultural imperialism" that decreases their likelihood of accessing traditional health care and social services (Genke 2004). Older gay men experienced additional stigma during the HIV/AIDS scares in the 1990s in mainstream medicine and continue to face the challenge today (Fenkl 2012). Sexual minorities see alternative medicine as more accepting because of its sex-positive approach, as opposed to the curative, biologically focused mainstream approach in Western medicine (Banu, Varela, and Fernandes 2011; Clark 2000; Genke 2004).

In addition to discrimination, sexual minorities face institutional barriers to adequate care in mainstream medicine (Orel 2014). Sexual minority individuals report lower rates of health insurance coverage (Matthews et al. 2005; Smith et al. 2010), substantially reducing their access to mainstream medicine, particularly preventative care. In addition, legal and medical decision making becomes a struggle for unmarried partners whose rights may not have been recognized or who may have trouble serving as health care proxies for their partners (Brotman et al. 2003).

Another reason to expect sexual minorities' increased alternative medicine usage is their higher prevalence of life-threatening or chronic illnesses. Previous research has found that individuals with HIV/AIDS are likely to use alternative medicine as treatment for their illnesses (Milan et al. 2008), along with Western medicine, partly because the latter alone does not provide adequate treatment at least for some patients. Because sexual minorities are at higher risk for HIV/AIDS (Fenkl 2012), they may be more likely to use alternative medicine as a treatment option. Sexual minority groups also have overall higher rates of depression and anxiety than heterosexuals (Fredriksen-Goldsen 2014), which are positively associated with alternative medicine usage (Matthews et al. 2005). These differences may also contribute to sexual minorities' higher usage of alternative medicine.

Finally, sexual minorities may be more open minded about unconventional behaviors than heterosexuals, which may increase their chance of using alternative medicine. Sexual minorities tend to have higher levels of socioeconomic status (SES) (Brown and Grossman 2014), which is positively associated with alternative medicine usage (McMahan and Lutz 2004; Smith et al. 2010). Further, holding a minority status encourages people to question taken-for-granted assumptions and consider new and alternative ideas (Banu, Varela, and Fernandes 2011). This process may apply to sexual minority status and alternative medicine use.

Summary, Research Questions, and Hypotheses

Previous studies on alternative medicine usage either focused on older adults or examined sexual orientation differences in the adult population as a whole, and very few studies incorporated both to determine whether older sexual minority and heterosexual individuals differ in this respect. Therefore, it is not clear whether the sexual orientation differences observed in the general adult population will apply to older adults. One could argue that older adults have an increased need for alternative medicine due to chronic pain as mentioned earlier, and the overall high rate in the older adult population may mute the sexual orientation difference in alternative medicine use. It is also possible, however, that the sexual orientation difference in alternative medicine use may increase in old age because the double stigma of being a sexual minority older adult creates a particularly high risk of facing discrimination in the mainstream medicine and turn sexual minorities to alternative medicine to a greater degree in old age.

Analyses use same-sex contact (SSC) as a measure of sexual orientation and test the following two hypotheses:

Hypothesis 1: SSC older adults will have higher rates of alternative medicine usage in the last twelve months than non-SSC older adults. Past research has found that sexual minority individuals are more likely to request and use alternative medicine than heterosexuals (London et al. 2003). We expect these findings to apply to the older adult population.

Hypothesis 2: The association between SSC and alternative medicine usage will be partly mediated by health status. In particular, past research has found that respondents who report higher numbers of health conditions and have worse health are more likely to use alternative medicine (Smith et al. 2010). Sexual minority older adults also have more health problems than heterosexual older adults (Fredriksen-Goldsen 2014), indicating that this factor at least partly accounts for the sexual orientation difference in alternative medicine use. We test this mediation in the analysis.

Methods

Data

This study used data from the first wave of the National Social Life, Health, and Aging Project (NSHAP), which is a longitudinal, population-based study of older Americans from age fifty-seven through age eighty-five. There are currently two waves of data available to researchers. This study only used Wave 1 NSHAP data because this wave contained a larger number of respondents reporting same-sex contact than Wave 2. In this wave, 249 respondents were missing data on at least one of the key variables, and they were dropped from analysis. The final sample included 2,519 respondents.

Focal Independent Variable (Same-Sex Contact). The NSHAP does not include any direct information on respondents' sexual identity. However, a dichotomous variable of SSC was created using information about respondent gender and sexual partner gender. When respondents reported having sex with anyone of their same gender within their lifetime, they were coded as SSC regardless of the number of sexual partners of the opposite gender. Respondents who did not report any instances of SSC served as the comparison. In the sample, 106 (approximately 4%) of respondents reported some SSC in their lifetime. The lifetime measure of SSC was chosen over the measure of recent experiences to encompass more individuals in the SSC group, particularly behaviorally bisexual people and those who had more fluid dating patterns, who may have happened to be dating someone of the opposite sex at the time of interview, as well as individuals who had SSC in the past but were sexually inactive at the time of study.

This measure generally allowed respondents more freedom to express non-heterosexual experiences by reducing the stigma attached to sexual minority identities such as gay and lesbian. This issue may be particularly important for older sexual minorities, who experienced or witnessed serious stigma when they were younger in less accepting times (Fenkl 2012). In addition, individuals who engaged in SSC only infrequently may not consider themselves a sexual minority, but they still differ from (other) heterosexually identified individuals in health status and thus need to be treated as sexual minorities in health research (Brown and Grossman 2014).

Although the SSC variable allowed us to measure same-sex experience more inclusively, there were two disadvantages. First, the timing of SSC was unknown, meaning that individuals who engaged in one act of SSC only at a young age were aligned with respondents who engaged in SSC acts throughout their lifetime. Second, because SSC was dichotomously coded to sustain cell sizes, respondents who had one SSC instance in their lifetime were also grouped with those who had had many. In robustness checks, however, no differences were found in alternative medicine use between respondents who engaged in one instance of SSC and those who engaged in two or more and three or more SSC acts (detailed results available upon request).

Dependent Variable (Alternative Medicine Usage). Respondents were asked a set of seven questions about whether or not they had used the following kinds of alternative medicine in the past twelve months: herbal supplement or remedy; high-dose or mega-vitamin; massage therapies; acupuncture; chiropractic treatments; meditation; religious or spiritual healing; and other types. A scale was created from these eight variables to count the total alternative medicine usage (range from 0 to 7; mean of .68).

Mediating Variable (Health Conditions) is an index created from nine health condition items. Respondents were asked whether a medical doctor had ever told them that they had any of the following health conditions: arthritis, ulcers, emphysema or COPD, asthma, stroke, hypertension, diabetes, Alzheimer's or dementia, cirrhosis, leukemia, lymphoma, skin cancer, cancer, poor kidney function, and thyroid problems. The summed scale represented the number of health conditions for each respondent and ranged from zero to nine. Initial analysis included other health measures (self-rated health, mental health, etc.), but were not significantly associated with SSC and did not alter the findings, so they were removed from the analysis.

Control Variables. *Race/ethnicity* consisted of the following four categories: white (72.8%), black (15.1%), and other (12.1%). *Education* measured the highest degree completed and consisted of the following four categories: less than high school education (21.7%); high school degree or equivalent (27.1%); some college education (28.7%); and a bachelor's degree or higher (22.6%). *Sex* was a dichotomous measure, consisting of males (46.4%) and females (53.6%). *Age* was a continuous variable ranging from fifty-seven to eighty-five years, with the average of 69.2 years. Respondents of ages fifty-seven to sixty years (12%) may not be commonly considered "older adults" but were kept in this study to preserve sample size.

Analytical Strategy

The analysis employed negative binomial regressions because the dependent variable—alternative medicine usage—was a count variable. Negative binomial regression was chosen over Poisson regression because the model's extra parameter allowed for smaller standard errors due to the overdispersed distribution of the count variable.

In addition to negative binomial models, several supplementary analyses were completed to test the robustness of the main results. First, the main dependent variable was broken down into dichotomous measures of each type of alternative medicine, and logistic regression models were used to examine how SSC and non-SSC older adult respondents compared across each of these types. Second, we ran propensity score matching models (Morgan and Harding 2006) to address concerns regarding selection into SSC and non-SSC groups because of preexisting differences. Propensity score matching models reduced this concern by creating an experiment-like design through matching SSC respondents with those who report no SSC by key sociodemographic and behavioral variables (Guo and Fraser 2015). This set of analysis used the "pscore" command in Stata 13 and matched respondents using four methods (nearest neighbor, radius, kernel, and stratification). The following set of variables was used to match respondents: gender, race, education, political attitudes, religious affiliation, number of years spent living in current neighborhood, having ever smoked or drank, and having ever been forced to have sex. Past studies found these variables predict nonheterosexual orientation (e.g., Nagamatsu et al. 2012).

Results

Descriptive Results

Descriptive statistics for all key variables are described below. Approximately 4.21 percent of the sample reported at least one instance of SSC during their lifetime. This number is higher than other studies of older adults that used sexual identities as a sexual orientation measure (e.g., 2% in Fredriksen-Goldsen et al. 2013). This difference is expected because sexual contact measures are more inclusive, as explained earlier.

Out of the total sample ($N=2,519$), respondents reported an average of .68 type of alternative medicines used in the past twelve months. As expected, SSC respondents reported more alternative medicine use (1.14) than non-SSC respondents (.66; $p<.001$). We also compared SSC respondents and non-SSC respondents on sociodemographic background. In both groups, the majority of respondents were white and female. SSC respondents were a bit younger (67.97 years of age) than non-SSC respondents (69.29 years of age; n.s.). SSC respondents were significantly more educated than non-SSC respondents ($p<.001$), with approximately 36.79 percent of SSC respondents reporting having a bachelor's degree or more, compared with only 21.92 percent of non-SSC respondents. The two groups differed significantly across marital status as well, with more non-SSC respondents (22.67%) reporting being widowed than SSC respondents (9.43%) and more SSC respondents reporting being single (16.04%) than non-SSC respondents (2.78%) ($p<.001$). Finally, SSC respondents reported slightly lower levels of chronic health conditions (2.01) than non-SSC respondents (2.25) although the difference was not significant. This result was contrary to past research that demonstrated greater chronic conditions for SSC (Milan et al. 2008). The discrepancy from previous research may be due to SSCs' reduced access to health care (Orel 2014) because our measure of chronic conditions was based on official diagnoses, instead of self-assessments.

Multivariate Results

Table 8.1 presents results from negative binomial models that predicted alternative medicine usage by SSC. As model 1 shows, SSC respondents were 73 percent more likely to use alternative medicine than non-SSC respondents (Incidence Rate Ratio [IRR] = 1.73, $p<.001$), thus providing support for hypothesis 1. Model 2 shows that the association between SSC and alternative medicine usage remained significant when controlling for race, education, gender, and age (IRR = 1.51, $p<.01$). Results in model 3 did not support hypothesis 2 that health status

TABLE 8.1

Negative Binomial Regression Analysis Predicting Alternative Medicine Usage by SSC

Independent variables	Model 1	Model 2	Model 3
Same-sex contact	.546***	.412**	.421**
	(.143)	(.135)	(.135)
Control variables			
Age		−.017***	−.020***
		(.004)	(.004)
Race[a]			
Black		−.672***	−.686***
		(.110)	(.110)
Other		.279**	.300**
		(.097)	(.096)
Education[b]			
Less than high school		−.014	−.037
		(.106)	(.106)
Some college		.466***	.461***
		(.086)	(.086)
Bachelor's degree or more		.667***	.678***
		(.090)	(.090)
Female		.367***	.329***
		(.064)	(.064)
Potential mediator			
Health conditions scale			.070***
			(.021)
Model alpha coefficient	1.171	.861	.848
Constant	−.414***	.269	.299
Model Chi^2	14.71	203.47	214.61
Pseudo R^2	.0026	.0356	.0376
$N = 2,519$			

Notes: For coefficients, standard errors are in parentheses.

[a] Compared with white respondents.

[b] Compared with respondents with a high school diploma or equivalent.

[c] Compared with married respondents.

* $p < .05$; ** $p < .01$; *** $p < .001$.

partially mediates the relationship between SSC and alternative medicine usage. Health status was significantly associated with alternative medicine usage (.07; $p < .001$) as expected, but adding the number of chronic health conditions caused the coefficient for SSC to slightly *increase* from model 2 (.41, $p < .01$) to model 3 (.42, $p < .01$), instead of reducing it. This finding was not surprising given that SSC older adult respondents reported slightly lower levels of health conditions than non-SSC older adult respondents, as discussed previously.

Supplemental Findings

Comparing Variation across Alternative Medicine Types. Although hypothesis 1 was supported in negative binomial regressions that predicted the total count of alternative medicines used, we were interested in whether all alternative medicines or some specific ones contributed to the association with SSC. Therefore, we conducted separate analyses for each alternative medicine (detailed results available by request). These analyses showed that more SSC respondents reported using each type of alternative medicine than non-SSC respondents, although not all differences reached statistical significance. For example, 20.75 percent of SSC respondents, compared with 12.65 percent of non-SSC respondents, used high-dose or mega-vitamins ($p < .05$). Similarly, 16.98 percent of SSC respondents, compared with only 8.54 percent of non-SSC respondents, used massage therapies ($p < .01$). SSC differences in meditation and "other types" were not significant.

Propensity Score Matching Models. Propensity score matching was conducted to examine whether the association between SSC and alternative medicine usage persisted after considering selection effects (Guo and Fraser 2015), as discussed in the methods section. All four matching methods yielded similar findings, but only the radius matching model showed significant average treatment effect among the treated (ATT) (i.e., ATT was greater than standard error*2). The ATT was .14 in the model based on radius matching. This result meant that SSC respondents would report using .14 more alternative medicines in the past twelve months than non-SSC respondents who were matched by age, race, gender, education, neighborhood, health and sexual behaviors, religious affiliation, and political beliefs.

Conclusions

This chapter focused on the older adult population and examined sexual orientation differences in alternative medicine usage within the last twelve months using SSC as a measure of sexual orientation. The analysis showed that SSC individuals were more likely to use alternative medicine in the past year than non-SSC individuals. This difference held true when controlling for race, gender, education, and age. Further, SSC individuals were more likely to report using every type of alternative medicine, although differences in some types did not reach statistical significance. Propensity score matching models indicated that selection was unlikely to account for the SSC difference in alternative medicine use.

The use of SSC as a sexual orientation measure may have helped detect the sexual orientation difference in alternative medicine use. The measure is more encompassing than the commonly used measure that focuses on sexual identity because it helps identify respondents who may not label themselves as a sexual minority. Previous research has never used SSC as a measure for testing sexual orientation differences in alternative medicine usage, and future research needs to test the difference in other age groups using the measure, in light of the current significant finding for older adults. In addition, future research should use SSC to test sexual orientation differences in other treatment-seeking behaviors and health outcomes for older adults because the measure may help detect sexual orientation differences that the commonly used identity measure has been unable to detect.

The sexual orientation difference was not explained by chronic health conditions, and we were unable to identify factors that contributed to the difference. We argued that one possible explanation is sexual minorities' experience of stigma in mainstream medicine. Older adult sexual minorities experience double stigma faced for their age and sexual orientation statuses (Fenkl 2012), and those who have experienced discrimination in mainstream medicine may be less likely to seek treatments from the system for their ailments, particularly those related to their sexual minority status such as STD tests or HIV/AIDS-related treatments (Fenkl 2012; Fredriksen-Goldsen and Muraco 2010). Alternative medicine provides them with a less stigmatizing option for health care. Future research should directly test discrimination in mainstream medicine as a potential mediator for sexual orientation difference in alternative medicine use.

There are three main limitations of the study. First, the small number of people reporting SSC (4%) did not allow us to address the diversity within the sexual minority population. Second, although the SSC variable allowed for a more inclusive measure of sexual orientation, the measure did not consider the total number of same-sex partners and the timing of SSC within respondents' life course, as we discussed before. More nuanced measures would provide additional insights in future research. Third, the study is cross-sectional, looking only at Wave I (2005) data, thus limiting the ability to establish the causal ordering. Propensity score matching models were used to try to offset this selection issue, but future analyses should directly test the reciprocal relationship using longitudinal data.

The current result calls for greater attention from research and health care communities because sexual minorities' greater usage of alternative medicine may indicate heteronormativity in traditional health care. Older adults already face larger numbers of health conditions that require medical attention, and fear of and discrimination at the hands of mainstream health care professionals may create stress and, in the long run, undermine their health, instead of improving their health. Even if sexual minorities receive effective treatments in alternative medicine, their constrained choices would still represent their disadvantages in health care access. Moreover, alternative medicine is not regulated to the same extent as mainstream medicine (Banu, Varela, and Fernandes 2011), which may reduce the level of monitoring sexual minority older adults receive for their health care. These issues highlight the need for more research to understand why sexual minorities use alternative medicine more frequently and what consequences it has for their health.

REFERENCES

Banu, Jameela, Erika Varela, and Gabriel Fernandes. 2011. "Alternative Therapies for the Prevention and Treatment of Osteoporosis." *Nutrition Reviews* 70 (1): 22–40.

Barnes, P. M., B. Bloom, and R. L. Nahin. 2008. "Complementary and Alternative Medicine Use among Adults and Children: United States, 2007." *National Health Status Report* 12: 1–23.

Brotman, S., B. Ryan, and R. Cormier. 2003. "What Are Older Gay Men Like? An Impossible Question?" *Journal of Gay and Lesbian Social Services* 13 (4): 55–65.

Brown, Maria T., and Brian R. Grossman. 2014. "Same-Sex Sexual Relationships in the National Social Life, Health, and Aging Project: Making a Case for Data Collection." *Journal of Gerontological Social Work* 57 (2–4): 108–129.

Clark, Peter A. 2000. "The Ethics of Alternative Medicine Therapies." *Journal of Public Health Policy* 21 (4): 447–470.

Fenkl, Eric A. 2012. "Aging Gay Men: A Review of the Literature." *Journal of LGBT Issues in Counseling* 6 (3): 162–182.

Fredriksen-Goldsen, Karen I. 2014. "Promoting Health Equity among LGBT Mid-Life and Older Adults." *Journal of the American Society on Aging* 38 (4): 86–92.

Fredriksen-Goldsen, Karen I., K. Hyun-Jun, S. E. Barkan, A. Muraco, and C. P. Hoy-Ellis. 2013. "Health Disparities among Lesbian, Gay, and Bisexual Older Adults: Results from a Population-Based Study." *American Journal of Public Health* 103 (10): 1802–1809.

Fredriksen-Goldsen, Karen I., and Anna Muraco. 2010. "Aging and Sexual Orientation: A 25-Year Review of the Literature." *Research on Aging* 32 (3): 372–413.

Genke, J. 2004. "Resistance and Resilience: The Untold Story of Gay Men Aging with Chronic Illness." *Journal of Gay and Lesbian Social Services* 17 (2): 81–95.

Guo, S., and M. W. Fraser. 2015. *Propensity Score Analysis: Statistical Methods and Applications.* 2nd ed. Thousand Oaks, CA: Sage.

London, A. S., C. E. Foote-Ardah, J. A. Fleishman, and M. F. Shapiro. 2003. "Use of Alternative Therapists among People in Care for HIV in the United States." *American Journal of Public Health* 93: 980–987.

Matthews, A. K., T. L. Hughes, G. P. Osterman, and M. M. Kodl. 2005. "Complementary Medicine Practices in a Community-Based Sample of Lesbian and Heterosexual Women." *Health Care Women International* 26: 430–447.

McMahan, Shari, and Rafer Lutz. 2004. "Alternative Therapy Use among the Young-Old (Ages 65–74): An Evaluation of the MIDUS Database." *Journal of Applied Gerontology* 23 (2): 91–103.

Milan, F. B., J. H. Arnsten, R. S. Klein, E. E. Shoenbaum, G. Moskaleva, D. Buono, and M. P. Webber. 2008. "Use of Complementary and Alternative Medicine in Inner-City Persons with or at Risk for HIV Infection." *AIDS Patient Care—STDs* 22: 811–816.

Morgan, S. L. and D. J. Harding. 2006. "Matching Estimators of Causal Effects: Prospects and Pitfalls in Theory and Practice." *Sociological Methods and Research* 35: 3–60.

Nagamatsu, Miyuki, Niwako Yamawaki, Takeshi Sato, Aki Nakagawa, and Hisako Saito. 2012. "Factors Influencing Attitudes toward Sexual Activity among Early Adolescents in Japan." *Journal of Early Adolescence* 33 (2): 267–288.

Orel, Nancy. 2014. "Investigating the Needs and Concerns of Lesbian, Gay, Bisexual, and Transgender Older Adults: The Use of Qualitative and Quantitative Methodology." *Journal of Homosexuality* 61 (1): 53–78.

Smith, Helen A., Alicia Matthews, Nina Markovic, Ada Youk, Michelle E. Danielson, and Evelyn O. Talbott. 2010. "A Comparative Study of Complementary and Alternative Medicine Use among Heterosexually and Lesbian Identified Women: Data from the ESTHER Project (Pittsburgh, PA, 2003–2006)." *Journal of Alternative and Complementary Medicine* 16 (11): 1161–1170.

Vaidya, Sharad, Charu Kapoor, Abhishek Nagpal, Ajay Jain, and Aswini Kar. 2013. "Acupuncture: An Alternative Therapy in Medicine and Dentistry." *European Journal of General Dentistry* 2 (3): 219–231.

PART THREE

Physical Health, Mortality, and Health Care

9

Activity Limitation Disparities between Same-Sex and Different-Sex Couples

RUSSELL L. SPIKER

This chapter addresses factors contributing to activity limitations—impairments in bathing mobility, dressing, eating, or toilet use—for same-sex and different-sex couples. I start by outlining the innovations of couple-level research for health disparities between same-sex and different-sex partnerships. Then, I outline two major social determinants of health for couples that may offer insight into disparities between same-sex and different-sex couples: assortative mating and shared resources as mechanisms of health concordance (Meyler, Stimpson, and Peek 2007). Next, I describe the results of multinomial logistic regression analysis of activity limitations on couples' characteristics. I conclude by discussing trends in couple health and providing suggestions for future research.

Background

Sexual minorities, especially those in couples, experience more activity limitations than heterosexuals (Conron, Mimiaga, and Landers 2010; Fredricksen-Goldsen, Kim, and Barkan 2012; Spiker, Reczek, and Liu 2016). The concentration of activity limitations among partnered sexual minorities warrants investigating couples and their characteristics. Studying couples provides information that studying individuals does not offer in isolation. As an example, consider the following: individual-level studies tell us that sexual minorities are more likely to have activity limitations than their heterosexual counterparts, or that people in same-sex relationships are more likely to have activity limitations than people in different-sex couples, but not the degree to which health disadvantages concentrate within couples. In turn, this study tells us about partners' linked lives, a relatively unexplored subject in sexual minority health research (Umberson et al. 2015). Individual-level data might indicate that same-sex partners are more likely to have lived with a partner who has activity limitations; alternatively, they might signal that sexual minority couples are more likely to have two limited partners. Both possibilities signal important disparities, but the latter possibility could indicate severe difficulties for a subset of couples. These crucial pieces of knowledge are relevant to researchers and policy makers who want to address the needs of same-sex partners. Thus, couple studies provide insight into health concordance between partners and its impact on health disparities. My research shows how partners' combined demographic and socioeconomic characteristics are associated with their health, providing additional insight into the shared experiences of same-sex and different-sex partners.

Population research demonstrates that sexual minority status is a direct risk for activity limitations (Conron et al. 2010; Fredricksen-Goldsen et al. 2012). These studies all suggest that, controlling for sociodemographic confounders, sexual minority individuals experience heightened risk of activity limitations compared with heterosexual individuals, leading to population health disparities. However, sexual minority populations are not monolithic and do not experience uniform risk of activity limitations. Same-sex cohabiting women experience higher rates of activity limitations than either same-sex cohabiting men or different-sex partnered individuals (Siordia 2014). Spiker and colleagues (2016) estimate that partnered lesbian women (combining both married and unmarried cohabitors) experience more than twice the risk of activity limitations than married straight women, married straight men, and never-married lesbians; single gay men have lower risk than never-married straight men and straight cohabiting men. I am not aware of any research explaining why same-sex partnered women experience heightened disadvantage.

Given a lack of couple-level research, the health concordance patterns of same-sex partners still need to be established. Recent research offers a clue: same-sex spouses report higher rates of concordance in chronic health conditions and self-rated health than different-sex spouses (Holway, Umberson, and Donnelly 2018) and that concordance is higher among same-sex married women than men. However, this research does not focus on activity limitations, and it includes same-sex spouses rather than cohabitors. Still, same-sex cohabitors may experience higher concordance in activity limitations than different-sex couples, which I investigate with the following hypothesis:

> *Hypothesis 1*: Same-sex couples will experience higher rates of activity limitations due to higher rates of both partners having activity limitations than different-sex spouses (hypothesis 1a [H1a]) and different-sex cohabitors (hypothesis 1b [H1b]). Same-sex couples will also have higher rates of activity limitations for one partner than different-sex spouses (hypothesis 1c [H1c]) but similar rates to different-sex cohabitors (hypothesis 1d [H1d]). Same-sex female couples will have higher rates of activity limitations than same-sex male couples (hypothesis 1e [H1e]). Couple

characteristics such as race, age, nativity status, and economic resources are expected to explain some of these differences.

Sexual Minority Research and Couple Health Concordance

Health concordance describes how intimate partners resemble one another in health outcomes and behaviors, but extant research focuses almost entirely on heterosexual spouses (Meyler et al. 2007). Concordance may play a key role in health disparities between couples because it drives partners to have similar health behaviors and outcomes. There are three major mechanisms of concordance: selection, shared resources, and interpersonal influence (social support and social contagion). Due to a lack of information on interpersonal influences in my data set, I focus on selection and shared resources and attend to interpersonal influences where necessary.

SELECTION. Selection is the process by which people choose partners, and is a source of health similarity. Individuals tend to select their partners based on desired characteristics given one's own tastes and characteristics (Becker 1991; Lillard and Panis 1996). This leads to demographic and health similarity between partners, which is strongest among spouses (Lillard and Panis 1996; Qian and Lichter 2007). Several studies show that same-sex cohabitors display more age and racial diversity and more economic homogeneity than different-sex spouses and cohabitors (Jepsen and Jepsen 2002; Schwartz and Graf 2009). Among heterosexual couples, dissimilarity in race, age, and nativity status (Kalmijn 1998; Schueths 2014; Teachman 2002) all increase relationship stress, and thus may affect stress-related health issues. It is not clear whether demographic matching is associated with health in similar ways for same-sex couples. Additionally, recent research suggests that same-sex spouses are more concordant on self-rated health, presence of chronic conditions, smoking behavior, and exercise than heterosexual spouses (Holway et al. 2018). This suggests that activity limitations concordance may be higher among same-sex cohabitors, but the previous study focused on same-sex spouses, not cohabitors, and did not directly measure activity limitations. To my knowledge, there are no existing data that allow an analysis of selection on health for the couples I study, so I restrict my analysis to demographic matching. I use age, race, and nativity status to capture selection. Due to different-sex spouses' greater demographic similarity than different-sex cohabitors or same-sex couples, I propose the following hypothesis:

> Hypothesis 2: Same-sex cohabitors' greater demographic dissimilarity accounts for some of the activity limitations disparity compared with different-sex spouses (hypothesis 2a [H2a]), but will not explain differences between same-sex and different-sex cohabiting couples

(hypothesis 2b [H2b]) because their demographic matching patterns are similar.

SHARED RESOURCES. Socioeconomic status influences partners' health by providing them with shared resources and stressors. Socioeconomic conditions are a known "fundamental cause" of health and illness (Phelan, Link, and Tehranifar 2010). Resources are a source of the "marital health boost" experienced by different-sex spouses over different-sex cohabitors (Light 2004; Meyler et al. 2007; Waite 1995), but same-sex cohabitors generally experience socioeconomic advantages over different-sex married couples. Same-sex couples generally have higher educational attainment, joint employment, and higher earnings parity (Black, Sanders, and Taylor 2007) than different-sex spouses or cohabitors. Same-sex couples have higher income-to-needs ratios than heterosexuals, in part due to smaller family size (Black et al. 2007). However, same-sex couples also have more educational heterogeneity (Jepsen and Jepsen 2002) and lower health insurance rates (Gonzales and Blewett 2014) than different-sex spouses, which may offset some of the other economic advantages. Given same-sex cohabitors' general resources advantages, I propose the following hypothesis:

> *Hypothesis 3*: Shared resources provide a buffer against activity limitations for same-sex cohabitors relative to different-sex couples (hypothesis 3a [H3a]), different-sex cohabitors' low resources explain their activity limitations risk relative to same-sex couples (hypothesis 3b [H3b]), and shared resources explain any differences between same-sex male and female cohabitors (hypothesis 3c [H3c]).

Method

Sample

Data come from the 1997–2015 Integrated Public Use Microdata Series National Health Interview Surveys (IPUMS-NHIS) (Blewett et al. 2016). The IPUMS-NHIS are cross-sectional household studies conducted annually by the National Center for Health Statistics. Data are generalizable to the noninstitutionalized population of the United States. I included partners from the ages of eighteen to sixty-five to account for the working-aged population of the United States, in keeping with previous research (Conron et al. 2010; Siordia 2014; Spiker et al. 2016), who had no missing data on unimputed variables.

Dependent Variable

The dependent variable is the incidence of activity limitations in a couple. The IPUMS-NHIS provides a summary variable (LANY) for whether a person reports needing assistance bathing or showering, getting into or out of beds or chairs, dressing, eating, or using the toilet. Values are "Limited in any way," "Not limited in any way," "Not limited or unknown," and "Unknown if limited." For each individual, I recorded 1="limited in any way" and 0="not limited in any way/not limited or unknown"; I deleted "unknown if limited" cases. I then added together both partners' limitations for the dependent variable: "neither partner limited," "one partner limited," or "both partners limited."

Independent Variables

Union Status. The focal independent variable, union status, measures partners' sex and marital status. I identified couples in which each partner reported the other as "unmarried partner" or "spouse" and coded them "same-sex" or "different-sex" based on partners' reported sex. I omitted same-sex spouses because there is an embargo on data between 2004 and 2007, which cut the already-limited sample size of same-sex spouses, and I did not have state-level identifiers to determine whether same-sex marriage was available to a couple (National Center for Health Statistics 2015). The final sample included 275,111 different-sex married couples, 33,401 different-sex cohabiting couples, 1,334 same-sex male cohabiting couples, and 1,510 same-sex female cohabiting couples.

Selection. Selection measures included racial composition (both white [reference], both black, both "other race," interracial), difference in partners' ages (single years), and nativity composition (both U.S. born [reference], one U.S. born, both foreign born).

ECONOMIC CHARACTERISTICS. I include two types of economic controls: shared resources and economic difference. Shared resources include partners' averaged educational attainment (using 0=less than high school; 1=high school or GED equivalent; 2=some college; 3=associate's degree or equivalent; 4=bachelor's degree or equivalent; 5=graduate or professional degree; insurance status (both partners insured [reference]; one partner insured; neither partner insured); employment status (both partners employed [reference]; one partner employed; neither partner employed); and the income-to-needs ratio, which compares total household income with the poverty threshold for a family of its size (0=0%–99%; 1=100%–199%; 2=200%–299%; 3=300%–399%; 4=400%–499%; 5=over 500%). Income-to-needs was recoded from the IPUMS-NHIS variable POVERTY2, harmonized with the five IMPOV imputation variables, and multiply imputed. Economic difference included difference in education (absolute value of the difference in partners' educational attainment) and earnings difference (the absolute value of the difference between partners' earnings using the following values supplied by the IPUMS-NHIS: 1=$1–$4,999; 2=$5,000–$9,999; 3=$10,000–$14,999; 4=$15,000–$19,999; 5=$20,000–$24,999; 6=$25,000–$34,999; 7=$35,000–$44,999; 8=$45,000–$54,999; 9=$55,000–$64,999; 10=$65,000–$74,999; 11=$75,000 and up). Earnings data were multiply imputed using the five EARNIMP variables provided by IPUMS-NHIS.

Controls

Region (Northeast [reference], North Central/Midwest, West, South), age (continuous, single years), and survey year (continuous, zeroed at 1997) were control variables across all regression models.

Analytic Plan

Analyses were survey-weighted and multiply imputed for missing income data using the mi estimate: svy: mlogit commands in Stata 14. I conducted bivariate analyses including tests for differences in proportions and means by union status (available by request) for each variable. The base outcome of the multinomial regressions was "neither partner limited." I used two-tailed $\alpha = .05$ for all comparisons. I regressed activity limitations on union status using these control and independent variable blocks: "base model" with no controls; controls only; controls + selection; controls + economic resources; "full model" with controls + selection + economic resources. The models presented in this chapter were chosen for parsimony; other models are available upon request. I rotated the union status reference groups to compare between all couple types.

Results

Bivariate Results

Bivariate results show differences between couple types on activity limitations, demographic characteristics, and economic resources. The results show 85.8 percent of different-sex married couples, 84.1 percent of different-sex cohabiting couples, 85.2 percent of same-sex male cohabiting couples, and 79.7 percent of same-sex female cohabiting couples report neither partner has activity limitations. For one limited partner, those numbers are 11.6 percent, 12.5 percent, 12.0 percent, and 15.3 percent, respectively. Different-sex cohabitors have higher rates of activity limitations for one or both partners than different-sex married couples. Same-sex female cohabitors have higher rates of activity limitations for one or both partners than all other couple types.

Same-sex couples are more demographically dissimilar than different-sex spouses. Same-sex male couples are most likely to be interracial (10.5%), followed by different-sex cohabitors (7.9%), same-sex female couples (6.5%), and different-sex spouses (3.8%). Same-sex male cohabitors have the highest average age difference (6.0 years), followed by same-sex female couples (5.4 years), different-sex cohabitors (4.7 years), and different-sex spouses (3.6 years). Same-sex female cohabitors are most likely to be both U.S. born (88.1%), followed by different-sex cohabiting couples (82.3%), same-sex male cohabitors (81.8%), and different-sex

spouses (78.5%). Same-sex male cohabitors are the most likely to have one partner foreign born and one U.S. born (13.4%), followed by different-sex cohabitors
(8.1%), different-sex spouses (8.0%), and finally same-sex female cohabitors (7.7%).

Overall, same-sex couples tend to have more socioeconomic resources than
different-sex couples. Same-sex male cohabitors are most likely to both be
employed (71.7%), followed by same-sex female cohabitors (70.1%), different-sex
cohabitors (63.0%), and different-sex spouses (61.3%). Different-sex cohabitors are
most likely to have neither partner employed (7.6%), followed by same-sex female
cohabitors (7.3%), same-sex male cohabitors (6.7%), and different-sex spouses
(6.1%). Different-sex spouses are most likely to have both partners insured (85.1%),
followed by same-sex female cohabitors (75.6%), same-sex male cohabitors
(72.9%), and different-sex cohabitors (52.9%). Different-sex cohabitors are most
likely to have only one partner insured (30.1%), followed by same-sex male cohabitors (18.2%), same-sex female cohabitors (17.2%), and different-sex spouses
(5.4%). Average educational attainment for same-sex male and same-sex female
couples was a bachelor's degree (mean of 2.9), some college for different-sex
spouses (mean of 2.4), and high school or equivalent for different-sex cohabitors (mean of 1.9). Same-sex male cohabitors have the highest average income-
to-needs ratio (380%), followed by same-sex female couples (340%), different-sex
spouses (330%), and different-sex cohabitors (250%).

Regression Results

Table 9.1 shows multinomial regression results with basic controls for three
regression models. Results pertaining to the hypotheses are discussed in the following text.

In model 1, compared with different-sex spouses, same-sex male and female
cohabitors have higher odds of activity limitations for one partner and same-
sex female cohabitors have higher odds of activity limitations for both partners.
These results are partially consistent with H1a and consistent with H1c. Compared with same-sex male cohabitors, same-sex female cohabitors have
45 percent higher odds of one limited partner ($p = .004$) and 111 percent higher
odds of two limited partners ($p = .003$); different-sex cohabitors have 46 percent
higher odds of one limited partner ($p < .001$) and 104 percent higher odds of two
limited partners ($p < .001$). These results are not consistent with H1b, consistent
with H1d for same-sex partnered women only, and consistent with H1e. Controlling selection (model 2) shows that racial composition works in expected ways
for health, but nativity status dissimilarity and age dissimilarity are associated
with lower odds of activity limitations for one or both partners. All dissimilarity is not negative for health. Selection eliminates the difference in activity limitations between same-sex male cohabitors and different-sex spouses, so
demographic differences may increase same-sex male cohabitors' risk of activity limitations. However, same-sex female cohabitors' odds of activity limitations

TABLE 9.1

Multinomial Logistic Regression of Activity Limitations on Union Status, Controls, Selection, and Shared Resources ($N = 311{,}356$)

Variables	Model 1				Model 2				Model 3			
	One limited		Both limited		One limited		Both limited		One limited		Both limited	
	OR	SE	OR	SE	OR	SE	OR	SE	OR	SE	OR	SE
Union status [ref.: Different-sex married]												
Same-sex male Cohabiting	1.24*[b]	.12	1.40[b]	.28	1.05[b]	.10	1.12[b]	.23	1.35**[b]	.14	1.51[b]	.35
Same-sex female Cohabiting	1.80***[a]	.15	2.95***[a]	.42	1.53***[a]	.13	2.41***[a]	.34	1.82***[a]	.15	2.95***[a]	.46
Different-sex Cohabiting	1.82***[a]	.04	2.86***[a]	.11	1.61***[a]	.04	2.42***[a]	.10	1.17***[b]	.03	1.32***[b]	.06
Controls												
Region [ref.: Northeast]												
North	1.24***	.03	1.37***	.07	1.17***	.03	1.28***	.07	1.09**	.03	1.11	.06
Central/Midwest	1.26***	.03	1.57***	.07	1.19***	.03	1.47***	.07	.99	.02	1.06	.05
South	1.16***	.03	1.24***	.07	1.21***	.03	1.29***	.07	1.10***	.03	1.17**	.06
West	1.06***	.00	1.10***	.00	1.05***	.00	1.10***	.00	1.05***	.00	1.08***	.00
Mean age Survey year	.98***	.00	.99**	.00	.98***	.00	.99*	.00	.98***	.00	1.00	.00
Selection												
Race [ref.: Both white]												
Both black					1.17***	.03	1.25***	.06	.97	.02	.81***	.04

	Model 1		Model 2		Model 3		Model 4	
Both other race	.83***	.03	.90	.08	.91*	.04	.81*	.07
Interracial	1.26***	.04	1.35***	.09	1.23***	.04	1.26**	.09
Nativity status [ref.: Both U.S. born]								
One U.S. born	.73***	.02	.62***	.04	.71***	.02	.64***	.04
Both foreign born	.49***	.01	.40***	.02	.3***	.01	.19***	.01
Age difference	.73***	.02	.62***	.04	1.02***	.00	1.03***	.00
Economic difference								
Difference in earnings					.99***	.00	.98***	.00
Difference in education					1.07***	.01	1.09***	.02
Shared resources					.85***	.01	.76***	.01
Mean education								
Insurance [ref.: Both insured]								
One insured					2.07***	.06	2.54***	.16
Neither insured					1.44***	.04	2.31***	.13
Employment [ref.: Both employed]								
One employed					3.41***	.06	3.59***	.16
Neither employed					3.70***	.09	15.7***	.71
Income-to-needs ratio					.92***	.00	.85***	.00

Note: Data from 1997–2015 IPUMS-NHIS. All data survey weighted. Missing earnings and income data imputed.

* *p* < .05; ** *p* < .01; *** *p* < .001; a differs from same-sex male cohabitors (*p* < .05); b differs from same-sex female cohabitors (*p* < .05).

for one or both partners compared with different-sex spouses are reduced, but not eliminated. These findings are consistent with H2a. Model 2 does not notably change differences between same-sex cohabitors and different-sex cohabitors, consistent with H2b.

In general, resources (model 3) work in the expected direction. Difference in education, lack of health insurance, and lack of employment are associated with higher odds of activity limitations. Higher education and income-to-needs ratios are associated with lower odds of activity limitations, as is greater difference in earnings. For same-sex cohabitors, holding resources constant reveals heightened disadvantages relative to different-sex spouses, with higher odds of one limited partner for same-sex male and female cohabitors and higher odds of two limited partners for same-sex female cohabitors. These results are consistent with H3a.

Differences between same-sex male cohabitors and different-sex cohabitors are reduced to nonsignificance by resource controls. Different-sex cohabitors are less likely to report activity limitations compared with same-sex female cohabitors (35% less likely for one partner [$p < .001$]; 55% less likely for both partners [$p < .001$]), consistent with H3b. Finally, compared with same-sex male cohabitors, same-sex female cohabitors show 35 percent higher odds of one limited partner ($p = .028$), and 96 percent higher odds of two limited partners ($p = .019$). These results do not support H3c.

Discussion

My study is the first to explore the prevalence of activity limitations for both partners in a couple, as well as the role of selection and shared resources as mechanisms in activity limitations disparities. Overall, sexual minority status is associated with higher risk of activity limitations. Selection on demographic characteristics may explain some of the activity limitations disparities between couples, but shared resources likely play a protective role for same-sex couples' activity limitations risk. Without holding selection and resources equal, all couple types have between 84.7 percent (same-sex cohabiting) and 88.4 percent (different-sex married) partners reporting concordance in activity limitations. However, for same-sex female cohabitors and different-sex cohabitors, a greater proportion of that concordance is concentrated in both partners having activity limitations than other couples. This may explain the lack of support for H1b and inconsistent support for H1d. As expected (H1c), same-sex couples have higher rates of activity limitations for one partner than different-sex spouses, and same-sex female couples have similar rates to different-sex cohabitors. Same-sex cohabiting women have greater rates of activity limitations for one or both partners than same-sex cohabiting men (consistent H1e). These results expand upon the findings of previous research (Fredricksen-Goldsen et al. 2012;

Siordia 2014; Spiker et al. 2016) by showing that same-sex partnered women's activity limitations disparities lead to concentrated disadvantages that elevate the possibility that both partners will experience activity limitations relative to same-sex male cohabitors and different-sex spouses. Results suggest that selection and shared resources play important roles in these disparities.

Selection

Selection patterns were consistent with prior research (Jepsen and Jepsen 2002; Schwartz and Graf 2009). Controlling for selection reduces the difference between same-sex male couples and different-sex spouses. The results suggest this dissimilarity is associated with activity limitations risk for same-sex cohabiting men and women relative to different-sex spouses, though more for men than for women (consistent with H2a).

Selection did not explain differences between same-sex and different-sex cohabitors (consistent with H2b), or between same-sex cohabiting men and women (consistent with H2c), likely because the couples were generally demographically similar to one another. Research on heterosexual couples shows that partner dissimilarity can create stress (Kalmijn 1998; Schueths 2014; Teachman 2002), and research suggests that couple-level stressors may amplify the health risks created by sexual minority stress, which is the social stress created by stigma against same-sex relationships (Frost et al. 2017; Meyer 2003). Demographic dissimilarity may also work differently for same-sex and different-sex couples, which could explain why same-sex cohabiting men's greater age and nativity status dissimilarity was not protective of their health, as would be suggested by the regression. Instead, interracial and nonnative couples may experience minority stress from multiple sources that increases health issues (Frost et al. 2017). Future research should further investigate this possibility.

Shared Resources

Shared resources appear to protect same-sex cohabitors against activity limitations relative to different-sex couples. The socioeconomic characteristics observed for same-sex couples are consistent with prior research (Black et al. 2007; Jepsen and Jepsen 2002; Schwartz and Graf 2009). With resources held constant, same-sex cohabiting men experience higher odds of activity limitations for one partner and same-sex cohabiting women experienced higher odds of activity limitations for one or both partners compared with different-sex spouses (consistent with H3a). Holding resources constant greatly reduced different-sex cohabitors' activity limitations risk relative to same-sex cohabitors (consistent with H3b). Notably, same-sex female cohabitors had significantly higher risk of activity limitations than different-sex cohabitors after resource controls. These findings suggest that shared resources are an important protector of same-sex couple health.

Holding resources equal did not explain differences in activity limitations risk between same-sex cohabiting men and women (inconsistent with H3c). Despite being fundamental causes of health disparities (Phelan et al. 2010), same-sex male cohabitors' greater resources do little to explain their advantage over same-sex female cohabitors. These results highlight the intersection of sexual minority status with other social statuses. Sex and sexual minority status may intersect in a few different ways. First, sexual minority women may face a "double disadvantage" being sexual minorities in a heterosexist society and women in a patriarchal society, leading to amplified stress (e.g., Frost et al. 2017). Second, concordance in health risk behaviors and apparently higher levels of social contagion among same-sex partnered women may also contribute (Holway et al. 2018). Finally, sexual minority women may use different selection criteria for partners due to acceptance of body and health diversity among sexual minority women, the higher incidence of activity limitations within their partner pool, or both. These possibilities should be investigated by future research.

Remaining Disparities

Controlling for selection and resources does not fully explain disparities between couples. Different-sex cohabiting couples remain more likely to have activity limitations than different-sex spouses after controlling for selection and resources, signaling that something else differentiates them. Throughout many of the models, different-sex cohabitors are more similar to same-sex cohabitors than to different-sex spouses. This may be due to the importance of marriage as an institution (e.g., Waite 1995). Additionally, processes such as social contagion and social control may drive disparities between married and unmarried couples. Future research that includes interpersonal interactions and compares same-sex spouses and same-sex cohabitors will help clarify the contributions of these factors.

Limitations

Consider these limitations when interpreting these results. First, the cross-sectional nature of the study makes causal inference uncertain, especially for socioeconomic status and health, which can impact one another. Second, this study infers sexual minority status from partnership and sex; these results should not be generalized to "gay"- and "lesbian"-identified populations. Third, due to cell size and data availability, certain variables (such as "racial composition") could be expanded in future research. Fourth, the sample of same-sex partnered men had relatively few couples in which both partners reported activity limitations ($n=40$), which may reduce significant differences between same-sex male couples and other couples. Finally, the lack of data on stress and interpersonal health influences is a shortcoming of available data; having such data in large population surveys would greatly improve future studies of sexual minority health.

Conclusions

My study demonstrates that sexual minority health disparities result from couple-level factors as well as individual-level factors. Sexual minority status is associated with couple-level activity limitations risk. Selection differences between same-sex and different-sex couples contribute to this disparity, possibly due to the proliferation of minority stress. Economic resources likely protect against sexual minority health disparities. Overall, same-sex cohabiting women experience a particularly high risk of activity limitations compared with other couples. This may occur due to the social stress associated with being both women and sexual minorities in a heterosexist and patriarchal society, or due to different processes in health behaviors and social control. Further research is necessary.

From these results, it is clear that a complete understanding of these disparities requires research on couples in addition to extant research on individuals. Sexual minority health disparities are gendered and associated with partners' combined social characteristics. Future research needs to investigate how gender, sexual minority status, union status, and health concordance affect other health outcomes. Such research will illuminate solutions that address the social roots of health disparities.

REFERENCES

Becker, Gary. 1991. *A Treatise on the Family.* Cambridge, MA: Harvard University Press.

Black, Dan, Seth G. Sanders, and Lowell J. Taylor. 2007. "The Economics of Lesbian and Gay Families." *Journal of Economic Perspectives* 21: 53–70.

Blewett, Lynn A., Julia A. Rivera Drew, Risa Griffin, Miram L. King, and Kari C. W. Williams. 2016. *IPUMS Health Surveys: National Health Interview Survey, Version 6.2.* Minneapolis: University of Minnesota.

Conron, Kerith J., Matthew J. Mimiaga, and Stewart J. Landers. 2010. "A Population-Based Study of Sexual Orientation Identity and Gender Differences in Health." *American Journal of Public Health* 100: 1953–1960.

Fredriksen-Goldsen, Karen I., Hyun-Jun Kim, and Susan E. Barkan. 2012. "Disability among Lesbian, Gay, and Bisexual Adults: Disparities in Prevalence and Risk." *American Journal of Public Health* 102: e16–21.

Frost, David M., Allen J. LeBlanc, Brian de Vries, Eli Alston-Stepnitz, Rob Stephenson, and Cory Woodyatt. 2017. "Couple-Level Minority Stress: An Examination of Same-Sex Couples' Unique Experiences." *Journal of Health and Social Behavior* 58: 455–472.

Gonzales, Gilbert, and Lynn A. Blewett. 2014. "National and State-Specific Health Insurance Disparities for Adults in Same-sex Relationships." *American Journal of Public Health* 104: E95–104.

Holway, Giuseppina Valle, Debra Umberson, and Rachel Donnelly. 2018. "Health and Health Behavior Concordance between Spouses in Same-Sex and Different-Sex Marriages." *Social Currents* 5: 319–327.

Jepsen, Lisa. K., and Christopher A. Jepsen. 2002. "An Empirical Analysis of the Matching Patterns of Same-Sex and Opposite-Sex Couples." *Demography* 39: 435–453.

Kalmijn, Matthijs. 1998. "Marriage and Homogamy: Causes, Patterns, Trends." *Annual Review of Sociology* 24: 395–421.

Light, Aubrey. 2004. "Gender Differences in the Marriage and Cohabitation Income Premium." *Demography* 41: 263–284.

Lillard, Lee A., and Constantijn W. A. Panis. 1996. "Marital Status and Mortality." *Demography* 33: 313–327.

Meyer, Ilan H. 2003. "Prejudice, Social Stress, and Mental Health in Lesbian, Gay, and Bisexual Populations: Conceptual Issues and Research Evidence." *Psychological Bulletin* 129: 674–697.

Meyler, Deanna, Jim P. Stimpson, and M. Kristen Peek. 2007. "Health Concordance within Couples: A Systematic Review." *Social Science & Medicine* 64: 2297–2310.

National Center for Health Statistics. 2015. *Changes to Data Editing Procedures and the Impact on Identifying Same-Sex Married Couples: 2004–2007 National Health Interview Surveys.* Washington, DC: U.S. Government Printing Office.

Phelan, Jo C., Bruce G. Link, and Parisa Tehranifar. 2010. "Social Conditions as Fundamental Causes of Health Inequalities: Theory, Evidence, and Policy Implications." *Journal of Health and Social Behavior* 51: S28–40.

Qian, Zhenchao, and Daniel T. Lichter. 2007. "Social Boundaries and Marital Assimilation: Interpreting Trends in Racial and Ethnic Intermarriage." *American Sociological Review* 72: 68–94.

Schueths, April. 2014. "'It's Almost like White Supremacy': Interracial Mixed-Status Couples Facing Nativism." *Ethnic and Racial Studies* 37: 2438–2456.

Schwartz, Christine R., and Nikki L. Graf. 2009. "Assortative Matching among Same-Sex and Different-Sex Couples in the United States." *Demographic Research* 21: 843–878.

Siordia, Carlos. 2014. "Disability Estimates between Same- and Different-Sex Couples: Microdata from the American Community Survey (2009–2011)." *Sexuality and Disability* 33: 107–121.

Spiker, Russell L., Corinne Reczek, and Hui Liu. 2016. "Activity Limitation Disparities by Sexual Minority Status, Gender, and Union Status." In *Applied Demography and Health in the 21st Century*, edited by M. N. Hoque, B. Pecotte, and M. A. McGehee, 183–200. New York: Springer.

Teachman, Jay D. 2002. "Stability across Cohorts in Divorce Risk Factors." *Demography* 39: 331–351.

Umberson, Debra, Mieke Beth Thomeer, Riannan A. Kroeger, Amy C. Lodge, and Minle Xu. 2015. "Challenges and Opportunities for Research on Same-Sex Relationships." *Journal of Marriage and Family* 77: 96–111.

Waite, Linda J. 1995. "Does Marriage Matter?" *Demography* 32: 483–507.

10

Same-Sex Unions and Adult Mortality Risk

A Nationally Representative Analysis

ANDREW FENELON

CHRISTINA DRAGON

CORINNE RECZEK

HUI LIU

Understanding the link between marriage and health has been a central area of inquiry for scholars and public health professionals interested in the social determinants of health. Married individuals experience better health and lower mortality risk than divorced, widowed, and never-married individuals, although this advantage is highly dependent on the extant social context. For example, the "marital advantage" in mortality partially reflects socioeconomic and health selection into and out of marriage, but it also has to do with the benefits of long-term legalized partnerships (Waite and Gallagher 2002). Legal marriage is associated with benefits in a number of domains, including providing a source of social support, bolstering economic circumstances, and improving health-related behaviors (Goldman, Korenman, and Weinstein 1995). Cohabiting couples are likely to receive some, but not all, of the benefits of marriage by virtue of lower levels of economic and social resources among cohabitors (Liu and Reczek 2012). Until recently, same-sex couples did not have access to legal marriage—and as a result to the legal protections of marriage—in most states, and thus most same-sex couples experienced cohabitation rather than marriage.

While the vast majority of the previous research on union status and health has focused on different-sex unions, it remains largely an open question regarding health in same-sex unions (Liu, Reczek, and Brown 2013). Individuals in same-sex unions receive many of the same social and economic benefits as those in different-sex unions (Wienke and Hill 2008). However, they are likely to face distinct challenges in many domains that relate to health (Umberson et al. 2015), as there is growing evidence that sexual minority populations (e.g., gay, lesbian, and bisexual-identified individuals) face unique health risks and that their health care needs are not always adequately addressed by the health care system (Clift and Kirby 2012; Gonzales and Blewett 2014). These unique health risks are also factors that are associated with mortality risk. A growing body of work has begun to explore whether the "marital advantage" in health extends to sexual minorities, although few of these studies examine the outcome of mortality, mainly due to data limitations.

In recent years, the emergence of nationally representative population-based research has been an important development in our understanding of the health and health care experience of those in same-sex unions (Institute of Medicine 2011). Same-sex cohabitors generally report poorer health than different-sex married but better health than different-sex cohabitors, despite having a socioeconomic advantage over both comparison groups (Denney, Gorman, and Barrera 2013; Liu, Reczek, and Brown 2013). Experiences of discrimination and homophobia have been shown to lead to deleterious health impacts in the short and long terms (Frost, Lehavot, and Meyer 2015). These effects include increased psychological distress and poorer mental health (Mays and Cochran 2001), increased risk of developing chronic conditions and disability (Gonzales and Henning-Smith 2014), reduced health care access (Gonzales and Blewett 2014; Gonzales and Henning-Smith 2017), and poorer health-related behaviors (Reczek, Liu, and Spiker 2014). These patterns may combine to raise the risk of early mortality for sexual minorities as a function of greater experiences of stigma in interpersonal and institutional relationships. Indeed, sexual minorities who experience greater levels of prejudice experience elevated mortality, driven by increased stress for individuals in high-stigma communities (Hatzenbuehler et al. 2014).

Although there are particular mortality risks that have been shown to be consistently higher among sexual minorities, such as suicide and HIV, until recently there was little evidence for a broad increase in all-cause mortality. A study using data from the 1990s found that men who reported same-sex sexual partners experienced elevated mortality risk in comparison with men who did not report same-sex partners, although this was driven by HIV-related mortality (Cochran and Mays 2011). As mortality from HIV was reduced, studies using more recent data found no excess mortality among men with same-sex partners, although women with same-sex sexual partners were at greater risk of suicide (Cochran and Mays 2015). However, a recent analysis demonstrates that sexual minority adults under age sixty experienced elevated all-cause mortality relative to heterosexuals, and this effect could not be explained by socioeconomic and demographic confounding (Cochran, Björkenstam, and Mays 2016). This finding is consistent with a small cohort study in Denmark that found elevated all-cause mortality risk for men and women in same-sex marriages following legalization (Frisch and Brønnum-Hansen 2009). These studies guide our expectations for the mortality experience of those in same-sex unions in the United

States; we expect that individuals in same-sex unions will experience a mortality disadvantage compared with those in different-sex unions. Specifically, we expect that same-sex cohabitors will have higher mortality risk than the different-sex married, but similar mortality experience to different-sex cohabitors. Additionally, we expect that socioeconomic status will not explain the mortality disadvantage of those in same-sex unions relative to the different-sex married.

Methods

Data

This chapter uses data from the National Health Interview Survey Linked-Mortality Files (NHIS-LMF) in years 1997–2009, with mortality follow-up through 2011. NHIS is a nationally representative multistage household survey collected annually by the National Center for Health Statistics. The survey includes a household component (containing information on the structure of the household) and a person component (containing information on the demographic and health characteristics of each household member). The vital status of each survey respondent is available through the end of 2011 based on a probabilistic linkage of NHIS to the National Death Index. Month of death is available for those who died. NHIS-LMF is one of the most commonly used sources of data for population-based studies of mortality differentials in the United States, and estimated mortality hazards are similar to those found in official U.S. life tables (Ingram, Lochner, and Cox 2008).

Variables and Sample

Studies examining health for those in same-sex unions and different-sex unions have typically compared same-sex cohabitors with individuals in different-sex cohabiting unions and different-sex married unions (Denney, Gorman, and Barrera 2013a; Liu, Reczek, and Brown 2013; Reczek, Liu, and Brown 2014a). We adopt this approach in our examination of differences in all-cause mortality risk. In 1997, NHIS began to collect information on unmarried partners as part of the household roster of the survey (Liu, Reczek, and Brown 2013). For each surveyed household, the "reference" person indicates his or her relationship to each household individual. Same-sex cohabitors are identified by matching the sex of the reference person and the sex of an individual identified as an unmarried partner. Using this approach, individuals are categorized by union type: different-sex married unions, different-sex cohabiting (unmarried) unions, or same-sex cohabiting (unmarried) unions. Although the populations in same-sex unions do not overlap wholly with gay, lesbian, and bisexual-identified individuals (i.e., they do not include those not in unions and do not measure sexual identity during our study period), they represent an important lens through which to observe mortality differences between sexual minorities and heterosexuals. Households containing "married spouses" of the same sex were excluded from the analysis. This is because a study by the National Center for Health Statistics (National Center for Health Statistics 2015) indicated that the potential for mis-classification of same-sex unions was highest for marriages. Even a very small number of different-sex married respondents with miscoded sex in NHIS could lead to a significant inflation of the number of same-sex marriages.

In addition to union status, we adjust for socioeconomic and demographic characteristics of individuals including age, sex, race-ethnicity (non-Hispanic white, non-Hispanic black, non-Hispanic other, Hispanic), education (less than high school, high school diploma, some college, bachelor's degree or more), family income-to-poverty ratio (<100%, 100–200%, 200–400%, 400%+), employment status (employed, unemployed, not in labor force), health insurance status (insured, uninsured, unknown), and year of interview.

Our sample includes all individuals in same-sex or different-sex unions eligible for linkage to the mortality file and who have non-missing values on the covariates. Because our focus is on individuals in same-sex or different-sex unions, unpartnered individuals (never married, divorced, widowed) are excluded from the sample. The total sample is 420,592 individuals from the age of twenty-five through the age of seventy-four at the time of interview. We restrict the sample adults twenty-five and above to ensure that most individuals in the sample have completed their education. We restrict the sample to adults under age seventy-five to reduce the number of potentially miscoded same-sex unions at older ages. Of the total sample, 385,285 respondents are in different-sex marriages, 32,371 are in different-sex cohabiting unions, and 2,936 are in same-sex cohabiting unions. The pooled sample provides a large enough number of deaths to calculate estimates of mortality hazards for very small populations, such as the population of those in same-sex unions. Nearly 24,000 deaths are observed in the sample through 2011, with 22,507 occurring to different-sex married individuals, 1,319 to different-sex cohabitors, and 117 to same-sex cohabitors. There is an insufficient number of deaths in the NHIS among those in same-sex unions to disaggregate differences by cause of death. However, the distribution of deaths across broad cause-of-death categories is similar between those in same-sex and different-sex unions.

Statistical Analysis

We use Cox proportional hazards models to estimate differences in all-cause mortality hazards by union type for individuals from the age of twenty-five through the age of seventy-four at the time of the survey. These models compare individuals in different-sex married unions (the reference group), different-sex cohabiting unions, and same-sex cohabiting unions. The initial model adjusts demographic characteristics (age, sex, race-ethnicity) and year of interview. The second model adds controls for socioeconomic characteristics, which may play an important role in mortality differences by union type (Liu, Reczek, and Brown 2013). All models account for the complex survey design of the NHIS, and respondents are weighted to adjust for eligibility status in the NHIS mortality linkage.

Results

Descriptive analysis of the NHIS sample suggests that those in same-sex and different-sex cohabiting unions are younger on average than those in different-sex marriages. Same-sex cohabitors are more likely to be non-Hispanic white than different-sex cohabitors and have higher socioeconomic status than the different-sex married. Same-sex cohabitors are more likely to have a bachelor's degree, more likely to be employed, and more likely to have incomes greater than 400 percent of the poverty line than are those in different-sex marriages, while different-sex cohabitors are disadvantaged on these measures. For example, 43 percent of individuals in same-sex cohabiting unions have at least a college degree, compared with 30 percent of the different-sex married and 17 percent of different-sex cohabitors. Different-sex cohabitors have the lowest socioeconomic status levels, with just 33 percent having incomes at 400 percent of the poverty line or above, compared with 47 percent of the different-sex married and 59 percent of same-sex cohabitors. Same-sex and different-sex cohabitors are also less likely than different-sex married to have health insurance coverage. The relatively high education and income levels of same-sex cohabitors compared with those in different-sex unions is consistent with the findings of other studies (Denney, Gorman, and Barrera 2013; Liu, Reczek, and Brown 2013), and suggests that they are likely to benefit in terms of health and mortality.

The hazard models in table 10.1 present hazard ratios of mortality for same-sex cohabitors and different-sex cohabitors relative to the different-sex married. Model 1 examines differences in mortality, controlling only for age, sex, race-ethnicity, and year of interview. Compared with the different-sex married, same-sex cohabitors experience 36 percent (95% Confidence Interval [CI]: 12%–65%) higher mortality risk, while different-sex cohabitors experience 43 percent (95% CI: 34%–52%) higher risk. The difference between same-sex and different-sex cohabitors (hazard ratio 1.08, not shown) is not statistically significant. Model 2 examines the role of socioeconomic and demographic characteristics, including covariates for education, family income, employment status, and health insurance status. The inclusion of these variables expands the mortality disadvantage of same-sex cohabitors and reduces the disadvantage of different-sex cohabitors. Relative to the different-sex married, same-sex cohabitors experience 49 percent (95% CI: 22%–82%) greater mortality risk and different-sex cohabitors exhibit 25 percent (95% CI: 17%–33%) greater risk. This reflects relatively higher SES among same-sex cohabitors and lower SES among different-sex

TABLE 10.1

Adjusted Hazard Ratios of Mortality for Those in Same-Sex and Different-Sex Unions Using NHIS Linked Mortality Files 1997–2009

	Model 1	*Model 2*
Union status		
Different-sex married	1.00	1.00
Same-sex cohabiting	1.36 (1.12–1.65)***	1.49 (1.22–1.82)**
Different-sex cohabiting	1.43 (1.34–1.52)***	1.25 (1.17–1.33)**
Age (years)	1.09 (1.09–1.09)***	1.08 (1.07–1.08)***
Male	1.55 (1.51–1.59)***	1.74 (1.69–1.79)***
Race-ethnicity		
Non-Hispanic white	1.00	1.00
Non-Hispanic black	1.49 (1.43–1.56)***	1.26 (1.20–1.31)***
Non-Hispanic other	1.14 (1.06–1.23)**	1.12 (1.04–1.21)***
Hispanic	1.16 (1.11–1.21)***	.85 (.81–.89)***
Education		
Less than high school		1.00
High school		.79 (.76–.82)***
Some college		.75 (.72–.78)***
College degree or more		.53 (.51–.56)***
Family income-to-poverty ratio		
<100% of poverty line		1.00
100%–199%		.92 (.87–.97)**
200%–399%		.75 (.72–.79)***
400%+		.62 (.59–.66)***
Employment status		
Employed		1.00
Unemployed		1.38 (1.22–1.57)***
Not in labor force		1.87 (1.79–1.93)***
Insurance status		
Covered		1.00

(continued)

Table 10.1. Adjusted Hazard Ratios of Mortality for Those in Same-Sex and Different-Sex Unions Using NHIS Linked Mortality Files 1997–2009 (continued)

	Model 1	Model 2
Not covered		.94 (.89–.99)*
Unknown		.91 (.68–1.20)
N	420,592	420,592

Source: National Health Interview Survey Linked Mortality Files 1997–2009 with follow-up through 2011.

Note: All models control for year of interview. Restricted to those individuals from age twenty-five through age seventy-four.

* $p < .05$; ** $p < .01$; *** $p < .001$.

cohabitors, with the different-sex married in between. Controls for socioeconomic covariates explain 38 percent of the mortality disadvantage of different-sex cohabitors versus different-sex married ($.38 = [\ln (1.43) - \ln(1.25)]/\ln[1.43]$). Net of socioeconomic covariates, same-sex cohabitors have 21 percent (95% CI: –2%–48%) higher mortality risk than different-sex cohabitors ($p = .07$). We find no evidence that the mortality disadvantage of same-sex cohabitors differs by sex (interaction p-value = .90, not shown).

Sensitivity Analysis

In classifications of same-sex couples that rely on household registers, the miscoding of sex can lead to misclassification of different-sex unions as same-sex unions (DeMaio, Bates, and O'Connell 2013). Because adults in same-sex unions represent a very small fraction of the sample, even a small rate of misclassification of different-sex unions as same-sex unions can result in a significant fraction of adults in same-sex unions actually being misclassified adults in different-sex unions. In order to examine the sensitivity of our results to errors in the coding of same-sex unions, we perform a series of checks on our analysis. We consider the possibility that errors in the identification of same-sex couples impact our estimates of the mortality disadvantage of same-sex couples. These sensitivity analyses present three scenarios. Scenario 1 performs the model with the survey years 2004–2007 excluded—since NHIS changed the method for correcting sex in the identification for same-sex married couples in these years (National Center for Health Statistics 2015). Scenario 2 restricts the sample to individuals from age twenty-five through age fifty-nine at baseline, since we might expect greater rate of misclassification (i.e., a greater fraction of observed same-sex couples reflect sex miscoding) among older couples. Scenario 3 restricts the sample to the "reference person," the individual who provides information on other household members. In each of these scenarios, the mortality disadvantage for same-sex cohabitors relative to the different-sex married remains statistically significant. In scenarios 1 and 2, the disadvantage expands relative to the main models, suggesting that to the extent that misclassification is occurring, it may be attenuating the mortality difference we observe in our main models. Our primary estimates thus represent a robust, if conservative, estimate of the mortality disadvantage of same-sex cohabitors.

Discussion

Despite the importance of understanding the health and mortality of sexual minorities in the United States, data limitations have largely precluded nationally representative studies of the mortality experience of this population. The current analysis provides one of the first nationally representative estimates of mortality differences between individuals in same-sex and different-sex unions, finding a mortality disadvantage for individuals in same-sex cohabiting unions relative to their counterparts in different-sex unions. Individuals in same-sex unions experienced considerably higher mortality risk than those in different-sex marriages, and this gap increases after adjustment for socioeconomic factors. Net of socioeconomic factors, same-sex cohabitors also experience slightly higher mortality risk than those in different-sex cohabiting unions, indicating that their baseline advantage relative to different-sex cohabitors reflects socioeconomic protection. These findings are consistent with those of previous research that found disadvantages for same-sex couples with respect to health behaviors, self-reported health, psychological distress, and access to health care (Denney, Gorman, and Barrera 2013; Gonzales and Henning-Smith 2015; Liu, Reczek, and Brown 2013). Our results suggest that the disadvantage of those in same-sex cohabiting unions in general health and health behaviors may translate into a corresponding disadvantage in mortality risk. Specifically, minority stress theory predicts that individuals in same-sex unions may respond to greater experiences of stress with coping mechanisms that include increased frequency of smoking and drinking, poorer diet, and reduced physical activity (Hatzenbuehler et al. 2008).

One important implication of our results is that resource differentials do not explain the mortality disadvantage of those in same-sex cohabiting unions. As a result, we are unable to frame this mortality disparity as reflecting fundamental causes or economic factors (Phelan, Link, and Tehranifar 2010). This recognition presents a challenge for addressing the elevated mortality risk of those in same-sex unions, and policy aimed at improving socioeconomic outcomes would not reduce this difference in mortality. But ruling out socioeconomic differences as an explanation presents an opportunity for researchers to identify additional mechanisms driving mortality disadvantages for sexual minorities, including minority stress theory. Existing research links relatively high levels of psychological distress and chronic disease among sexual minorities to high rates of stigma and chronic stressors faced by sexual minorities (Meyer 2003). Institutional and interpersonal stigma, discrimination, and homophobia faced by sexual minorities directly arouse minority stress and in turn may lead to poorer physical health and to mental health problems (Institute of Medicine 2011). Our results suggest that this stress further leads to an increase in the risk of early death for adults in same-sex unions.

A strength of our study is the consideration of the role of unions, which can highlight the importance of both relationship status and minority status in impacting the mortality experience of those in same-sex and different-sex unions. The minority status of those in same-sex unions stands out as an important influence on their mortality disadvantage, particularly given their lack of access to the benefits of legal marriage until recently. Although same-sex marriage became legal in many states during the 2010s, the vast majority of same-sex couples in our sample lived for most of their lives during periods in which they were unable to legally marry their partners. To the extent that legal marriage itself offers protections for couples that provide health benefits, same-sex couples may be at a disadvantage (Haas and Whitton 2015). A recent article demonstrated that same-sex couples living in states that have legalized same-sex marriage report better health than those states without marriage equality (Kail, Acosta, and Wright 2015). Moreover, lack of legal access to marriage for the large majority of respondents during the survey years makes issues of socioeconomic or health selection into marriage potentially less salient for same-sex couples. Same-sex cohabitors in our sample are more likely than different-sex cohabitors to include long-term, committed couples resembling marriage relationships, making their mortality disadvantage all the more striking.

Some of the mortality disadvantage of same-sex cohabitors relative to the different-sex married may reflect differences in health-related behaviors. Previous research indicates that same-sex cohabitors, both men and women, are more likely to be cigarette smokers than those in different-sex marriages (Reczek, Liu, and Brown 2014). Women in same-sex unions are more likely to be obese than women in different-sex unions, while the opposite is true for men (Boehmer, Bowen, and Bauer 2007). Individuals in same-sex cohabiting unions also tend to report heavier alcohol use than those in different-sex marriages. Men and women in same-sex unions in the NHIS data set also appear to be somewhat "protected" from unhealthy behaviors by relatively high education, and would have a larger gap in health-related behaviors with the different-sex married without this advantage (Reczek, Liu, and Brown 2014). The mortality disadvantage of same-sex couples may also be explained by disparities in access to health care or the quality of services received. Same-sex couples are less likely than those in different-sex marriages to have employer-sponsored health insurance coverage (Gonzales and Blewett 2014), and they are also less likely to gain access to dependent coverage through their partners. There is also evidence that sexual minorities are less likely to receive adequate care in a doctor-patient context. Individuals in same-sex couples report that they are less likely than individuals in different-sex unions to report that it is easy to see a specialist and are more likely to report unmet medical care needs (Buchmueller and Carpenter 2010; Kreps et al. 2014). Future research should build on the present study to assess the potential mechanisms driving differences in mortality outcomes between same-sex and different-sex couples.

Limitations

Research on this topic is generally limited by the misclassification of same-sex couples in the NHIS as a function of the coding of sex. For example, if sex is miscoded for one member of a couple, different-sex unions will be inaccurately coded as same-sex unions and vice versa. An informal analysis of same-sex married couples in the 2004–2007 NHIS by the Division of Health Interview Statistics at the National Center for Health Statistics found that a significant number of same-sex "married" couples likely were different-sex couples with miscoded sex for one individual (National Center for Health Statistics 2015). However, no similar assessment was done for same-sex cohabiting couples. Our sensitivity analyses suggest that to the extent that misclassification of same-sex couples is occurring in NHIS, it may attenuate our estimate of the mortality difference.

We are also unable to consider differences by cause of death given a small number of deaths observed for same-sex cohabitors ($N=117$). Comparing the mortality disadvantage of adults in same-sex unions across causes of death can help to distinguish potential explanations for the disadvantage, but few data sources contain a sufficient sample size to consider cause of death. Future research should leverage additional potential data sources to incorporate an analysis of causes of death.

Conclusions

This study explored the mortality risk of individuals in same- and different-sex unions in the United States, and presented new insight into the potential effects of stress and stigma on the health and well-being of sexual minority individuals. In doing so, this study adds to the emerging body of research on the health and well-being characteristics of individuals in same-sex unions, representing an important step in broadening our understanding of the linkages between social support, family relationships, resources, and health (Umberson et al.

2015). Through the lens of relationships, we demonstrate those in same-sex unions have an elevated risk of early death compared with those in different-sex unions, a disadvantage that cannot be explained by differences in educational and economic resources. Disadvantages in health translate into shorter life spans for those in same-sex unions compared with those in different-sex unions. These questions have gained increased importance as legal marriage was extended to same-sex couples nationwide in 2015. Future research should use this change as an opportunity to identify the potential benefits that come from legal recognition while remaining mindful of the challenges still faced by sexual minorities.

REFERENCES

Boehmer, Ulrike, Deborah J. Bowen, and Greta R. Bauer. 2007. "Overweight and Obesity in Sexual-Minority Women: Evidence from Population-Based Data." *American Journal of Public Health* 97 (6): 1134–1140.

Buchmueller, Thomas, and Christopher S Carpenter. 2010. "Disparities in Health Insurance Coverage, Access, and Outcomes for Individuals in Same-Sex Versus Different-Sex Relationships, 2000–2007." *American Journal of Public Health* 100 (3):489.

Clift, Joseph B., and James Kirby. 2012. "Health Care Access and Perceptions of Provider Care among Individuals in Same-Sex Couples: Findings from the Medical Expenditure Panel Survey (MEPS)." *Journal of Homosexuality* 59 (6):839–850.

Cochran, Susan D., Charlotte Björkenstam, and Vickie M. Mays. 2016. "Sexual Orientation and All-Cause Mortality among US Adults Aged 18 to 59 Years, 2001–2011." *American Journal of Public Health* 106 (5): 918–920.

Cochran, Susan D., and Vickie M. Mays. 2011. "Sexual Orientation and Mortality among US Men Aged 17 to 59 Years: Results from the National Health and Nutrition Examination Survey III." *American Journal of Public Health* 101 (6): 1133–1138.

Cochran, Susan D., and Vickie M. Mays. 2015. "Mortality Risks among Persons Reporting Same-Sex Sexual Partners: Evidence from the 2008 General Social Survey—National Death Index Data Set." *American Journal of Public Health* 105 (2): 358–364.

DeMaio, Theresa J., Nancy Bates, and Martin O'Connell. 2013. "Exploring Measurement Error Issues in Reporting of Same-Sex Couples." *Public Opinion Quarterly* 77 (S1): 145–158.

Denney, Justin T., Bridget K. Gorman, and Cristina B. Barrera. 2013. "Families, Resources, and Adult Health: Where Do Sexual Minorities Fit?" *Journal of Health and Social Behavior* 54(1): 46–63.

Frisch, Morten, and Henrik Brønnum-Hansen. 2009. "Mortality among Men and Women in Same-Sex Marriage: A National Cohort Study of 8333 Danes." *American Journal of Public Health* 99 (1): 133–137.

Frost, David M, Keren Lehavot, and Ilan H Meyer. 2015. "Minority Stress and Physical Health Among Sexual Minority Individuals." *Journal of Behavioral Medicine* 38 (1):1–8.

Gonzales, Gilbert, and Lynn A. Blewett. 2014. "National and State-Specific Health Insurance Disparities for Adults in Same-Sex Relationships." *American Journal of Public Health* 104 (2): e95–e104.

Gonzales, Gilbert, and Carrie Henning-Smith. 2015. "Disparities in Health and Disability among Older Adults in Same-Sex Cohabiting Relationships." *Journal of Aging and Health* 27(3): 432–453.

Gonzales, Gilbert, and Carrie Henning-Smith. 2017. "The Affordable Care Act and Health Insurance Coverage for Lesbian, Gay, and Bisexual Adults: Analysis of the Behavioral Risk Factor Surveillance System." *LGBT Health* 4 (1):62–67.

Haas, Stephen M, and Sarah W Whitton. 2015. "The Significance of Living Together and Importance of Marriage in Same-Sex Couples." *Journal of Homosexuality* 62 (9): 1241–1263.

Hatzenbuehler, Mark L., Anna Bellatorre, Yeonjin Lee, Brian K. Finch, Peter Muennig, and Kevin Fiscella. 2014. "Structural Stigma and All-Cause Mortality in Sexual Minority Populations." *Social Science & Medicine* 103: 33–41.

Hatzenbuehler, M. L., S. Nolen-Hoeksema, and S. J. Erickson. 2008. Minority Stress Predictors of HIV Risk Behavior, Substance Use, and Depressive Symptoms: Results from a Prospective Study of Bereaved Gay Men. *Health Psychology* 27(4): 455–462.

Ingram, Deborah D., Kimberly A. Lochner, and Christine S. Cox. 2008. "Mortality Experience of the 1986–2000 National Health Interview Survey Linked Mortality Files Participants." *Vital and Health Statistics.* Series 2, *Data Evaluation and Methods Research* (147): 1–37.

Institute of Medicine. 2011. *The Health of Lesbian, Gay, Bisexual, and Transgender People: Building a Foundation for Better Understanding.* Washington, DC: National Academies Press.

Kail, Ben Lennox, Katie L. Acosta, and Eric R. Wright. 2015. "State-Level Marriage Equality and the Health of Same-Sex Couples." *American Journal of Public Health* 105 (6): 1101–1105.

Kreps, Gary L., Allan D. Peterkin, Karina Willes, Mike Allen, Jimmie Manning, Katy Ross, Juliann C. Scholl, Gina Castle Bell, Gilbert Gonzales, and Ryan Moltz. 2014. *Health Care Disparities and the LGBT Population.* Plymouth, UK: Lexington Books.

Liu, Hui, and Corinne Reczek. 2012. "Cohabitation and US Adult Mortality: An Examination by Gender and Race." *Journal of Marriage and Family* 74 (4): 794–811.

Liu, Hui, Corinne Reczek, and Dustin Brown. 2013. "Same-Sex Cohabitors and Health: The Role of Race-Ethnicity, Gender, and Socioeconomic Status." *Journal of Health and Social Behavior* 54 (1): 25–45.

Mays, Vickie M., and Susan D. Cochran. 2001. "Mental Health Correlates of Perceived Discrimination among Lesbian, Gay, and Bisexual Adults in the United States." *American Journal of Public Health* 91 (11): 1869–1876.

Meyer, Ilan H. 2003. "Prejudice as Stress: Conceptual and Measurement Problems." *American Journal of Public Health* 93 (2): 262–265.

National Center for Health Statistics. 2015. *Changes to Data Editing Procedures and the Impact on Identifying Same-Sex Married Couples: 2004–2007 National Health Interview Survey.* Hyattsville, MD: Division of Health Interview Statistics, National Center for Health Statistics.

Phelan, J. C., B. G. Link, and P. Tehranifar. 2010. "Social Conditions as Fundamental Causes of Health Inequalities: Theory, Evidence, and Policy Implications." *Journal of Health and Social Behavior* 51: S28–S40.

Reczek, Corinne, Hui Liu, and Dustin Brown. 2014. "Cigarette Smoking in Same-Sex and Different-Sex Unions: The Role of Socioeconomic and Psychological Factors." *Population Research and Policy Review* 33 (4): 527–551.

Reczek, Corinne, Hui Liu, and Russell Spiker. 2014. "A Population-Based Study of Alcohol Use in Same-Sex and Different-Sex Unions." *Journal of Marriage and Family* 76 (3): 557–572.

Umberson, Debra, Mieke Beth Thomeer, Rhiannon A. Kroeger, Amy C. Lodge, and Minle Xu. 2015. "Challenges and Opportunities for Research on Same-Sex Relationships." *Journal of Marriage and Family* 77 (1): 96–111.

Waite, Linda J., and Maggie Gallagher. 2002. *The Case for Marriage: Why Married People Are Happier, Healthier and Better Off Financially.* New York: Broadway Books.

Wienke, Chris, and Gretchen J Hill. 2008. "Does the 'Marriage Benefit' Extend to Partners in Gay and Lesbian Relationships? Evidence from a Random Sample of Sexually Active Adults." *Journal of Family Issues* 30 (2): 259–289.

11

Access to Health Care for Partnered and Nonpartnered Sexual Minorities

MATT RUTHER

NING HSIEH

Previous research on sexual minorities' access to health services has shown that compared with heterosexuals, lesbians, gays, and bisexuals (LGB) are disadvantaged in multiple aspects of health care access, such as insurance coverage, receiving timely care when needed, and having regular places for health care (Buchmuller and Carpenter 2010; Heck et al. 2006; Hsieh and Ruther 2017; Ponce et al. 2010). However, some of the studies predate the implementation of the Affordable Care Act (ACA) and the legalization of same-sex marriage, which may have enhanced health care access among sexual minorities through, for example, gaining dependent health coverage from the spouse's employer. Other studies examine the general situation faced by LGB using more recent data, but few of them have addressed how union or marital status may influence health care access across sexual orientation groups. In this chapter, we compare several aspects of access across groups of different sexual orientation and union status post-ACA and post–marriage equality. Our purpose is to demonstrate whether disparities in health care identified in prior research remain and highlight the current health care environment for sexual minority populations.

Many studies have shown that marriage is related to better health outcomes—largely operating through a mechanism of gaining economic and psychosocial resources as well as changing health behaviors (Bachman et al. 2002; Carr and Springer 2010; Reczek and Umberson 2012; Umberson 1992; Waite and Gallagher 2000). While the vast majority of studies examine only heterosexual populations, the general consensus is that these protective benefits will accrue similarly to partners in same-sex marriages (or equivalent partner arrangements) as they do to married heterosexuals (Buffie 2011). However, lower rates of marriage or equivalent relationships may prevent sexual minorities from achieving the health advantage of these relationships.

Partnership rates among lesbians (51%–61%) and gay men (37%–46%) are lower than they are among their heterosexual counterparts (62%), although lesbians have notably higher partnership rates than gay men (Carpenter and Gates 2008). The lower partnership rates among sexual minorities may be due to the perceived lack of benefits accruing from such relationships as the result of legal barriers (e.g., the Defense of Marriage Act [DOMA]) (Badgett, Gates, and Maisel 2008), familial, religious or other social pressure, or a reluctance to self-identify as LGB in the survey setting due to social desirability. Because legally bound partnerships are important for claiming spousal benefits including health coverage and social security, sexual minorities in general may have poorer access to health insurance and health care services compared with heterosexuals. However, the disadvantage of acquiring health care resources through partnership may be compensated for by higher socioeconomic status. As previous studies noted, same-sex partnered men and women report higher levels of educational attainment, income, and full-time employment than opposite-sex partnered men and women (Gonzalez and Blewett 2014; Gonzalez and Henning-Smith 2017). Therefore, sexual minorities may purchase health services out of pocket or through health plans provided by their own employers more often than through spousal health plans. Yet, it is unclear how partnership status is related to access to care among sexual minorities in comparison with their straight counterparts when socioeconomic factors are taken into account.

LGB Insurance Rates and Other Access to Care Outcomes

Previous studies show that LGB individuals are disadvantaged in several aspects of health care access, an effect that exists for both single and partnered sexual minorities (Buchmuller and Carpenter 2010; Heck et al. 2006; Ponce et al. 2010). According to evidence from the California Health Interview Survey in the early 2000s, Ponce and colleagues (2010) find that single lesbians were less likely to be insured than were single heterosexual women, although there were no significant differences in the type of insurance present. Single gay men were no less likely than single straight men to have insurance, and likewise exhibited no difference with single heterosexual men in the type of insurance present.

Relative to their married heterosexual counterparts, partnered lesbians and gay men are less likely to have health insurance, report greater difficulty in seeing health care specialists, and experience greater delays in obtaining necessary care (Ash and Badgett 2006; Buchmueller and Carpenter 2010; Clift and Kirby 2012; Dahlhamer et al. 2016; Gonzalez and Blewett 2014; Heck et al. 2006; Ponce et al. 2010). Liu, Reczek, and Brown (2013) show that—among both men and women—individuals in married opposite-sex couples exhibit higher insurance rates than individuals in partnered same-sex couples, who in turn exhibit higher insurance rates than individuals in partnered opposite-sex couples. Although this observation is not controlled for socioeconomic status or other demographic factors, it suggests the importance of the legal distinction of marriage in health care access.

At least some of the disparities between partnered gay men and lesbians and married heterosexuals are likely explained by the greater access to employee-sponsored insurance (ESI) for dependents enjoyed by opposite-sex married couples. For example, Ash and Badgett (2006) find higher rates of ESI for employees with a same-sex partner, but lower rates of ESI for dependents of the employees. In spite of the higher rates of own-ESI, individuals in same-sex relationships have lower rates of health coverage (than those in an opposite-sex relationship) not only because of lack of ESI for dependents but also because they are no more likely to rely on other sources of insurance such as Medicaid, other government coverage, and private insurance.

Consistently, Ponce et al. (2010) also find higher uninsurance rates—more than double—for partnered lesbians and gay men relative to married heterosexuals, a disparity likely attributable to historical differences in both marriage laws and domestic partnership benefits. Partnered or married lesbians exhibited higher uninsurance rates than similar heterosexual women and a lower likelihood of having employer-sponsored dependent benefits. Among partnered or married men, gay men had a lower likelihood of dependent coverage than did heterosexual men, and had a significantly higher risk of having public coverage and of being uninsured. This study also illustrates that the uninsurance disparity between lesbians and straight women is larger than the uninsurance disparity between gay and straight men, a finding consistent with other studies (Buchmuller and Carpenter 2010; Heck et al. 2006).

While the study sample in Ponce et al. (2010) was limited to California residents, comparable results are found with nationally representative samples. Gonzalez and Blewett (2014) show that males in same-sex relationships are less likely than married opposite-sex males to have ESI and more likely to have Medicaid or similar government insurance; unmarried males in opposite-sex partnerships are least likely to have ESI. Similarly, females in same-sex relationships are less likely than married opposite-sex females to have ESI, but more likely to have Medicaid. Moreover, these disparities were largest in states with bans on same-sex marriage or with no provisions for same-sex marriage.

Although a focus on the dichotomous insured versus uninsured question is the most commonly used measure of health care access, other outcomes likewise show disparities between sexual minorities and heterosexuals. In an analysis of MEPS data from 1996 to 2007, Clift and Kirby (2012) find that individuals in same-sex couples are less likely to report ease in seeing a specialist or getting medical care when desired and more likely to report delays in obtaining prescription medications. Individuals in same-sex couples are also less likely to report that their doctor or health care provider displayed respect or spent adequate time with them.

Blosnich (2017) notes that although sexual minority individuals reported lower satisfaction with health care received, this lower satisfaction is generally mitigated when demographic and socioeconomic characteristics (including partnership) are accounted for. However, lesbians, gay men, and bisexuals continued to report lower satisfaction with some specific types of coverage, notably that which was individually purchased or offered through the Veterans Health Administration or other military healthcare. In a race-stratified analysis, Hsieh and Ruther (2017) also report no differences between LGB individuals and heterosexuals in satisfaction with health care received.

In all, the prior literature suggests continued disparities in insurance rates among partnered gay and lesbians and married heterosexuals, likely related to differences in employer-sponsored coverage. However, there are no observable insurance rate disparities between unmarried same-sex partners and unmarried opposite-sex partners, or between single gay men and heterosexual men. There is little research on other aspects of access to care, although the limited evidence suggests a higher likelihood of delaying care for sexual minorities, even after controlling for differences in sociodemographic factors and economic status.

Effects of ACA, Medicaid Expansion, and Recent Supreme Court Decisions on LGB Insurance Rates

Access to health care for LGB individuals and persons in same-sex partnerships is expected to be markedly influenced by full implementation of the Affordable Care Act (Obamacare) and recent Supreme Court decisions in *United States v. Windsor* (2013) and *Obergefell v. Hodges* (2015). These Court decisions reposition same-sex marriage as equal to opposite-sex marriage, thereby extending many health insurance benefits to dependents in same-sex partnerships. These ongoing shifts in social policy and attitudes necessitate a current look at health care access for LGB persons and same-sex partnered individuals.

Ponce et al. (2010) suggest two ways in which married heterosexuals are advantaged in access to health insurance—at least historically—relative to same-sex partners. Firstly, more employers extend coverage to the dependents in marital relationships than to the dependents in unmarried partnerships, regardless of the sex of the partners. Secondly, prior to *United States v. Windsor*, health insurance benefits for married heterosexuals were tax-exempt, while the same benefits for married gays and lesbians were taxable. This latter point is not a minor one: Badgett (2007) found that under the Defense of Marriage Act, employees paid, on average, $1,069 in additional federal income taxes when they added a same-sex spouse to an employer health plan.

The potential effects of national legislation—such as the decisions in *United States v. Windsor* and *Obergefell v. Hodges*—on access to health care can be identified from changes to health care access outcomes in a state with prior similar legislation in place. Using a difference-in-differences approach, Buchmueller and Carpenter (2012) analyze California Health Interview Survey data over a period (2001–2007) during which employers became obligated to offer same-sex partners the same benefits as opposite-sex partners. Likely due to the fact that lesbians are more likely to take advantage of same-sex benefits than are gay men (Badgett, Gates, and Maisel 2008; Gates, Badgett, and Ho 2008), the authors find some evidence that the benefit reform lessened the disparity in health insurance coverage between lesbians and straight women. They assert that although a direct causative linkage cannot be made, it is possible that the effect was the consequence of the expansion of dependent employer-sponsored benefits. There was no corresponding reduction in the health insurance disparity between gay men and straight men. This study also demonstrated that extending employment benefits to same-sex partners may have subsequent effects on both the partnership rates and employment rates of the same-sex partnered population. The California data show that the employment reforms increased partnership rates and decreased employment rates of lesbians; no analogous effect was found for gay men.

Although the full effects of ACA and marriage equality on the health outcomes and access to health care of same-sex partnered populations may not be known for years, recent evidence suggests that disparities in insurance rates have declined in light of these changes. Skopec and Long (2015) report that between the summer of 2013 and the winter of 2014—during which time major provisions of the ACA came into effect—there were net gains in the rate of insurance coverage among LGB adults. These increases occurred among both public and private coverage pools. Gonzalez and Henning-Smith (2017) observe that relationship status elicits no effect on the likelihood of LGB adults being uninsured in the 2014 Behavioral Risk Factor Surveillance System (BRFSS), and Hsieh and Ruther (2017) find no differences between rates of uninsurance for sexual minority and straight populations in 2013–2015 NHIS data.

In spite of the gains in the percentage insured, sexual minority populations still remain disadvantaged in other aspects of access to care. In Health Reform Monitoring Survey data from winter 2014, LGB adults continued to report greater problems accessing health care and affording health care, relative to straights (Skopec and Long 2015). Sexual minorities also remain more likely than straights to have delayed or unmet care for financial reasons or nonfinancial reasons (e.g., scheduling, transportation, etc.), and some nonwhite sexual minority groups have higher rates of using the emergency department as their usual source of care (Hsieh and Ruther 2017).

Although early indications of the effects of recent legislative and judicial reforms on access to care disparities between LGB and heterosexual populations are promising in some respects, additional questions remain. It is not clear, for example, whether unmarried same-sex couples presently exhibit access to health care equivalent to legally married same-sex spouses, or whether the financial and nonfinancial barriers to care shown by sexual minorities are the same for partnered and nonpartnered LGBs. There is also limited information on whether partnership mitigates any of the perceived dissatisfaction with care displayed by sexual minorities.

The goal of this chapter is to illustrate—in the context of the recent social, political, and legal changes to the status of same-sex partners and the health care system itself—the contemporary association between an individual's partnership status and access to health care, particularly as it pertains to the LGB population. According to the literature mentioned previously, we develop several research questions regarding disparities in insurance coverage, delayed or unmet care, satisfaction with care received, and type of health insurance:

1. Are married heterosexuals more likely to be insured than married LGBs, partnered LGBs and heterosexuals, and never married LGBs?
2. Are married heterosexuals less likely to have delayed or unmet care for financial or nonfinancial reasons than other groups?
3. Do married heterosexuals feel more satisfied with care they received than other groups?
4. How does the type of primary health insurance vary across comparison groups?

Data and Methodology

This study uses pooled data from the 2014–2016 National Health Interview Surveys (NHIS). The NHIS collects nationally representative samples of the civilian noninstitutionalized population in the United States, using a multistage sampling framework. Although sexual identity questions were first asked in the 2013 NHIS, this sample is not used here. The U.S. Supreme Court case *U.S. v. Windsor*—which held that the federal government must recognize same-sex marriages approved by individual states—was decided in June of 2013, and the major provisions of the Affordable Care Act came into force at the beginning of 2014. The effects of these major changes in the access to health care of married and partnered same-sex couples would thus not have been observable until 2014, at the earliest, and the inclusion of the 2013 sample could confound these effects.

The current study compares adults aged eighteen and older who self-identify as straight with those who identify as gay, lesbian, or bisexual. The initial data set included 51,659 adults who either identified as straight and partnered or married or identified as lesbian, gay, or bisexual. Of these, 742 were missing values on one or more of the explanatory or outcome variables used in the study; these records were excluded from the analysis. Because the income variable contained a larger number of missing records ($n = 8,199$ of the 50,917 remaining), all analyses were carried out using the imputed family income point estimates available in the NHIS data along with the *mi* functions in Stata 14 (StataCorp 2015). The NHIS imputed income variables are generated from a prediction equation that incorporates several demographic and health status variables, and are based on five imputations; the income point estimates are top-coded at the 95th percentile. The analytic sample for the model of health care satisfaction only included individuals who reported receiving health care in the previous twelve months ($n = 46,053$).

The analysis examines four access to health care outcomes as dependent variables using logistic regression models. *No insurance* indicates that the respondent is not covered by any health insurance at the time of survey. *Delayed/unmet care for cost reasons* summarizes three questions about the need for health care in the past twelve months: whether the respondent had unmet care for financial reasons, whether the respondent had delayed care for financial reasons, or whether the respondent was unable to afford specific services (e.g., specialists) due to financial reasons. A respondent is considered to have delayed or unmet care if the answer to any of these questions is yes. *Delayed care for noncost reasons* indicates that the respondent has delayed medical care in the past twelve months because he or she "could not get though on the phone, could not get an appointment soon enough, waited too long to see the doctor, doctor's office was not open when you could get there, or did not have transportation." Finally, *lower satisfaction with health care* indicates whether the respondent is less than "very satisfied" with the health care that he or she received in the past twelve months; the comparison group is individuals who are very satisfied with their health care.

In addition, the source of health insurance (dependent variable) is evaluated using a multinomial logistic regression model. The source of insurance was categorized using a hierarchical classification system in which respondents were assigned to a single source of care category based on the primary insurer, to account for the fact that respondents may have multiple sources of care. The source of care was assigned in the following order: (1) Medicare; (2) ESI (either own insurance or as a dependent), Veterans Health Administration, or other military care; (3) Medicaid or insurance obtained through similar government resources; (4) privately purchased insurance. Respondents who were not insured were excluded from this analysis. A multinomial model compares a nominal set of outcomes against some predetermined base outcome. In this analysis, the base outcome is whether the respondent has only privately purchased insurance.

For all regression analyses, models assess access to health care disparities by sexual identity and partnership status (independent variables), as categorized into five mutually exclusive groups: married heterosexual, partnered heterosexual, married LGB, partnered LGB, and never married LGB. Individuals who are divorced, separated, or widowed are excluded from the sample. Never married heterosexuals were excluded from the analysis, as we intend to focus on the comparisons between married or partnered LGB and married or partnered heterosexual and between married or partnered LGB and never married LGB.

All analyses were conducted using the *svy* command in Stata with the sample design weights to account for the multilayered survey design of the NHIS. The results of the analyses are presented as odds ratios or—for the multinomial logit model—relative risk ratios, along with the associated 95 percent confidence intervals. In all models, the reference group is married heterosexuals.

In addition to differences in partnership status, all analyses were controlled for the effects of age, gender, race, Hispanic ethnicity, educational attainment, self-rated health (a proxy for health care needs), household income, employment status, perceived financial strain, and survey year. Perceived financial strain is a continuous composite scale created using the Stata *alpha* function, which indexes (Cronbach's alpha = .93) the respondent's level of worry about having enough money for normal monthly bills, housing costs, maintaining a decent standard of living, normal medical care, medical expenses for a serious illness or accident, and retirement. Higher values of the summary scale (which ranges from 0 to 4) indicate greater financial worry.

Results

The results from the analysis of partnership status on access to care outcomes are shown in table 11.1. Models 1–4 display the odds ratios from the logistic regression models of not having health insurance, delaying health care for cost or noncost reasons, and satisfaction with care. Models 5–7 display the relative risk ratios from the multinomial logistic regression model of source of insurance coverage. All results are from multivariate analyses controlling for partnership status, age, gender, race, education, income, employment status, financial worry, self-rated health, and survey year.

Relative to married heterosexuals, married or partnered LGBs are no less likely to have health insurance coverage (model 1). Never married LGBs are also no less likely to have health insurance coverage. However, the odds of a partnered heterosexual lacking health insurance are approximately 60 percent greater than a similarly situated married heterosexual. Non-Hispanics, older persons, females, less healthy individuals, and higher-income individuals have increased odds of having health insurance, while unemployed persons and persons with higher levels of financial worry are less likely to have health insurance. In addition, health insurance coverage rates increase over the years 2014 to 2016, an expected result given the implementation of ACA provisions at the beginning of this period.

TABLE 11.1

Odds of Reporting Barriers to Health Care Access and Type of Health Insurance Coverage Obtained

	No health insurance (model 1)		Delayed/unmet care for cost reasons (model 2)		Delayed care for noncost reasons (model 3)	
	OR	95% CI	OR	95% CI	OR	95% CI
Partnership status						
Married heterosexuals	(ref.)		(ref.)		(ref.)	
Partnered heterosexuals	1.60***	[1.41,1.81]	1.32***	[1.19,1.47]	1.18*	[1.04,1.34]
Married LGBs	1.03	[.64,1.64]	1.59**	[1.18,2.15]	1.37	[.99,1.88]
Partnered LGBs	1.14	[.68,1.91]	1.95***	[1.45,2.62]	1.50*	[1.06,2.12]
Never-married LGBs	.99	[.74,1.31]	1.44**	[1.14,1.80]	1.72***	[1.37,2.16]
Survey year						
2014 NHIS	(ref.)		(ref.)		(ref.)	
2015 NHIS	.73***	[.66,.81]	.98	[.90,1.07]	1.16**	[1.06,1.28]
2016 NHIS	.69***	[.62,.78]	.99	[.90,1.08]	1.35***	[1.21,1.50]
Race						
White	(ref.)		(ref.)		(ref.)	
Black	1.05	[.89,1.23]	.88*	[.77,.99]	1.07	[.94,1.22]
Hispanic	2.16***	[1.92,2.43]	.73***	[.65,.81]	1.07	[.95,1.21]
Other race	1.23*	[1.03,1.46]	.67***	[.58,.78]	1.00	[.85,1.18]
Age	.97***	[.97,.98]	.99***	[.98,.99]	.99***	[.99,1.00]
Female	.74***	[.68,.81]	1.26***	[1.18,1.35]	1.31***	[1.21,1.41]
Educational attainment						
No HS diploma	(ref.)		(ref.)		(ref.)	
HS diploma/GED	.65***	[.57,.74]	.95	[.85,1.07]	1.02	[.88,1.18]
Some college	.43***	[.38,.49]	1.10	[.98,1.23]	1.18*	[1.02,1.36]
Bachelor's degree or more	.29***	[.25,.34]	1.02	[.90,1.15]	1.32***	[1.14,1.54]

Less than very satisfied with care received (model 4)		Medicare vs. privately purchased insurance (model 5)		ESI vs. privately purchased insurance (model 6)		Medicaid vs. privately purchased insurance (model 7)	
OR	95% CI	OR	95% CI	OR	95% CI	OR	95% CI
(ref.)		(ref.)		(ref.)		(ref.)	
1.00	[.92,1.09]	1.00	[.79,1.25]	.64***	[.54,.74]	1.61***	[1.34,1.94]
1.25	[.95,1.65]	1.25	[.53,1.53]	.77	[.53,1.10]	.98	[.54,1.80]
1.18	[.88,1.60]	1.18	[.33,2.09]	.90	[.51,1.57]	1.24	[.62,2.51]
.84	[.70,1.01]	.84	[.85,2.37]	.61**	[0.42,0.88]	.76	[.50,1.14]
(ref.)		(ref.)		(ref.)		(ref.)	
1.19***	[1.12,1.27]	1.19***	[.81,1.05]	.90*	[0.81,0.99]	1.07	[.93,1.23]
1.11**	[1.03,1.19]	1.11**	[.79,1.04]	.84***	[0.76,0.92]	1.17*	[1.01,1.35]
(ref.)		(ref.)		(ref.)		(ref.)	
1.06	[.96,1.17]	1.06	[1.79,2.87]	2.13***	[1.78,2.57]	2.66***	[2.11,3.36]
1.13**	[1.04,1.24]	1.13**	[1.52,2.24]	1.34***	[1.15,1.56]	2.38***	[1.96,2.89]
1.48***	[1.35,1.64]	1.48***	[1.03,1.57]	1.06	[.89,1.25]	2.26***	[1.80,2.84]
.99***	[.98,.99]	.99***	[1.05,1.07]	.96***	[.96,.96]	.94***	[.94,.95]
.88***	[.83,.93]	.88***	[.95,1.18]	.94	[.86,1.01]	1.15*	[1.02,1.29]
(ref.)		(ref.)		(ref.)		(ref.)	
1.05	[.95,1.16]	1.05	[.70,1.00]	1.32***	[1.12,1.54]	.65***	[.54,.77]
1.02	[.92,1.13]	1.02	[.60,.89]	1.31***	[1.12,1.52]	.53***	[.44,.64]
1.05	[.94,1.18]	1.05	[.78,1.14]	1.26**	[1.06,1.49]	.37***	[.29,.46]

(continued)

Table 11.1. Odds of Reporting Barriers to Health Care Access and Type of Health Insurance Coverage Obtained (continued)

	No health insurance (model 1)		Delayed/unmet care for cost reasons (model 2)		Delayed care for noncost reasons (model 3)	
	OR	95% CI	OR	95% CI	OR	95% CI
Self-rated health						
High self-rated health	(ref.)		(ref.)		(ref.)	
Medium-high Self-rated health	.92	[.83,1.03]	1.31***	[1.18,1.45]	1.41***	[1.25,1.59]
Medium self-rated health	.93	[.82,1.06]	1.80***	[1.63,1.98]	1.80***	[1.59,2.05]
Medium-low self-rated health	.83*	[.69,1.00]	2.84***	[2.49,3.23]	2.51***	[2.14,2.94]
Low self-rated health	.63**	[.46,.86]	2.94***	[2.37,3.65]	3.36***	[2.65,4.26]
Income (imputed)	.99***	[.98,.99]	.99***	[.99,.99]	1.00	[1.00,1.00]
Work status						
Employed	(ref.)		(ref.)		(ref.)	
Unemployed	1.84***	[1.53,2.21]	1.37***	[1.16,1.61]	1.24*	[1.04,1.47]
Retired	.26***	[.19,.35]	.83*	[.72,.96]	1.28**	[1.08,1.51]
Disability	.35***	[.27,.45]	1.63***	[1.35,1.96]	1.70***	[1.35,2.13]
Other not working	1.54***	[1.35,1.75]	1.14*	[1.02,1.28]	0.97	[.84,1.12]
Financial worry	1.86***	[1.76,1.96]	2.74***	[2.62,2.87]	1.50***	[1.43,1.58]
N	50,917		50,917		50,917	

Note: ESI = employer-sponsored insurance.

* p < .05; ** p < .01; *** p < .001.

Less than very satisfied with care received (model 4)		Medicare vs. privately purchased insurance (model 5)		ESI vs. privately purchased insurance (model 6)		Medicaid vs. privately purchased insurance (model 7)	
OR	95% CI	OR	95% CI	OR	95% CI	OR	95% CI
(ref.)		(ref.)		(ref.)		(ref.)	
1.29***	[1.20,1.38]	1.29***	[1.00,1.39]	1.31***	[1.19,1.45]	1.32**	[1.10,1.57]
1.65***	[1.53,1.78]	1.65***	[1.13,1.55]	1.62***	[1.45,1.80]	1.88***	[1.59,2.22]
2.04***	[1.83,2.27]	2.04***	[1.22,1.80]	1.65***	[1.41,1.94]	2.25***	[1.81,2.79]
2.16***	[1.77,2.63]	2.16***	[.99,1.91]	1.75***	[1.30,2.37]	2.73***	[1.93,3.88]
1.00***	[1.00,1.00]	1.00***	[1.00,1.00]	1.01***	[1.01,1.01]	.97***	[.97,.98]
(ref.)		(ref.)		(ref.)		(ref.)	
1.12	[.96,1.30]	1.12	[.98,2.45]	.61***	[.45,.82]	2.73***	[2.01,3.71]
1.11*	[1.01,1.23]	1.11*	[1.58,2.31]	.44***	[.39,.49]	.88	[.71,1.09]
.93	[.82,1.06]	0.93	[5.59,9.38]	.77*	[.60,.98]	3.23***	[2.49,4.19]
1.10	[1.00,1.21]	1.10	[.68,1.20]	.58***	[.50,.68]	1.59***	[1.29,1.96]
1.85***	[1.79,1.92]	1.85***	[1.02,1.18]	.83***	[.78,.87]	1.02	[.95,1.09]
46,053		50,917		50,917		50,917	

Although there is no observable difference in insurance coverage rates between married straights and married or partnered same-sex couples, same-sex couples are more likely to have delayed or unmet health care for financial reasons (model 2). Partnered heterosexuals and never married LGBs are similarly more likely to have delayed or unmet care as a result of cost. These effects are present even after accounting for differences in income, employment status, and financial worry, and are large in magnitude. For example, married LGBs are almost 60 percent more likely than comparable married heterosexuals to have delayed or unmet care for financial reasons.

Partnered LGBs, never married LGBs, and partnered heterosexuals are also more likely than married heterosexuals to have delayed health care for noncost reasons, such as problems scheduling an appointment or arranging transportation (model 3). Although the odds ratio is notably larger than one, the difference between married same-sex and married opposite-sex couples is only marginally significant ($p < .06$).

Model 4 shows the results from the analysis of factors affecting satisfaction with care. There are no statistically significant differences in being less satisfied with care based on partnership status, regardless of sexual identity, although both married and partnered LGBs display marginally higher dissatisfaction with care. Dissatisfaction is higher among Hispanics, younger persons, males, less healthy individuals, and wealthier individuals. Interestingly, the rate of dissatisfaction with the health care received has gone up over time, possibly the result of increased congestion in the health care system.

The final three models in table 11.1 present the results from the analysis of type of insurance coverage, for those respondents who reported having any coverage. There are no partnership differences in the likelihood of having Medicare relative to having directly purchased insurance, an unsurprising result given the near universality of Medicare coverage for seniors. Although all partner types exhibit lower odds than married heterosexuals of having ESI relative to directly purchased insurance, only for partnered heterosexuals and never married LGBs is this likelihood statistically significant. There are no significant differences between married heterosexuals and married or partnered LGBs in the likelihood of having ESI. Finally, in the comparison of having Medicaid or similar coverage relative to directly purchased insurance, only partnered heterosexuals are more likely than the other groups to exhibit a higher likelihood of this coverage than coverage purchased directly. Married, partnered, and never married LGBs all report similar rates of Medicaid coverage as do married heterosexuals.

Conclusions

Partnered sexual minorities have historically exhibited disparities in access to health care relative to heterosexual individuals, due at least in part to differences in the availability of insurance coverage for married and partnered sexual minorities (Ash and Badgett 2006; Ponce et al. 2010). Recent shifts in society's view of same-sex relationships—symbolized by the repeal of DOMA and the inclusionary language of the ACA—may have had some effect on the presence or magnitude of these disparities. The goal of this chapter is to illustrate the contemporary association between an individual's partnership status and access to health care, particularly as it pertains to the LGB population.

The results in table 11.1 show that there are no differences in the likelihood of having health insurance between married heterosexuals and married or partnered sexual minorities, and no differences in the likelihood of having health insurance between married or partnered sexual minorities and never married sexual minorities. Although uncontrolled models (not shown) indicate higher insurance rates for partnered and never married LGBs, these differences are fully explained by social and demographic characteristics of the individuals. Only partnered heterosexuals exhibit higher uninsurance rates than married heterosexuals after accounting for these individual-level differences. The fact that partnered opposite-sex couples have higher uninsurance rates but partnered same-sex couples do not is at least partly explained by the larger confidence intervals for the LGB populations. Adjusted Wald tests of the estimated coefficients in the first column of table 11.1 indicate no statistically significant differences between opposite-sex partnered individuals, same-sex partnered individuals, and never married LGBs.

These results—which relied on data collected over the 2014–2016 period—contrast with those found in prior studies based on pre-2010 data that suggest more disadvantage in health coverage among LGBs (Ash and Badgett 2006; Buchmuller and Carpenter 2010; Heck et al. 2006; Ponce et al. 2010). Although specific causes are not tested here, the fact that the DOMA repeal and ACA implementation occurred just prior to the period covered by this sample lends credence to the notion that these legislative measures were at least partly responsible for the reduction in disparities between married heterosexuals and the sexual minority groups.

Column 6 in table 11.1 further indicates that the reduction in uninsurance disparities between married heterosexuals and married or partnered sexual minorities is related to an increase in the presence of ESI among sexual minorities. Although Ponce and colleagues (2010) do not directly compare the likelihood of having ESI versus directly purchasing insurance, their results suggest that partnered sexual minorities are more likely to purchase coverage directly than to receive it through an employer. In particular, partnered LGBs are notably less likely to have dependent ESI than are their heterosexual counterparts. Although the present study does not distinguish between own- versus dependent-ESI coverage due to data limitation, the results show that partnered and married sexual minorities are now no less likely than married heterosexuals to have

ESI coverage from any source. However, never married LGBs remain significantly more likely to have directly purchased insurance rather than to obtain coverage through an employer.

In many studies, access to health care is defined by this single measure of health insurance coverage. However, whether someone has insurance and whether that person has the resources and ability to use that insurance are two very different questions. Because an underlying objective in most health studies is to identify ways to improve health outcomes, the mere presence of insurance coverage is an insufficient metric with which to gauge; health service utilization is equally as important in achieving health outcome improvements. As such, additional measures of access to care—whether care is delayed for cost or noncost reasons and level of satisfaction with care received—are also considered here.

It is in these other measures of access to care in which disparities between the sexual minority and straight populations surface, specifically in the likelihoods of delaying care for cost or noncost reasons. All sexual minorities, regardless of partnership status, exhibit greater odds of delaying care for financial reasons than do married heterosexuals. Given that prior studies have shown the higher socioeconomic status of some sexual minority groups—and the fact that income, employment, and educational attainment are accounted for in all models—this difference remains unexplained. In the case of never married LGBs and partnered heterosexuals—both of whom are more likely to directly purchase health coverage rather than obtain it from an employer—this disparity may arise from the reduction in disposable income resulting from directly purchasing coverage. However, this explanation would not account for the differences for married and partnered sexual minorities, neither of whom exhibit different coverage types than married heterosexuals.

The financial difficulties reported by coupled LGBs might be the result of differences in the cost of medical and health services in those areas in which these populations might cluster. Sexual minorities are more likely to live in high-cost, high-amenity areas (Black et al. 2002), places in which health care might also be more expensive. To the extent that observed differences in income and financial worry do not compensate for these higher costs, the costs may discourage necessary health care acquisition. Unfortunately, the NHIS does not include geographic information below the regional level. A similar regional explanation might account for the higher likelihood of noncost delays shown by partnered and never married LGBs.

Recent studies have also noted that cultural barriers to health care use, such as disrespectful or insensitive attitudes among health care providers, lack of trust between patients and providers, and difficulty in finding LGBTQ-friendly providers (especially in nonurban areas), are all important factors of delayed or forgone use of health services among sexual minorities (Hsieh and Ruther 2017; McNair,

Hegarty, and Taft 2012). Considering the recent enactment of religious exemption laws in several states, where health care providers may deny services to sexual minorities in the name of religious freedom (Moreau 2018; Pear and Peters 2018), even sexual minorities who have adequate health insurance coverage may not receive care they need due to legal discrimination based on sexual orientation. More complication may be introduced if the current administration scales back or removes part of the ACA. For example, Medicaid expansion is largely funded by the federal government and has increased insurance coverage in many states (Rudowitz and Antonisse 2018); a withdrawal of the Medicaid expansion may affect those currently benefiting, including some low-income individuals.

Although the NHIS is a well-respected and nationally representative survey, it still presents limitations in studies of the sexual minority population. Notably, although the NHIS has a large sample size, the number of LGB respondents remains fairly small. The relatively small size of the sexual minority respondents in the sample reduces the power of the analyses for those groups, resulting in wider confidence intervals than might otherwise exist. Aggregating the gay, lesbian, and bisexual populations into a "sexual minority" group improves the size of that sample, but the mingling of these potentially different populations may introduce inconsistencies and overgeneralization into the results. The study is also unable to separately analyze individuals who identify with other sexual identities or as transgender.

Despite these limitations, the present study shows that disparities in health care access by sexual orientation continue. While marriage equality and ACA have recently improved insurance coverage rates among sexual minorities, economic and noneconomic obstacles to health care utilization remain challenging to many sexual minorities, married or unmarried. The disparities in health care access may also continue contributing to the long-observed disadvantages in health outcomes among sexual minority communities.

REFERENCES

Ash, M. A., and M.V.L. Badgett. 2006. "Separate and Unequal: The Effect of Unequal Access to Employment-Based Health Insurance on Same-Sex and Unmarried Different-Sex Couples." *Contemporary Economic Policy* 24 (4): 582–599.

Bachman, J. G., P. M. O'Malley, J. E. Schulenberg, L. D. Johnston, A. L. Bryant, and A. C. Merline. 2002. *The Decline of Substance Use in Young Adulthood: Changes in Social Activities, Roles, and Beliefs.* Mahwah, NJ: Lawrence Erlbaum Associates.

Badgett, M.V.L. 2007. "Unequal Taxes on Equal Benefits: The Taxation of Domestic Partner Benefits." Williams Institute, UCLA School of Law, University of California. Retrieved from http:/williamsinstitute.laww.ucla.edu/wp-content/uploads/Badgett-UnequalTaxes OnEqualBenefits-Dec-2007.pdf.

Badgett, M. L., G. J. Gates, and N. C. Maisel. 2008. "Registered Domestic Partnerships among Gay Men and Lesbians: The Role of Economic Factors." *Review of Economics of the Household* 6 (4): 327.

Black, D., G. Gates, S. Sanders, and L. Taylor. 2002. "Why Do Gay Men Live in San Francisco?" *Journal of Urban Economics* 51: 54–76.

Blosnich, J. R. 2017. "Sexual Orientation Differences in Satisfaction with Healthcare: Findings from the Behavioral Risk Factor Surveillance System, 2014." *LGBT Health* 4 (3): 227–231.

Buchmueller, T., and C. S. Carpenter. 2010. "Disparities in Health Insurance Coverage, Access, and Outcomes for Individuals in Same-Sex versus Different-Sex Relationships, 2000–2007." *American Journal of Public Health* 100 (3): 489–495.

Buchmueller, T. C., and C. S. Carpenter. 2012. "The Effect of Requiring Private Employers to Extend Health Benefit Eligibility to Same-Sex Partners of Employees: Evidence from California." *Journal of Policy Analysis and Management* 31 (2): 388–403.

Buffie, W. C. 2011. "Public Health Implications of Same-Sex Marriage." *American Journal of Public Health* 101 (6): 986–990.

Carpenter, C., and G. J. Gates. 2008. "Gay and Lesbian Partnership: Evidence from California." *Demography* 45 (3): 573–590.

Carr, D., and K. W. Springer. 2010. "Advances in Families and Health Research in the 21st Century." *Journal of Marriage and Family* 72 (3): 743–761.

Clift, J. B., and J. Kirby. 2012. "Health Care Access and Perceptions of Provider Care among Individuals in Same-Sex Couples: Findings from the Medical Expenditure Panel Survey (MEPS)." *Journal of Homosexuality* 59 (6): 839–850.

Dahlhamer, J. M., A. M. Galinsky, S. S. Joestl, and B. W. Ward. 2016. "Barriers to Health Care among Adults Identifying as Sexual Minorities: A US National Study." *American Journal of Public Health* 106 (6): 1116–1122.

Gates, G., M.V.L. Badgett, and D. Ho. 2008. "Marriage, Registration, and Dissolution by Same-Sex Couples in the US." Williams Institute, UCLA School of Law, University of California. Retrieved from http://repositories.cdlib.org/uclalaw/williams/gates_1.

Gonzalez, G., and L. A. Blewett. 2014. "National and State-Specific Health Insurance Disparities for Adults in Same-Sex Relationships." *American Journal of Public Health* 104 (2): e95–e104.

Gonzalez, G., and C. Henning-Smith. 2017. "The Affordable Care Act and Health Insurance Coverage for Lesbian, Gay, and Bisexual Adults: Analysis of the Behavioral Risk Factor Surveillance System." *LGBT Health* 4 (1): 62–67.

Heck, J. E., R. L. Sell, and S. Sheinfeld Gorin. 2006. "Health Care Access among Individuals Involved in Same-Sex Relationships." *American Journal of Public Health* 96 (6): 1111–1118.

Hsieh, N., and M. Ruther. 2017. "Despite Increased Insurance Coverage, Nonwhite Sexual Minorities Still Experience Disparities in Access to Care." *Health Affairs* 36 (10): 1786–1794.

Liu, H., C. Reczek, and D. Brown. 2013. "Same-Sex Cohabitors and Health: The Role of Race-Ethnicity, Gender, and Socioeconomic Status." *Journal of Health and Social Behavior* 54 (1): 25–45.

McNair, R. P., K. Hegarty, and A. Taft. 2012. "From Silence to Sensitivity: A New Identity Disclosure Model to Facilitate Disclosure for Same-Sex Attracted Women in General Practice Consultations." *Social Science & Medicine* 75 (1): 208–216.

Moreau, J. 2018. "129 Anti-LGBTQ State Bills Were Introduced in 2017, New Report Says." *NBC News* (January 12, 2018). Retrieved from https://www.nbcnews.com/features/nbc-out/129-anti-lgbtq-state-bills-were-introduced-2017-new-report-n837076.

Obergefell v Hodges. 2015. 135 S Ct 2584.

Pear, R., and J. W. Peters. 2018. "Trump Gives Health Workers New Religious Liberty Protections." *New York Times* (January 18, 2018). Retrieved from https://www.nytimes.com/2018/01/18/us/health-care-office-abortion-contraception.html.

Ponce, N. A., S. D. Cochran, J. C. Pizer, and V. M. Mays. 2010. "The Effects of Unequal Access to Health Insurance for Same-Sex Couples in California." *Health Affairs* 29 (8): 1539–1548.

Reczek, C., and D. Umberson. 2012. "Gender, Health Behavior, and Intimate Relationships: Lesbian, Gay, and Straight Contexts." *Social Science and Medicine* 74: 1783–1790.

Rudowitz, R., and L. Antonisse. 2018. "Implications of the ACA Medicaid Expansion: A Look at the Data and Evidence (Issue Brief May 2018)." Henry J. Kaiser Family Foundation. Retrieved from http://files.kff.org/attachment/Issue-Brief-Implications-of-the-ACA-Medicaid-Expansion-A-Look-at-the-Data-and-Evidence.

Skopec, L., and S. K. Long. 2015. "Lesbian, Gay, and Bisexual Adults Making Gains in Health Insurance and Access to Care." *Health Affairs* 34 (10): 1769–1773F.

StataCorp. 2015. *Stata Statistical Software: Release 14*. College Station, TX: StataCorp LP.

Umberson, D. 1992. "Gender, Marital Status, and the Social Control of Health Behavior." *Social Science & Medicine* 34: 907–917.

United States v Windsor. 2013. 133 S. Ct. 2675.

Waite, L., and M. Gallagher. 2000. *The Case for Marriage: Why Married People Are Happier, Healthier, and Better Off Financially*. New York: Doubleday.

12

Law and Same-Sex Couples' Experiences of Childbirth

EMILY KAZYAK

EMMA FINKEN

In 2017, the Supreme Court ruled in *Pavan v. Smith* that states must allow married same-sex couples to both be listed as parents on their child's birth certificate. Although the ruling garnered less media attention than the Court's 2015 *Obergefell v. Hodges* decision on marriage, it nonetheless illustrates a significant issue pertinent to the families who are the focus of this chapter: lesbian same-sex couples who had children via donor insemination before 2015. Indeed, prior to this ruling, these couples faced an unequal legal climate insofar as only the biological mother could be listed on the birth certificate and thus be legally recognized as a parent; the nonbiological mother had no legal recognition of her parenthood. Couples often pursued a second-parent adoption so that the nonbiological mother could be legally recognized as a parent. Yet this option was not available to all couples; state laws allowed, denied, or made uncertain same-sex couples' access to pursuing this legal recognition for the nonbiological mother (Dalton 2001; Kazyak 2015). Drawing on data from interviews with twenty-one lesbian parents, we analyze how the unequal and varied legal context shapes their health care experiences related to childbirth.

Our analysis is informed by social science research that focuses on "the relevance of law in everyday life" (Erlanger 2005). We follow in what Richman (2009) defines as the "constitutive" theoretical tradition that seeks to understand the mutually constitutive relationship between laws on the books and how law is imagined and experienced in daily life. This theoretical perspective focuses on "everyday people's" engagement with the law and legal categories and argues that the law serves as an interpretive framework through which people understand themselves and others in everyday life (Ewick and Silbey 1998). People may embrace, reject, or rework legal categories in social interactions (Baumle and Compton 2015). Guided by this constitutive theoretical framework in sociolegal studies, in our chapter, we ask: how is the law present in lesbian women's health care experiences? We focus on pregnancy, childbirth, and postpartum health care.

We draw on data from interviews with both biological and nonbiological mothers in three states with different second-parent adoption laws (Nebraska/ unavailable, Iowa/guaranteed, Missouri/uncertain). We address how the legal variation (i.e., the nonbiological mother could do a second-parent adoption in some but not all states represented in the sample) mattered to their decision-making processes related to health care. Namely, we find that those living in states with unavailable or uncertain access discussed the option of giving birth in a different state that had guaranteed access.

We also address how the legal inequity faced by all of the couples (i.e., the nonbiological mother was not immediately legally recognized as a parent in any state) mattered to their health care experiences. We find that this lack of legal equity permeated how lesbian women expected to be treated within health care settings. All couples, regardless of state, experienced fear that they would be discriminated against as a result of their sexual orientation and that this would be worse for the nonbiological mother especially, given her lack of legal rights. Our analysis illustrates that the decisions LGBTQ people make about their health care and their experiences within health care settings are embedded in a broader legal context. Additionally, our analysis highlights the role that health care providers may play in alleviating LGBTQ people's apprehension about health care settings.

Methods

Data Collection and Analysis

Data come from twenty-one interviews with lesbian parents. All interviewees had a child within the context of a same-sex couple using donor insemination and both biological mothers and nonbiological mothers were interviewed. The interviews were conducted in 2012–2013 by the first author as part of a larger project about how lesbian couples experience, understand, and make decisions about second-parent adoption. Participants were recruited from three states that had different laws regarding second-parent adoption for same-sex couples at the time the interviews were conducted: Iowa (guaranteed access), Missouri (uncertain access), and Nebraska (unavailable access). Participants were recruited through a purposive, convenience sample with several starting points so as not to overrely on particular social networks. Starting points included regional LGBTQ organizations in each state (such as PFLAG) as well as churches with welcoming LGBTQ-friendly stances. The first author also recruited through national LGBTQ organizations (such as Equality Resource Council and LGBTQ parenting groups on websites such as Babycenter.com) and through a public Facebook page.

The first author conducted all of the interviews in-person, over the phone, or over Skype. Prior to the interview, people completed a short survey that included demographic questions. The survey also included questions about their relationship with their child and their experiences with the law (e.g., whether they were recognized as a legal parent). The interviews were semistructured and covered questions about how they gained information about the legal climate in which they were living, their decision-making process about whether or not to do a second-parent adoption, and their experiences regarding the law in both interpersonal and institutional interactions.

Once the data were collected, the interviews were transcribed in full and coded using QSR-Nvivo software. The first author began analyses by reading through the transcripts and taking notes on interesting emerging themes, what Emerson, Fretz, and Shaw (1995) refer to as "open coding." During this process, the first author was struck by how salient the law was in people's narratives about their pregnancy, labor and delivery, and postpartum care. After doing open coding and generating themes, the first author trained two graduate student research assistants to code the interviews using them. After the interview data were coded, the first author wrote analytic memos that linked themes, which were developed into the findings in the following text in collaboration between the authors. The memos allowed us to assess whether variation among the participants existed with regard to each topic (e.g., were people in states with guaranteed access less likely to talk about the law?). In order to ensure confidentiality, pseudonyms are used. The quotes were edited for the sake of both confidentiality and clarity, but the meaning and words have not been otherwise changed.

Profile of Participants

The sample includes participants from each state in roughly equal proportions (see Table 12.1). Respondents were diverse in terms of whether they lived in urban, rural, or suburban areas, as well as their class status, but less so with regard to race and ethnicity, as the sample is predominately white (see Kazyak 2015 for more discussion of demographics of the sample). In all but one family, one parent was biologically related and one parent was not biologically related to their children (in one family, each parent had given birth). With regard to legal status, half of the sample (10 participants) pursued a second-parent adoption and half (11 participants) did not pursue a second-parent adoption (but one participant was in the process). Those who did a second-parent adoption include two couples who were living in Nebraska but did a second-parent adoption in another state. Six people in the sample do not have a legal tie to their child(ren).

TABLE 12.1

Interviewee Demographics

Pseudonym	State	Bio-mom?	Legally recognized as parent?	State law second-parent adoption
Anne	Nebraska	No	No	Unavailable
Barbara	Nebraska	No	Yes, through 2nd parent adoption	Unavailable
Tiffany	Nebraska	Yes	Yes, since birth	Unavailable
Victoria	Missouri	Yes	Yes, since birth	Uncertain
Grace	Missouri	No	No	Uncertain
Cathy	Missouri	No	Yes, through 2nd parent adoption	Uncertain
Harriet	Missouri	Yes	Yes, since birth	Uncertain
Darcie	Iowa	No	Yes, through 2nd parent adoption	Guaranteed
Linda	Iowa	Yes	Yes, since birth	Guaranteed
Elizabeth	Iowa	No	No	Guaranteed
Melanie	Missouri	Yes	Yes, since birth	Uncertain
Jan	Nebraska	Mix	Yes, since birth and through 2nd parent adoption	Unavailable
Tanya	Nebraska	Mix	Yes, since birth and through 2nd parent adoption	Unavailable
Shawna	Missouri	Yes	Yes, since birth	Uncertain
Joyce	Missouri	No	No	Uncertain
Pamela	Iowa	Yes	Yes, since birth	Guaranteed
Robyn	Iowa	No	Yes, through 2nd parent adoption	Guaranteed
Erin	Nebraska	Yes	Yes, since birth	Unavailable
Phoebe	Nebraska	No	No	Unavailable
Ellen	Nebraska	Yes	Yes, since birth	Unavailable
Nikki	Nebraska	No	No	Unavailable

Results

Health Care Decision-Making Processes: Deciding Where to Give Birth

In this section we discuss how the state legal context influenced women's health care decisions about where to give to birth. The availability of second-parent adoptions differed across states at the time of the study, and this variation influenced lesbian women's experiences. Specifically, for the women residing in Nebraska and Missouri, states where second-parent adoption was either unavailable or contingent on county within the state, respectively, the law was quite salient in their decision-making process about where to give birth. No one in Iowa discussed the legal context as part of their decision-making process about where to give birth.

Consider the experiences of Cathy and Harriet who live in Missouri, a state with, as they put it, "confusing" and "ambiguous" laws. When describing where they gave birth, Cathy said: "We were told that as long as you deliver in the county as opposed to the city, you can apply for second-parent adoption, but you can't do that in the city." Since the laws in the county "didn't coincide" with the laws in the city where they lived, Cathy explained, "we delivered in the county to be able to do the adoption."

Other couples who lived in Missouri and also Nebraska couples had contemplated driving to Iowa, a state with guaranteed access to second-parent adoption for same-sex couples. Victoria who lived in Missouri commented: "We've talked about driving over [state] lines into Iowa for her to have this baby." The possibility of giving birth in Iowa also emerged in the interview with Ellen and Nikki, a couple living in Nebraska. As Ellen discussed their decision to give birth in Nebraska instead of Iowa, she stated: "I feel like if we lived closer to the border it would have been one thing to just like hop over to Iowa to the hospital." Since they did not live close to Iowa's border, they ultimately decided to not "go through all that" and Ellen gave birth in Nebraska.

Although the law did not ultimately influence where Ellen and Nikki or Victoria and Grace ultimately gave birth, the fact that it was part of their decision-making process illuminates how lesbian women weigh their options with a consideration of a broader legal context. Such references to the law and availability of second-parent adoption did not emerge in the narratives of lesbian women living in Iowa. Since these couples were guaranteed access to second-parent adoption regardless of where in the state they delivered their child, they did not have to consider different hospitals in different parts of the state or a different state entirely as they decided where to give birth.

Expectations for Treatment in Health Care Settings

In this section, we focus on the expectations that women had about how they would be treated in health care settings. We find that overall women's expectations were quite low insofar as they articulated fears that they would be discriminated against and concerns that their family's lack of legal equity would translate into poor treatment by health care providers. The narratives of fear and concern were consistent in interviewees across states. We argue the lack of variation across states reflects the fact that even in states that guarantee access to second-parent adoption, these families nonetheless faced the scenario where the nonbiological mother would not have legal ties to her child until that second-parent adoption took place. Thus, all couples experienced the pregnancy and labor and delivery and postpartum care without that legal protection. We divide this section into two parts. First, we discuss how lesbian women were fearful about how the nonbiological mom would be treated within health care settings. Of course, a sense of fear and anxiety when approaching childbirth is not necessarily unique to lesbian women (Melender 2002). However, these couples had additional worries that stemmed from the lack of legal equity. We highlight how their expectations for health care settings were so fraught with fear by noting how each family thought about "worse case hypothetical scenarios" they might encounter. Second, we discuss the strategies that lesbian women used to try to mitigate their fear, which further illustrates the degree to which the lack of legal equity for their family (and especially for the nonbiological mom) factored into their expectations for how they would be treated in health care settings.

Fear for Nonbiological Mom and Worst-Case Hypothetical Scenarios

Participants discussed having a lot of fear about how the nonbiological mother would be treated during labor and delivery. For example, Cathy said: "My biggest fear would be somebody [in the hospital] telling me I couldn't go somewhere or see my son or see my wife." Joyce also recalled a sense of anxiety as the nonbiological mother. Among the things she was nervous about included "Are you going to let me into the delivery room? If she has a C-section, are you going to let me in there? Will I be able to go down and hold my baby? Am I going to be the one who's allowed to have that bracelet, allowing me to you know go get my baby from the nursery if I want to?" Explicitly explaining how her fears were rooted in the law, Joyce noted: "My worse fear was . . . I'll want to go get my baby, I'll have no rights to [my son] and they won't let me see him." The lack of legal equity Joyce experienced translated into medical situations being "terrifying for me on my end not being the biological parent." The questions, concerns, and fear raised by Cathy and Joyce echoed those that other nonbiological moms raised. As Joyce's quote illustrates, their fear for how they would be treated stemmed from the fact that they knew they were not legally recognized as a parent, and thus they were unsure if they would have access to certain things (e.g., having a bracelet that would allow them to go to the nursery to hold their baby).

The fear that permeated people's expectations for how the nonbiological mother would be treated in health care settings is also illustrated what we call "worst case hypothetical scenarios." These were scenarios they had imagined that typically involved either the biological mother or the child dying. As couples entertained these scenarios, they expressed fear about whether the nonbiological mother would either be able to retain custody of their child or be able to be with her spouse. Again, these fears stemmed from the lack of legal equity these families experienced insofar as the nonbiological mom would be considered a legal stranger.

In discussing her thinking through of the worst-case scenario of her wife dying in childbirth, Victoria mused: "Would they just let me keep the baby?" She had even considered whether she needed to become a foster parent so she could immediately petition to keep the baby in the event of such a situation. This concern that the nonbiological parent would not be able to retain custody of their child in the event of the biological parent's death was echoed by every interviewee. People also discussed the fear of not being able to make medical decisions for their child if this worst-case scenario occurred. Linda described the fear from the perspective of being the biological-related mother, saying: "What if something happened to me, who would speak for the child?" Her wife echoed the concern that "I might not have access to my child's medical records, because I don't have a legal relationship with him." In sum, the lack of legal protection for the nonbiological mom that families in all states experienced translated into families thinking through worst-case scenarios and being fearful about treatment in health care settings. Next, we turn to the strategies families used to help mitigate those fears.

Strategies Used to Lessen Fears about Health Care Settings

One strategy the lesbian women used was obtaining as much legal protection for the nonbiological mother as possible and bringing that documentation to the hospital. Examples include making living wills, making sure their relationship status was solidified and recognized, and having the nonbiological mother become a health proxy. Cathy combated her anxieties about her legal status using several of these methods: "[Wife] did a living will. And there was another [health] proxy, so that I can make decisions for her and so that everything would be deferred to me personally. She . . . printed off generic documents from [the insurance providers] and we both signed them and had them notarized and turned them in to our doctors and the hospital where we delivered so everything was scanned in and in our charts." Others also took protective measures for the nonbiological mother: Harriet said "[the hospital staff] asked for both our proxy and living will. So we gave it to them and they put it in the file." Likewise, Erin and Phoebe detailed the various measures they had taken to ensure that the nonbiological mother had as many legal protections as she could. They explained: "We carry a pin on us at all times" that contains electronic copies of documents like a power of attorney. Phoebe explained they carry it at all times "because if anything were to happen and we are at the hospital and she can't answer for herself or [their son] then I just show them the papers." All of these examples illustrate the degree to which the law permeated lesbian women's expectations for how their families and the nonbiological mother in particular would be treated in health care settings.

A second strategy used by couples that had done a second-parent adoption was to make sure health care providers were aware that the nonbiological mother was legally recognized as a parent and thus had the legal ability to make medical decisions for her child. For instance, Jan and Tanya were the one couple living in Nebraska who had done a second-parent adoption in another state. Jan, the nonbiological mother, explained that when they moved, she was very clear with their new pediatrician that she is the "adoptive mother." In explaining why she "made a point to say I'm the adoptive mother," she said that she "wanted to convey to them I have legal standing here [and let them know that] I can make legal decisions for this child, so don't bother to question me." This strategy further illustrates the fear that without health care providers having that awareness, the nonbiological mother may be denied treatment decisions. Next, we discuss whether their expectations were realized as we detail their actual experiences within health care settings.

Experiences in Health Care Settings

In general, the fears that lesbian women had about how their family and how the nonbiological mother would be treated by health care providers were not often realized. As we outline, many reported overall positive interactions. We also do discuss, however, instances of negative interactions with health care providers.

Positive Experiences

Several women recalled their positive experiences at the hospital during pregnancy, labor and delivery, and other parenting-related health care services. Melanie noted: "I think the hospital was really amazing. . . . Everybody who came in, I introduced her as my wife [to them], that sort of thing, [so] I didn't set it up where there would be any sort of issue." Referencing her experience as a nonbiological mother, Darcie said: "I can't say that I've ever been treated as the lesser parent from doctors." Others mentioned experiences they had where they thought that health care providers made an extra effort to be inclusive and supportive. For instance, Harriet explained: "Our OB's office was really nice. . . . If anything we felt extra special. . . . I felt like the nurses just loved us . . . [because the nurses thought] what's better than one mom? Two." Phoebe also described an experience that was "really nice" and made her feel that the doctor's office "did a really good job" being supportive. She retold the experience of their first appointment when her spouse was eight weeks pregnant: "One nurse said, 'Oh, you're a support for someone? [and I replied] 'Yeah,' . . . and the nurse was looking through the paperwork and she looked at me and said 'You're more than her support person, you're her wife, why didn't you say anything? That's awesome! Congratulations to you, too!'" Both of these stories speak to the positive impact that health care practitioners can have in terms of being inclusive and supportive of same-sex couples and LGBTQ people.

Negative Experiences

Other couples experienced less supportive health care providers and settings. For instance, Victoria said that she has told the doctor's office "about a million times" that she and Grace were married, but they nonetheless "would enter her as my sister because we have the same last name." Jan also shared an experience at a pediatrician's office where the pediatrician informed her: "My nurse was kind of uncomfortable with your status, so I'm going to be handling this." Jan recalled being angry at both the nurse's reaction and at the doctor for telling her about the nurse's reaction and has since switched pediatricians.

Two additional stories illustrate how lesbian experiences within health care settings can be negative (even without a specific health care provider being unsupportive) due to the lack of legal equity their families faced. Erin and Phoebe described their experiences at a hospital where they had their child as positive overall, but did note "the only thing that was maybe not good . . . they make you watch videos before they let us leave the hospital and one of them is talking about how you have to get married so you can have your rights as a father." Although their interactions with health care providers were positive, that the hospital promoted a video that ignored same-sex couples and highlighted their family's legal inequity (i.e., they did not have the option to get married or have rights granted to the nonbiological parent) indicates how lesbian women can experience health care settings (not providers per se) as unsupportive.

Darcie and Linda described the experience of filling out their child's birth certificate application in the hospital as an extremely invalidating and emotionally charged experience. Darcie explained that having to only list the biological mother coupled with having to identify her as unmarried to avoid having to list a father "was much more emotional than we ever imagined" and in fact referred to it as "gut wrenching." Linda explained why it was so emotional: "Not only are we not acknowledging the nonbiological mother, we're not acknowledging your marriage either." Linda and Darcie said that even when the hospital staff person came in with the birth certificate application, they both "just bust[ed] out crying." Their story underscores how negative health care experiences that stem from legal inequity can occur even without any one health care provider being discriminatory or unsupportive.

In sum, people's stories indicate how medical providers can mitigate or compound stress that comes with an unequal legal landscape. Couples in all states reported both positive and negative interactions with health care providers.

Discussion

As LGBTQ people increasingly have children after coming out and/or in the context of a same-sex marriage, it is important to address their expectations and experiences surrounding parenting. Given that pregnancy and birth are medicalized processes (Simonds, Rothman, and Norman 2007), examining how lesbian same-sex couples experience childbirth sheds light on issues pertaining to health and same-sex couples. Our overarching goal in this chapter is to underscore that decisions related to health care and experiences with health care practitioners cannot adequately be understood without accounting for the legal context within which those decisions and experiences occur. In other words: legal inequity for LGBTQ people matters to their health care experiences. For lesbian couples having children via donor insemination, the lack of guaranteed legal recognition of the nonbiological mother permeated their expectations for health care settings. Their accounts underscore the feelings of fear and anxiety experienced when anticipating interacting with health care practitioners. Future work should address whether lesbian couples still approach health care with a sense of fear and anxiety given changes in laws. Since changes in the laws do not always translate evenly to changes in practices, questions remain, for instance, about whether the Supreme Court 2017 decision has affected how states process birth certificates. Moreover, newly passed religious freedom laws in some states that allow health care providers to be exempt from working with LGBTQ people may continue to negatively impact the experiences of lesbian couples (Kazyak, Burke, and Stange 2018; Miller 2018).

It is important to note that in most cases, people's fears were not actually realized. By and large lesbian women in our study reported overall positive interactions with health care providers. Yet the fact that these positive experiences stood out to them, not to mention their discussions of what they anticipated, helps to highlight that they did not start with the expectation of inclusive and supportive health care treatment. Our work indicates that it is important to recognize the role that health care providers might play in mitigating the stress and fear that lesbian women experience. The law and legal categories were central to how lesbian women approached health care settings. Yet for some health care providers, the law and legal categories were seemingly not important to how they interacted with and treated same-sex couples (i.e., they recognized the nonbiological mother as a parent during labor even though she was consider a "legal stranger" by law). These accounts illustrate how people may reject legal categories in social interactions (Ewick and Silbey 1998).

Conclusions

The focus on lesbian same-sex couples navigating health care settings relating to childbirth is an interesting case to consider as well because sexuality is salient and visible in a way that is not necessarily the case in other health care situations that LGBTQ people experience. Research indicates that LGBTQ people are not always out to their health care provider, citing the fear of discrimination (Eliason and Schope 2001). Despite their fear, in the case of lesbian same-sex couples having a child, the people interviewed for this study nonetheless wanted to be out and visible about their sexuality and family. For Erin and Phoebe, the process of having a child together actually facilitated their first time coming out to a stranger, in this case the OB/GYN with whom they were working. Interviewees made it a point to research doctors and pediatricians who were LGBTQ-friendly, often relying on other LGBTQ friends and LGBTQ community organizations. Couples likewise discussed making an effort to include the nonbiological mother in all health care interactions and to talk with the staff at doctors' offices and hospitals about their status as a two-mom family. Thus similar to instances in other settings, same-sex couples with children may actually make LGBQ sexuality more visible in health care settings (Bernstein 2015). In fact it is precisely because of this visibility that couples described the fear they had. Although our chapter focuses only on lesbian same-sex couples having children, we argue that this case study provides insights into thinking about same-sex unions and health more broadly. Our work raises questions about what strategies couples might utilize to combat fear experienced in health-related contexts. Likewise, people's narratives highlight work that health care practitioners and health care offices can do to alleviate stigma and discrimination that LGBTQ people experience.

REFERENCES

Baumle, Amanda, and D'Lane Compton. 2015. *Legalizing LGBT Families: How the Law Shapes Parenthood*. New York: New York University Press.

Bernstein, Mary. 2015. "Same-Sex Marriage and the Future of the LGBT Movement." *Gender & Society* 29 (3): 321–337.

Dalton, Susan. 2001. "Protecting Our Parent–Child Relationships: Understanding the Strengths and Weaknesses of Second-Parent Adoption." In *Queer Families, Queer Politics: Challenging Culture and the State*, edited by M. Bernstein and R. Reimann, 201–220. New York: Columbia University Press.

Eliason, Michele J., and Robert Schope. 2001. "Does 'Don't Ask Don't Tell' Apply to Health Care? Lesbian, Gay, and Bisexual People's Disclosure to Health Care Providers." *Journal of the Gay and Lesbian Medical Association* 5 (4): 125–134.

Emerson, Robert M., Rachel I. Fretz, and Linda L. Shaw. 1995. *Writing Ethnographic Field Notes*. Chicago: University of Chicago Press.

Erlanger, Howard. 2005. "Organizations, Institutions, and the Story of Shmuel: Reflections on the 40th Anniversary of the Law and Society Association." *Law and Society Review* 39 (1): 1–10.

Ewick, Patricia and Susan S. Sibley. 1998. *The Common Place of Law: Stories from Everyday Life*. Chicago: University of Chicago Press.

Kazyak, Emily. 2015. "'The Law's the Law, Right?' Sexual Minority Mothers Navigating Legal Inequities and Inconsistencies." *Sexuality Research and Social Policy* 12 (3): 188–201.

Kazyak, Emily, Kelsy Burke, and Mathew Stange. 2018. "Logics of Freedom: Debating Religious Freedom Laws and Gay and Lesbian Rights." *Socius* 4: 1–18.

Melender, Hanna-Leena. 2002. "Experiences of Fears Associated with Pregnancy and Childbirth: A Study of 329 Pregnant Women." *Birth: Issues in Perinatal Care* 29 (2): 101–111.

Miller, Susan. 2018. "3 Years after Same-Sex Marriage Ruling, Protections for LGBT Families Undermined." *USA Today*. https://www.usatoday.com/story/news/nation/2018/06/04/same-sex-marriage-ruling-undermined-gay-parents/650112002/.

Obergefell v. Hodges, 135 S. Ct. 2071, 576 U.S., 191 L. Ed. 2d 953 (2015).

Pavan v. Smith 137 S. Ct. 2075 (2017).

Richman, Kimberly D. 2009. *Courting Change: Queer Parents, Judges, and the Transformation of American Family Law*. New York: New York University Press.

Simonds, Wendy, Barbara Katz Rothman, and Bari Meltzer Norman. 2007. *Laboring On: Birth in Transition in the United States*. New York: Routledge.

13

Married in Texas

Findings from an LGBTQ Community Needs Assessment

KARA SUTTON

RICHARD K. SCOTCH

The political, legal, and social landscape for lesbian, gay, bisexual, transgender, and queer (LGBTQ) people is changing rapidly in the United States and around the world, yet research on the needs and concerns of the LGBTQ population has been limited. Like other conservative states in the United States, the State of Texas has been slow to recognize marriage equality. Although same-sex marriage was not explicitly prohibited until the early 1970s, the Texas legislature enacted prohibitions on same-sex marriage on four separate occasions between 1973 and 2005 (Equality Texas 2015). However, with the 2015 Supreme Court decision in *Obergefell v. Hodges*, as in every state, Texas laws against same-sex marriage were overturned. Since the decision, many couples have exercised their right to marry. With marriage equality now firmly established by the Supreme Court as a legal right, and more Americans openly identifying themselves as LGBTQ, more extensive information about the characteristics and experiences of same-sex couples within the LGBTQ community may provide insight into the perspective of these couples. According to previous studies, approximately 740,000 or 3.6 percent of Texas residents identify as LGBTQ with over 46,000 households reporting as same-sex households (Gallup 2013; Williams Institute 2016), most centrally located within large metropolitan areas. However, little research has been conducted about LGBTQ Texas residents or their service needs.

In this chapter, we provide some findings from a recent needs assessment study of LGBTQ individuals in the State of Texas, as well as some comments on the significance of our research. The needs assessment, conducted statewide in 2017, involved an online survey of 858 individuals, as well as a separate survey of service providers focused on the LGBTQ community and qualitative interviews and focus groups. Since the survey included substantial proportions of respondents who were married, unmarried but in relationships, and single, it allows comparisons among people across these varying relationships to suggest the impact of marriage for LGBTQ individuals in Texas.

The needs assessment study was commissioned by the Texas Pride Impact Funds, a foundation committed to advance positive change for LGBTQ communities across Texas. Its purpose was to develop actionable findings for use by funders and providers of LGBTQ-focused services in Texas, but the results may be of interest to anyone concerned with the status of LGBTQ individuals in the United States. Texas is the second most populous state in the United States, and thus is worthy of attention by itself, but it also provides an interesting mix of traditional political conservatism in rural and suburban areas with a substantial high technology economy in several dynamic urban centers. Social conditions in contemporary Texas may be a useful bellwether for much of the twenty-first-century American heartland.

Methods and Data

In 2017, the Texas Pride Impact Funds commissioned a needs assessment survey on the state's LBGTQ community from a research team at the University of Texas at Dallas led by the authors. The purpose of the assessment was to understand the key concerns and unmet needs of the LGBTQ community in Texas. The study examined the demographic composition of respondents and their self-reported economic stability, education, legal and civic participation, and physical and mental well-being. Particular attention was paid to include previously understudied special populations such as communities of color, senior citizens, transgendered people, and residents of rural communities.

Multiple methods and information sources were used to conduct the assessment, including online surveys of individual community members and LGBTQ-focused service providers, as well as qualitative interviews with LGBTQ community leaders. The surveys, completed in July 2017, assessed needs, concerns, service use, and gaps for Texas's LGBTQ community. Respondents were recruited through existing contacts known to leaders within the sponsoring Texas Pride Impact Funds and the research team, as well as various LGBTQ-oriented media outlets.

The survey was conducted through a snowball sampling technique that employed word of mouth to recruit respondents, since strategies for eliciting more representative responses from the entire population of LGBTQ Texans were not practical for our project. The research team reached out to service providers, activist groups, and media outlets that could be identified which focused on the LGBTQ community in Texas for their assistance in recruiting people to participate in the survey, but that process may have meant that individuals who were not already engaged in that community were unlikely to have been invited to participate. As a result, we cannot be confident that those participating in this survey were typical of all self-identified LGBTQ individuals in Texas, let alone those whose sexual or gender identity is, for whatever reason, not clearly established. Despite repeated efforts to include as diverse a sample as possible, those who are socially isolated were less likely to have been contacted, while our survey is likely to be overly representative of LGBTQ individuals who are well connected to the larger LGBTQ community and who readily identify with that community.

In addition to the survey of individual community members, a separate survey was conducted of service providers focused on the LGBTQ community. Again, participants were recruited through a snowball sample utilizing the social network of the research team, the Texas Pride Impact Funds leadership, and early respondents. Representatives from a total of seventy-eight organizations responded to this provider survey; the results, which concerned service provision and unmet needs, were not directly relevant to this chapter, and are reported elsewhere (Texas Pride Impact Funds 2017).

Finally, two focus groups and ten personal interviews with key informants were conducted by the two principal investigators in communities around the state. These respondents also were identified by Texas Pride Impact Funds leaders as well as by contacting local and statewide advocacy organizations. They included people identified as LGBTQ community leaders and others knowledgeable about LGBTQ community needs, including leaders of several LGBTQ community-based groups and other community activists. Interviews and focus groups were held in major metropolitan areas and several smaller communities around the state.

Results: General

A total of 858 respondents completed the community member survey, of whom 47.3 percent reported their gender as male, 41.5 percent as female, 4.2 percent as transgender male, and 5.7 percent as transgender female. Sexual orientation was reported as gay by 46.9 percent of respondents, as lesbian by 34.2 percent respondents, and as bisexual by 12.9 percent, with other orientations reported by the remaining 6.0 percent. Of the 845 respondents reporting their relationship status, 30.3 percent responded that they were legally married, 20.6 percent that they were dating and cohabiting, 13.4 percent that they were dating but not cohabiting, and 35.7 percent that they were single.

Respondents were nearly uniformly split between those who reported being unmarried and/or living alone (49.1%) and those who were married or cohabitating (50.9%). Of those living independently, 35.7 percent considered themselves single, whereas the remaining 13.4 percent reported a dating but not cohabitating relationship status. Among the same-sex couples residing together,

30.2 percent were legally married, a group more likely to be female and to average an approximate 8.2 years older than their nonmarried counterparts.

Approximately 60 percent of female respondents reported marriage or cohabitation, 14 percentage points higher than male respondents. On the other hand, transgender females held lower rates, with only 32.8 percent reporting marriage or cohabitation, nearly 9 percentage points lower than transgender males. Of those reporting legal marriage, 76.9 percent identified as Caucasian, with Native Americans and Spanish/Latino respondents reporting the highest rates of single status (48.3% and 43.4%, respectively). African American respondents were represented proportionally within each relationship category. Married individuals were more likely to reside in urban areas, while respondents in suburban regions were more likely to be single. (Suburban residents across all relationship statuses were less likely to participate openly in their communities as LGBTQ.) Qualitative results further revealed that suburban residents reported needing to travel great distances in order to socialize, engage, and contribute with others and foster a sense of "no longer needing to hide." Combined, these data along with lower overall mental health self-ratings among single respondents suggest that urban residence may better meet the needs and preferences of many LGBTQ people, regardless of relationship and life stages.

Legally married individuals in the survey scored reported higher economic status than unmarried respondents, showing significantly higher levels of education, income, and overall financial security. When asked about individual financial standing, nearly 72 percent of those who were legally married reported positive statuses, with only 5 percent indicating negative outcomes of either falling behind financially or struggling to make ends meet compared with approximately 30 percent of single or noncohabiting respondents. Over 52 percent of those making over $70,000 per year were legally married, while 69.1 percent of single respondents earned $50,000 per year or less. Educational attainment followed a similar pattern, showing graduate and professional degree attainment most likely among the legally married, with 43.6 percent holding either a master's or terminal degree, an average 17 percentage points greater than for other relationship statuses.

Legally married respondents and those who were living together reported the highest full-time employment rates (71.2% and 68.4%, respectively), an average of 18.2 percent higher than single and/or noncohabiting LGBTQ community members. Unmarried respondents and those living alone reported substantially higher rates of unemployment and part-time employment, approximately 45 percentage points higher than LGBTQ couples living together.

Family composition and community variations also were shown to affect income security among respondents. Even when controlling for household size, the presence of children, and educational attainment levels, living together as

TABLE 13.1

Percent Reporting Experiencing Event in the Last Year by Relationship Status

	Single (%)	Dating, not cohabitating (%)	Dating, cohabitating (%)	Legally married (%)
Postponed medical care due to insufficient resources	43.0	48.29	33.8	25.1
Skipped or delayed paying bills due to insufficient resources	28.1	30.1	21.1	21.2
Experienced food insecurity	25.5	33.8	18.2	11.6
Experienced housing insecurity	16.5	23.5	7.2	2.3
Experienced homelessness	24.9	44.8	14.8	5.8
Received food assistance	19.8	22.2	13.5	7.5
Received housing subsidies	9.4	14.8	4.7	1.3
Experienced unemployment	17.1	25.3	12.8	4.1
Inadequate transportation to services I need	24.1	24.4	13.0	8.4
Provided care for elderly or individual with a disability in my home	26.7	13.1	17.8	16.9
Experienced inadequate legal assistance for LGBTQ issues	20.7	20.9	12.2	11.1

Experienced LGBTQ-sensitive child custody issues	7.3	15.6	3.9	8.0
Been treated for substance abuse	2.1	0.0	2.1	1.8
Been treated for mental health issues	34.7	41.8	30.7	23.3
Considered suicide	13.5	17.4	5.4	6.8
Tested for HIV/AIDS	30.61	37.27	35.06	27.87
Tested for STDs, other than HIV/AIDS	36.6	43.0	35.8	30.7
Experienced domestic partner abuse	14.8	12.6	5.3	4.9
Experienced sexual assault	9.9	16.5	1.4	1.8
Experienced sex/gender workplace discrimination	26.1	24.2	21.4	12.4
Experienced harassment due to sex/gender identity	27.2	46.2	19.9	16.9
N	305	113	177	258

Column percentages shown

Source: Impact Texas LGBTQ Needs Assessment: A Report Prepared by the University of Texas at Dallas for the Texas Pride Impact Funds, October 2017.

either married or unmarried improved income security. Additionally, individuals reporting being legally married reported were nearly four times as likely to have health insurance through a spouse or partner compared with those dating but cohabiting.

Survey results were complemented by qualitative data from interviews and focus groups conducted with Texas LGBTQ community leaders and other key informants. A common theme from these data was that a persistent challenge reported among LGBTQ individuals in the state was social isolation and stigma, factors that were lessened by the achievement of legal marriage equality and by the social support received from strong long-term relationships.

Access to social service providers did not vary in any significant manner by relationship status or living arrangement, suggesting marriage and cohabitation are not associated with a reduction of barriers to social service providers for this sample. On the other hand, when asked specifically about LGBTQ social service providers, being married or dating and cohabitating were associated with increased rates of access to gender-specific health and mental health LGBTQ-oriented services, possibly suggesting that the benefits of marriage or living together might assist with awareness of or encouragement for utilization of these services. Similar but reduced effects were true for transgender respondents who were married or cohabitating, though being legally married showed no advantage.

Married survey respondents also reported experiencing food and housing insecurity less frequently than those in other relationship statuses, and married people were less likely to delay medical care and payment for medical care due to insufficient resources. Furthermore, married people were about one-third less likely to experience homelessness compared with single-status individuals, were significantly less likely to be unemployed, and were one-third less likely to have received mental health treatment, controlling for age and ethnicity. Cohabitation also was strongly associated with reduced domestic partner abuse and sexual assault than for single people, although reported domestic partner abuse was even lower among those legally married.

Results: Health Issues

The LGBTQ communities across the United States face disproportionate risk to their well-being and continue to experience greater health challenges as a minority group (Choi and Meyer 2016; Kates et al. 2018; Martos 2017; Orel 2014; Pew Research Center 2013), which has been attributed in part to isolation resulting from discrimination and social stigma (Institute of Medicine 2011). Legal recognition and social acceptance of same-sex marriage have been shown to increase health care utilization and reduce adverse health outcomes (Hatzenbuehler, McLaughlin, and Slopen 2010).

Survey respondents overwhelming expressed concern about health care, universally ranking access to routine health care as their number one priority need, independent of relationship status. Respondents were asked to select their top five priorities from a list of forty-two issues covering economic security, housing, education, legal, safety, social, spiritual, and health-related topics. Overall, 31.3 percent of respondents reported access to routine health care as their top priority requiring attention within the LGBTQ community, followed by health care provider LGBTQ competency (10.1%) as the second leading priority. Nearly 70 percent of respondents chose health-related concerns as their top need; other issues identified included access to behavioral health care (6.2%), LGBTQ senior aging issues (5.5%), transgender health (4.8%), HIV education and care (4.2%), access to specialized health care (3.4%), and women's health (3.3%). Only 10.7 percent of respondents reported a lack of health insurance. These selections remained consistent when controlling for marital status and living arrangement, as well as for race, gender, and age, and without exception, access to routine health care emerged as the highest priority facing the LGBTQ community.

Marital status and living arrangement were associated with variation in provider-patient interaction. For those cohabiting, 83 percent of respondents who were legally married and 77 percent of those living together reported being open with their doctors about their gender identity and sexuality, compared with 61 percent of respondents who were single or dating but not cohabitating. Marriage, rather than cohabitation alone, was more strongly associated with positive health outcomes.

Residents who were single or not cohabitating reported the highest need for access to both routine and behavioral health care. Lack of access to specialized health care was most frequently cited as a need among married respondents, a finding that might be correlated with the average increased age of the marital subgroup. Among those reporting a disability, which includes both physical and mental disabilities, over 40 percent were single individuals, nearly twice the rate of disability among married respondents and over twice the rate of those in dating relationships both with and without cohabitation. While type of disability was not ascertained, those reporting a disability and singlehood also reported mental health issues at significantly higher rates, suggesting a positive effect of dating and marriage on mental health and well-being. While the transgender community was the most underserved in terms of availability and competency of health resources, this was independent of relationship status or living arrangement.

Concern for LGBTQ aging issues was high among each category of relationship status, but there was increasing concern for long-term care across the categories of single, dating but not cohabitating, dating and cohabitating, and legally married, possibly corresponding to similar increased average age across those categories. Unmarried or noncohabitating LGBTQ seniors reported being more at risk for isolation and poor mental health compared with cohabiting or married respondents, probably due to fewer options for informal care and social support. There were more positive health outcomes reported for those cohabitating compared with single or dating but not cohabiting respondents. Married individuals over fifty-six years of age reported higher rates of "excellent" mental health than did respondents from any other relationship status.

Cohabitation, whether married or unmarried, is associated with higher positive self-reported health scores for general mental and physical health, even controlling for age. Individuals who were single or dating without cohabitation were more likely to report poor mental and physical health relative to couples living together. Of the respondents who are in cohabitating relationships, 54.2 percent reported "very good" and "excellent" mental health, 15.5 percent higher than respondents who were single or dating while living independently of their partner. Similarly, respondents who were married or living together with their partner cited their physical health status as either "very good" or "excellent," an average 12.9 percent higher than those who were unmarried and living alone. Of concern was that one in five legally married, and nearly one in four cohabitating, respondents reported "poor" or "fair" mental health status, lower for noncohabitating respondents yet still a meaningful rate of perceived unwellness. The survey did not offer any obvious insight, however, into the source of these perceptions. The lower levels of reported health needs among the married, however, may be related to their higher levels of insurance coverage, educational attainment, and earned income.

Among the health measures, married and cohabitating respondents assigned lower priority to HIV education and care than noncohabitating respondents. Nearly all other health topics (including less immediate health needs like healthy living and prenatal care) showed uniformly high levels of importance among respondents across relationship status subgroups, as did concerns with gender transition and transgender health issues, with only slightly larger percentages from legally married respondents rating these issues as "not important" or "slightly important."

Providing care for an elderly or disabled individual in the home was more common among single individuals, with 42.7 percent reporting having provided this type of care at least once in their lifetime, over twice the percentage of those who were in noncohabitating dating relationships, and 9.5 percentage points above respondents who were living with spouses or partners. There were very low rates of reported substance use; those respondents who did report being affected by substance use were primarily single, male, middle-aged (30–49 years), and located in large urban areas. The importance of drug and alcohol use varied by relationship type, with married individuals more likely to report problems with alcohol use compared with other statuses, and single individuals more likely to rank drug use issues of greater importance than other relationship statuses.

There were no significant relationship-level effects on those who were treated for substance abuse in the last year.

Conclusions

Our findings lend support to the idea that the institution of marriage in general, and marriage equality in particular, can be a stabilizing force for its participants, and perhaps for the larger society. We believe that the most significant set of findings from our survey were that married respondents reported more positive results on many quality of life issues. Married and cohabitating respondents reported greater financial and social stability than others. Married respondents also were older, had greater educational attainment, had better self-reported health outcomes, and had fewer problems related to disability, stress, and mental health issues.

Since this is cross-sectional data, we cannot conclude whether marriage is a stabilizing force among same-sex couples, or more stable individuals were more likely to marry, or if marriage and stability were attributes that developed as our respondents aged. In any case, however, we believe that our findings are consistent with claims made by many marriage equality advocates, that the institutionalization of marriage equality will have positive results for those affected.

ACKNOWLEDGMENTS

The authors would like to thank the Texas Pride Impact Funds (TPIF) for its support of this needs assessment project. Views expressed in this chapter are those of the authors and not of TPIF. We also would like to thank the student members of our research team, all students at the University of Texas at Dallas, particularly our lead research assistants, Jennera Berry and Keaton Johnson from the Applied Sociology graduate program, for their contributions to the needs assessment. We also would like to thank the respondents to our surveys and our interviewees and focus group participants who were willing to share their experiences and concerns with us. Unless alternative citation is provided, all data cited in this chapter are taken from Texas Pride Impact Funds, 2017.

REFERENCES

Choi, S. K., and I. H. Meyer. 2016. *LGBT Aging: A Review of Research Findings, Needs, and Policy Implications*, 1–54. Los Angeles: Williams Institute. Retrieved from https://williamsinstitute.law.ucla.edu/wp-content/uploads/LGBT-Aging-A-Review.pdf.

Equality Texas. 2015. *Texas' First Anti-Marriage Law*. Retrieved from https://www.equalitytexas.org/texas-first-anti-marriage-law-2/.

Gallup. February 2013. *LGBT Percentage Highest in D.C., Lowest in North Dakota*. Washington, DC: Gallup Politics. Retrieved from http://www.gallup.com/poll/160517/lgbt-percentage-highest-lowest-north-dakota.aspx.

Hatzenbuehler, M. L., K. A. McLaughlin, and N. Slopen. 2014. "Stressful Life Events, Sexual Orientation, and Cardiometabolic Risk among Young Adults in the United States." *Health Psychology* 33 (10): 1185–1194.

Institute of Medicine. 2011. *The Health of Lesbian, Gay, Bisexual, and Transgender People: Building a Foundation for Better Understanding.* Washington, DC: National Academies Press.

Kates, J., U. Ranji, A. Beamesderfer, A. Salganicoff, and L. Dawson. 2018. *Health and Access to Care and Coverage for Lesbian, Gay, Bisexual, and Transgender Individuals in the U.S.* Retrieved from http://files.kff.org/attachment/Issue-Brief-Health-and-Access-to-Care-and-Coverage -for-LGBT-Individuals-in-the-US.

Martos, A. J., P. A. Wilson, and L. Meyer. 2017. *Lesbian, Gay, Bisexual, and Transgender (LGBT) Health Services in the United States: Origins, Evolution, and Contemporary Landscape.* PLoS ONE 12 (7): 1–18. https://doi.org/10.1371/journal.pone.0180544.

Orel, N. A. 2014. "Investigating the Needs and Concerns of Lesbian, Gay, Bisexual, and Transgender Older Adults: The Use of Qualitative and Quantitative Methodology." *Journal of Homosexuality* 61 (1): 53–78. Retrieved from http://www.tandfonline.com/doi /abs/10.1080/00918369.2013.835236.

Pew Research Center. 2013. *A Survey of LGBT Americans: Attitudes, Experiences and Values in Changing Times.* Pew Social Trends, Washington, DC. Retrieved from http://www .pewsocialtrends.org/files/2013/06/SDT_LGBT-Americans_06-2013.pdf.

Texas Pride Impact Funds. 2017. *Impact Texas LGBTQ Needs Assessment: A Report Prepared by the University of Texas at Dallas for the Texas Pride Impact Funds.* Richardson: University of Texas at Dallas.

Williams Institute. 2016. *LGBT People in Texas.* UCLA School of Law. Los Angeles, CA: The Regents of the University of California. Retrieved from http://williamsinstitute.law .ucla.edu/wp-content/uploads/Texas-fact-sheet.pdf.

PART FOUR

Relationship Quality, Experience, and Identity

14

Social Context and the Stability of Same-Sex and Different-Sex Relationships

KARA JOYNER
WENDY MANNING
BARBARA PRINCE

Scholarly and media interest in sexual minorities has risen dramatically over the course of the past decade, along with the visibility of relationships between partners of the same biological sex (or gender identity). Limitations in survey and census data make it difficult to examine trends in the prevalence of same-sex relationships. However, parallel measures of sexual orientation in data sets such as the Census and the General Social Survey indicate that the percent of same-sex couples in the population has increased substantially over recent decades (Black et al. 2000; Lofquist et al. 2012). Scholars have long compared the dynamics of same-sex and different-sex couples because such comparisons reveal the importance of institutions in the stability of contemporary relationships (Lau 2012). For instance, the finding that same-sex couples are less stable than different-sex couples is thought to reflect the fact that they have not (until recently) been able to legally marry and benefit from the legal protection and social prestige that marriage offers. Comparisons of same-sex and different-sex couples are also motivated by a concern with child well-being in different family contexts. Several of the studies that use population-based samples to compare the outcomes of same-sex and different-sex couples focus on relationship stability. Generally speaking, these studies find that same-sex male couples (hereafter male couples) and same-sex female couples (hereafter female couples) have higher rates of dissolution than different-sex couples (Manning and Joyner 2018).

The finding that same-sex couples are more unstable than different-sex couples is consistent with a minority stress perspective that emphasizes the unique challenges faced by sexual minorities (Meyer 2003). A handful of recent studies have identified several distinct couple-level minority stressors that emanate from the marginalized status of same-sex couples. Male and female couples report numerous stressors, especially fears and experiences of rejection, devaluation, and discrimination (Frost et al. 2017). Studies concerning health and well-being more generally have highlighted characteristics of neighborhoods and communities that indicate the climate of acceptance for sexual minorities. Two commonly used indicators of climate include the concentration of same-sex couples and patterns of voting for Republican or Democratic candidates. Data from the National Longitudinal Study of Adolescent to Adult Health (Add Health) offer an unprecedented opportunity to consider whether the stability of same-sex unions differs according to these indicators.

Background

Stability of Same-Sex Relationships

Studies comparing the stability of same-sex and different-sex couples use population-based samples drawn from the United States and several European countries, including Norway, Sweden, Britain, and the Netherlands. These studies have primarily focused on co-residential unions. The relative stability of same-sex couples depends on whether partners are in a legally married, formalized (registered partnership, domestic partnership), cohabiting, or dating relationship. Legalized same-sex relationships are found to be just as stable as legalized different-sex relationships (e.g., Rosenfeld 2014), if not more stable (e.g., Ross, Gask, and Berrington 2011). Same-sex cohabiting relationships are found to be less stable than different-sex cohabiting relationships (e.g., Lau 2012). Gaps in the stability of same-sex and different-sex relationships appear to be weakening over time and in some recent studies are not significant (e.g., Manning, Brown, and Stykes 2016). Most prior studies find that female couples are less stable than male couples, a finding that runs counter to the notion that women are more relational than men.

The findings of prior studies examining same-sex couple stability are potentially biased by differential selection into co-residential relationships. The process of forming same-sex co-residential unions appears to be gendered, with fewer gay men than lesbian women classified as married or cohabiting at the time of interview (Carpenter and Gates 2008; Rosenfeld 2014). Tracking the stability of relationships from their point of initiation, rather than co-residence, removes the bias posed by differential selection into more established relationships. The Add Health data provided Joyner, Manning, and Bogle (2017) the opportunity to assess the stability of same-sex and different-sex relationships following their formation (e.g., first date or sexual encounter) rather than co-residence. Their key finding was that male couples had substantially higher rates of dissolution than female couples and different-sex couples, even after controlling for sociodemographic indicators. This suggests that research on the stability of same-sex couples needs to account for selection into co-residential unions, especially for male couples.

Minority Stress

Studies on the dynamics of same-sex relationships draw from perspectives that emphasize minority stress as it relates to sexual minorities (e.g., Otis et al. 2006). According to the minority stress perspective, gays, lesbians, and bisexuals experience a higher prevalence of negative mental and physical outcomes than do heterosexuals as a consequence of their stigmatized status in society (Meyer 2003). The perspective has been extended to address stressors that stem from the stigmatization of same-sex relationships. Recently, Frost and colleagues (2017) conducted interviews with a wide range of male and female couples (e.g., dating, cohabiting and legally recognized) that were engaged in a sexual relationship and identified seventeen distinct couple-level stressors. They found that the majority of couples reported experiencing during the course of their relationship fears of rejection, devaluation, and discrimination (75%), in addition to experiences of these stressors (70%). Other couple-level stressors included (in order of frequency) consequences of unequal legal recognition of their relationship (62.5%), hiding their relationship (50.0%), internalized stigma (47.5%), coming out as a same-sex couple (43.3%), seeking safety and community (38.3%), not being perceived as a couple (30.0%), having children or not (25.8%), navigating benefits for same-sex couples (20.8%), limitations to participation in family (17.5), managing stereotypes of what same-sex couples are like (15.8%), and feeling public scrutiny (15.0%).

Quantitative studies of couple-level stressors point to some gender differences: women in same-sex relationships experience more stress than men due to family reactions, whereas men in these relationships experience more stress due to violence and harassment (Todosijevic, Rothblum, and Solomon 2005). Much of the qualitative and quantitative research concerning the minority stress perspective focuses on stigma processes at the individual and interpersonal levels. For example, Frost and colleagues (2017) found that the sources of the stressors experienced by same-sex couples were most often the family of one or both partners, rather than wider structural factors. This could reflect that couples in this study were recruited from San Francisco and Atlanta, cities with relatively high concentrations of same-sex couples.

Structural Stigma

Another way scholars have extended the minority stress perspective is by considering structural factors that influence the stigma process. Hatzenbuehler and Link (2014, 2) define structural stigma as "societal-level conditions, cultural norms, and institutional policies that constrain the opportunities, resources, and well-being of the stigmatized." Hatzenbuehler, his colleagues, and other researchers have pioneered a variety of indicators of structural stigma that correspond to states, counties, neighborhoods, and schools, and they have examined how these indicators are associated with the health and psychological well-being of sexual minorities.

A common indicator of structural stigma is the concentration of gays and lesbians in a census tract, zip code area, county, or state, as captured by the percentage of same-sex couple households in a neighborhood. Hatzenbuehler and his colleagues routinely use same-sex couple concentration as one of but many indicators in their measures of structural stigma to explain variation in the health and psychological well-being of sexual minorities (e.g., Hatzenbuehler 2011). Researchers are increasingly highlighting the role of same-sex couple concentration at the neighborhood level in differentiating the outcomes of sexual minorities (e.g., Carpiano et al. 2011). For instance, Felson and Adamczyk (2018) found using data from the New York City Community Health Survey that disparities in psychological distress between heterosexuals and sexual minorities were smaller in areas known to be beacons of gay subculture (e.g., the West Village) than in other places.

Another indicator of structural stigma is county-level political variables, such as voting for the Republican presidential candidate (e.g., Everett 2014) or registering as a Democrat (e.g., Hatzenbuehler 2011). With some exceptions (e.g., Everett 2014), county-level political indicators are often bundled together with other county-level indicators of structural stigma, such as same-sex couple concentration (Hatzenbuehler 2011). Oswald and colleagues (2010) argue that aggregate voting patterns serve as indicators of "community climate," defined as the level of support for LGBT people in a specific locale. Republican legislators, candidates, and voters are less likely than their Democratic counterparts to view sexual minorities positively or support legal protections for this population (e.g., McVeigh and Diaz 2009). Given the high correlation between indicators such as the percent of individuals in an area voting for the Republican candidate and the percent voting for the Democratic candidate, studies typically measure Republican or Democratic voting.

Research on the quality of same-sex relationships has rarely incorporated measures of structural stigma and has instead included measures of perceived or internalized stigma. Recent meta-analytic reviews of this research have found evidence of small but significant associations between minority stress and relationship quality (e.g., Cao et al. 2017). Recently, Fischer, Kalmijn, and Steinmetz (2016) compared the social well-being (i.e., social integration) of individuals in same-sex and different-sex couples across European countries with different levels of normative and legal tolerance. They measured normative tolerance at the country level based on attitudes toward homosexuality and other indicators, and they measured legal tolerance at this level based on supportive laws for gays and lesbians. Fischer and colleagues (2016) found evidence that gaps in well-being between individuals in same-sex and different-sex coresidential unions decreased as levels of normative and legal tolerance in their countries increased.

In tolerant countries, individuals in same-sex couples actually fared slightly better than their counterparts in different-sex couples. They additionally found that normative tolerance was more critical than legal tolerance in reducing gaps between same-sex and different-sex unions and that level of tolerance was more critical for male couples than for female couples.

To our knowledge, only one study comparing the stability of same-sex and different-sex relationships has included a measure of structural stigma. Using data from the 2008 panel of the Survey of Income and Program Participation (SIPP), Manning, Brown, and Stykes (2016) compared the stability of same-sex cohabiting, different-sex cohabiting, and different-sex married couples. In their sample, same-sex cohabiting couples experienced levels of stability that were similar to those of different-sex cohabiting couples. They also found evidence of a structural stigma effect: levels of instability for same-sex cohabiting couples were greater in states with a constitutional ban against same-sex marriage. They documented a similar effect for different-sex cohabiting couples. Thus, their indicator may not only capture structural stigma for same-sex couples but also proxy for other contextual factors associated with union stability. Hatzenbeuler (2014) argues that inferences about the effects of structural stigma are stronger when indicators of stigma are associated with the outcomes of stigmatized groups but not nonstigmatized groups.

Current Investigation

This study uses data from Add Health to examine the influence of structural stigma on the stability of the most recent romantic and/or sexual relationships reported by respondents during its fourth wave (conducted between 2007 and 2009). Add Health followed a cohort of respondents from adolescence to young adulthood. As most respondents were born between 1976 and 1982, they were between the ages of twenty-five and thirty-two at the time of the Wave 4. We distinguish three groups of respondents on the basis of their own sex (marked by the interviewer) and the sex of their most recent partner (marked by the respondent): different-sex relationships, female relationships, and male relationships. Based on our prior work (Joyner et al. 2017), we expect that men in same-sex relationships will exhibit the highest likelihood of dissolution and respondents in different-sex relationships will show the lowest likelihood, with women in same-sex relationships falling somewhere between these two groups. On the basis of the minority stress perspective, we hypothesize that same-sex couples will enjoy greater stability when they reside in neighborhoods with greater concentrations of same-sex couples. Similarly, we anticipate greater stability among same-sex couples in bluer counties (i.e., those with lower shares of votes cast for Republican candidates), assuming support for same-sex couples is greater in these counties.

We examine the effects of our two indicators of structural stigma on stability of most recent relationships using survival analysis. We first discuss estimates based on life table methods that reveal the proportion of different-sex relationships, female relationships, and male relationships that dissolve prior to the fifth year. We calculate an additional set of life table estimates for male couples who reside in census tracts with low, medium, and high concentrations of same-sex couples. Alternatively, we calculate a set of estimates for male couples who live in counties with low, medium, and high levels of Republican voting. Next, we present relative odds ratios based on discrete-time logistic regression models that adjust for survey design effects. These models include not only controls for neighborhood context (i.e., tract-level urban residence and residential stability) but also key sociodemographic indicators tied to relationship stability: race-ethnicity, age, race-age homogamy, living with two biological parents in adolescence, family socioeconomic status in adolescence, prior sexual partnerships, and duration.

Data and Sample

Add Health is a longitudinal school-based study (Harris et al. 2009). To select the schools in its sample, Add Health used a database provided by Quality Education Data for its primary sampling frame. Using rosters from each school, Add Health selected a nationally representative (core) sample of 12,105 adolescents in grades seven to twelve to participate in the first in-home interview. Add Health additionally selected oversamples of four racial groups: 1,038 black adolescents from well-educated families, 334 Chinese adolescents, 450 Cuban adolescents, and 437 Puerto Rican adolescents. The first in-home interview was conducted between April and December of 1995. The response rate for the in-home sample was 79 percent. A second in-home interview was conducted roughly one year later but did not include respondents who had subsequently graduated from high school. In 2001 and 2002, Add Health reinterviewed 15,197 of the Wave 1 in-home respondents (with a response rate of 77.4%). The database for Wave 3 consists of a rich contextual data file that includes variables measured at the block, tract, county, and state levels based on data from the 2000 Census. The Wave 3 database additionally includes a file with variables measuring voting patterns in 2000 (and in other years) at the state and county levels. This database includes measures of context that correspond to the period roughly one year prior to the Wave 3 interviews.

Between 2007 and 2009, Add Health conducted the fourth wave of in-home interviews with 15,701 of the original 20,745 respondents (with a response rate of 80.3%). By the time of the fourth in-home interview, respondents were between the ages of twenty-four and thirty-two. Add Health used state-of-the-art survey methods (i.e., computer-assisted self-interviews and partner rosters) to identify all the partners with whom respondents had experienced a "romantic or sexual relationship" since 2001. Respondents were also asked to report any romantic or sexual relationships that eventuated in pregnancy, cohabitation, or marriage, regardless of the time frame. Respondents were then asked to provide basic demographic information on their relationships, in addition to their partners, including their gender, age, and race-ethnicity. Add Health asked respondents about the entire length of most recent relationships but did not collect this information for other relationships listed.

Our sample includes Add Health respondents who were interviewed at Waves 3 and 4 ($N = 13,034$). As our models adjust for survey design effects, we restrict our sample to the 12,286 respondents with the cluster variable (psuscid), strata variable (aregion), and longitudinal weight (gswgt134). We further limit our sample to 11,991 respondents who reported having had a current or recent romantic or sexual relationship at Wave 4. For respondents who report multiple relationships, we focus on the most recent relationship. We then exclude eighty-one respondents who did not provide information enabling us to classify the relationship (i.e., information on the type of relationship and gender of their partner). We next remove 235 respondents with missing information on duration of the relationship. Finally, we exclude 221 respondents who did not have contextual data (i.e., residential geocodes) at Wave 3 (described later in this chapter). Among this group, 140 men and 138 women are classified as having a same-sex partner, and 11,176 respondents are classified as having a different-sex partner. These three groups are defined on the basis of the sex composition of the relationships rather than reports of their sexual orientation identity. Thus, they potentially include respondents who self-identified as bisexual. While these sample sizes are not large, they are greater than those reported in many other data sets and offer nationally representative data on young adults from a specific age group, cohort, and period. (See Joyner et al. 2017 for the sample sizes of same-sex couples in previous studies of same-sex couple stability).

Dependent Variable

Relationship Stability. To examine the dissolution of most recent relationships following their formation, we use discrete-time logistic regression models that estimate the monthly probability that couples dissolve. These models require information on whether the relationship was current at the time of Wave 4 and the monthly duration of the relationship at the time of dissolution or interview. To obtain information on the duration of the relationship, Add Health asked respondents, what is "the total amount of time that you (have been/were) involved in a romantic or sexual relationship with {initials}"? Respondents were allowed to report in days, months, and years. Responses to total months were added to days (divided by 31) and years (divided by 12) to construct the monthly duration of relationship. Note this indicator of duration represents the *total* amount of time they have been a "couple." Respondents who do not dissolve their relationship are censored at the month of interview. As few respondents contribute years of exposure beyond the seventh year, we limit the period of risk by censoring respondents whose relationships extended beyond seven years at eighty-four months. To measure how the likelihood of dissolution differs over the risk period, we include in the models a time-varying variable for month as risk along with a squared term for this variable.

Individual Characteristics

Our models include a number of time-constant variables, including age at Wave 4 race-ethnicity, adolescent family structure, and family socioeconomic status (SES). Race of respondent was collected from the first wave of the study and recoded to a series of dummy variables (non-Hispanic black, Hispanic, and non-Hispanic other), with non-Hispanic white acting as the reference group. Based on the household roster, adolescent family structure distinguishes whether the respondent was living with both biological parents at the first wave. Family SES is based on a measure developed by Bearman and Moody (2004) that incorporates information on parental education and occupation from Wave I. Relationship history variables include respondents' prior marriage status (I if respondent was previously married and zero otherwise) and logged number of other sexual partners during their lifetime. To measure heterogamy, we utilize information that respondents provided on partners to develop measures of whether they were a different race than respondent (using the categories non-Hispanic white, non-Hispanic black, Hispanic, non-Hispanic Asian, non-Hispanic Native American, and non-Hispanic other for respondent and partner) and the age difference (absolute value) between partners.

Contextual Variables

The Wave 3 contextual data file includes variables measured at the neighborhood level, defined as the census tract of respondents, in addition to the county and state levels. Our key neighborhood-level variables are urban residence, residential stability, and concentration of same-sex cohabitating unions. We also include an indicator of county-level voting patterns.

URBANIZED RESIDENCE. As a measure of urban residence, we distinguish whether or not respondents live in a census tract that is entirely urbanized. Cities have several features that potentially reduce social and institutional control over the dynamics of relationships (i.e., their size, density, heterogeneity), especially the transience of their populations.

RESIDENTIAL STABILITY. Studies of marital dissolution highlighting contextual influences often include a measure of residential stability to capture social integration. Toward this end, we include a tract-level measure that averages two variables: the percent of the population five years or older living within the same housing unit for five or more years and the percentage of occupied housing units that are owner occupied. The alpha score for respondents' scores on this scale is .78.

SAME-SEX COUPLE CONCENTRATION. We use the percent of households headed by same-sex unmarried partners in respondent's tract as an indicator of social support for same-sex couples.

COUNTY-LEVEL VOTING PATTERNS. As an alternative indicator of support for same-sex couples, we measure the percent of votes cast in respondent's county for the Republican presidential candidate during the 2000 election (McVeigh and Diaz 2009). This variable has a near perfect correlation with the percent of votes cast for the Democratic presidential candidate (not shown).

Findings

Descriptive Statistics

Individuals with same-sex relationships differ from their counterparts with different-sex relationships in terms of factors potentially associated with stability. Contrasts of the demographic variables for the three groups of respondents indicate some significant differences ($p < .05$). In comparison to respondents with different-sex partners, men with same-sex partners were more likely to dissolve their relationships and to report a duration for their relationships that was shorter. They were less likely to be previously married and more likely to have a different-race partner. They also indicated that they had a greater number of previous sex partners. Women with same-sex partners indicated that they had shorter-duration relationships and more previous sex partners in comparison to respondents with different-sex partners.

We used life table methods to determine the weighted proportion of different-sex couples, male couples, and female couples that dissolved prior to the fifth year (not shown). Roughly, about one-fifth of respondents with different sex partners had dissolved their relationships by year five in comparison to one-quarter of women and one-half of men with different sex partners. Estimates were similar when the sample was not restricted to respondents who conducted a Wave 3 interview (i.e., Joyner et al. 2017). We also computed additional estimates of dissolution that separated the different groups of couples by same-sex couple concentration, and alternatively, Republican voting. For ease of interpretation, we distinguished three groups of respondents for each of these contextual variables based on tertiles. The life table estimates revealed that the chances of dissolution for male couples (but not other couple types) differed monotonically by our focal contextual variables, with greater stability in census tracts with higher concentration of same-sex couples and lower stability in counties with greater Republican voting. These life table estimates were unadjusted and thus failed to control for variables that could be associated with these contextual variables and dissolution.

We examined the association between our focal variables and relationship dissolution in multivariate survival models (not shown). The first model included indicator variables for male and female couples with different-sex couples as the comparison group, in addition to a linear term for same-sex couple concentration. As suggested earlier in this chapter, this model also included controls for the baseline hazard, individual characteristics, and tract-level variables (i.e., urbanized residence and residential stability). To take into account the fact that the effect of same-sex couple concentration differed according to couple type, the model included interaction terms for the concentration variables and the two couple-type indicators. Results from this model revealed that the main effect of same-sex concentration, which pertained to different-sex couples, failed to significantly increase the likelihood of dissolution. They also revealed that the effect of same-sex concentration was significantly different for male couples but not female couples. The second model was identical to the first but substituted Republican voting for same-sex concentration. The pattern of results for this model was similar to that of the first model. The main effect of Republican voting (representing the effect for different-sex couples) was not significant, nor was the interaction term for female couples. However, the effect of Republican voting was significantly different for male couples.

Figure 14.1 displays the relative odds of dissolution based on these two models. Figure 14.1A corresponds to the first model, while figure 14.1B corresponds to the second model. The range for the *x*-axis in both figures is restricted to reflect the distributions of these contextual variables. Figure 14.1A reveals differences between male couples and different-sex couples become less pronounced as the percent of households headed by same-sex couples in the census tracts of respondents decreases. Couples with two men that reside in tracts with no same-sex couples have odds of dissolution that are over five times greater than those of different-sex couples. Yet, in census tracts with a high concretion of same-sex couples, differences between male couples and different-sex couples are minuscule. Figure 14.1B shows a similar (but reversed) pattern, with differences between male couples and different-sex couples becoming less pronounced as Republican voting in the counties of respondents decreases.

Several other variables had significant associations with the stability of most recent relationships (not shown). The odds of dissolution declined over the risk period. In comparison to whites, blacks and other respondents (a group that combines non-Hispanic Asians, Native Americans, and other) had higher odds of relationship dissolution. The odds of dissolution decreased with

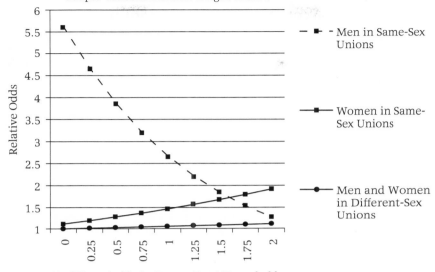

A. Relative Odds of Dissolution by Couple Type and Same-Sex Couple Concentration in Neighborhood

- - ■ - - Men in Same-Sex Unions

——■—— Women in Same-Sex Unions

——●—— Men and Women in Different-Sex Unions

% of Households in Census Tract Households Headed by Same-Sex Couples

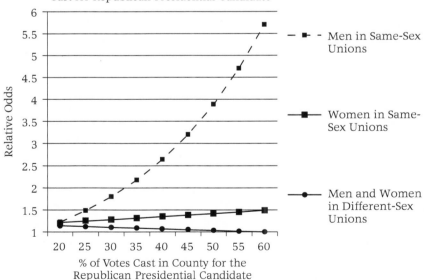

B. Relative Odds of Dissolution by Couple Type and Votes Cast for Republican Presidential Candidate

- - ■ - - Men in Same-Sex Unions

——■—— Women in Same-Sex Unions

——●—— Men and Women in Different-Sex Unions

% of Votes Cast in County for the Republican Presidential Candidate

FIGURE 14.1. Dissolution by Couple Type and Select Contextual Variables

Notes: Relative odds computations are based on discrete-time logistic regression models that include a linear and squared term for duration in months as well variables described in the text. The models adjust for survey design effects.

age. Interestingly, higher values of family SES were associated with higher odds of dissolution. Individuals were more likely to dissolve their relationship if they had accumulated more sex partners prior to the relationship. As expected, differences in both the race and age of partners translated into higher odds of dissolution.

Conclusions

Data from Wave 4 of Add Health allowed us to track the stability of relationships from the moment they were formed and to compare same-sex and different-sex relationships. Data from Wave 3 of Add Health enabled us to examine the effects of social context on the stability of couples. As most of the relationships reported at Wave 4 began after Wave 3, our measurement of context preceded the period of risk for dissolving a union. Our results first corroborated patterns based on a previous study (Joyner et al. 2017) that used only data from Wave 4 of Add Health: Male couples, but not female couples, had significantly higher dissolution rates than different-sex couples. We were able to extend this prior study by examining how the dissolution rates of male couples differed according to social context.

Relative odds based on survival models that included contextual variables demonstrated that when men in same-sex relationships resided in neighborhoods with relatively large concentrations of same-sex cohabiting couples, or when they lived in counties with a small minority of votes cast for the Republican candidate, they experienced likelihoods of dissolution similar to those observed for men and women in different-sex relationships. The majority of the male couples in our sample lived in neighborhoods with small or moderate concentrations of sexual minorities in their census tract or were residents of counties with a majority (>50%) of votes cast for the Republican presidential candidate. As male couples in these contexts experienced very high likelihoods of dissolution, they drove much of the gap in stability observed between men in same-sex couples and respondents in different-sex couples.

While we move beyond prior work with our focus on structural stigma, our study has some limitations. We relied on an existing contextual data set that did not distinguish the proportion of households headed by male versus female couples. Male couples geographically cluster to a much greater extent than do female couples (Black et al. 2000). Were we to use sex-specific measures of same-sex couple concentration, our results for male couples could have been stronger. Another issue is that we measure same-sex couple concentration at the tract level. While studies routinely use census tracts to define neighborhoods, these administratively defined units may not capture the spatial experiences of individuals. We were limited to two indicators of social context. Future studies should consider additional indicators of structural stigma, such as state-level antidiscrimination laws. Another limitation is that we did not capture the mechanisms by which our two key contextual variables influenced the stability of male couples. Carpiano et al. (2011) argue gay neighborhoods provide "a place where gay men can visibly display their gay identity, avoid having to justify themselves to others, and develop romantic and platonic relationships without fear" (p. 76). Our sample represents a narrow age band (ages 25–32) of young adults in the 2007–2008 period; thus, it does not represent the experiences of all gays and lesbians.

Minority stress and structural stigma have been argued to be important factors determining the health and well-being of sexual minorities. However, few studies have been able to empirically evaluate how indicators of structural stigma are associated with the dynamics of same-sex couples (e.g., Manning, Brown, and Stykes 2016). Data from Add Health provided us a unique opportunity to extend a nascent body of research on how stigma is associated with the quality and stability of same-sex couples by measuring structural stigma (Cao et al. 2017). Furthermore, these data allowed us to contribute to a body of studies examining the effects of same-sex couple concentration and Republican voting on psychological well-being and physical health (Everett 2014; Hatzenbuehler 2011). Future research will benefit from developing innovative ways to measure structural stigma and considering differences in the experiences of men and women. Supportive relationships are critical to health and well-being. To ensure that sexual minorities benefit relationships in the same ways as sexual majorities, it is necessary to develop interventions that ameliorate structural stigma.

ACKNOWLEDGMENTS

Direct correspondence to Kara Joyner (kjoyner@bgsu.edu). This research was supported in part by the Center for Family and Demographic Research, Bowling Green State University, which has core funding from the Eunice Kennedy Shriver National Institute of Child Health and Human Development (R24HD050959). This research uses data from Add Health, a program project directed by Kathleen Mullan Harris and designed by J. Richard Udry, Peter S. Bearman, and Kathleen Mullan Harris at the University of North Carolina at Chapel Hill, and funded by grant P01-HD31921 from the Eunice Kennedy Shriver National Institute of Child Health and Human Development, with cooperative funding from twenty-three other federal agencies and foundations. Special acknowledgments are due to Ronald R. Rindfuss and Barbara Entwisle for assistance in the original design. Information on how to obtain the Add Health data files is available on the Add Health website (http://www.cpc.unc.edu/addhealth). No direct support was received from grant P01-HD31921 for this analysis.

REFERENCES

Bearman, Peter S., and James Moody. 2004. "Suicide and Friendship among American Adolescents." *American Journal of Public Health* 94 (1): 89–95.

Black, Dan, Gary G. Gates, Seth Sanders, and Lowell Taylor. 2000. "Demographics of the Gay and Lesbian Population in the United States: Evidence from Available Systematic Data Sources." *Demography* 37 (2): 139–154.

Cao, Hongjian, Nan Zhou, Mark Fine, Yue Liang, Jiayao Li, and W. Roger Mills-Koonce. 2017. "Sexual Minority Stress and Same-Sex Relationship Well-Being: A Meta-Analysis of Research Prior to the U.S. Nationwide Legalization of Same-Sex Marriage." *Journal of Marriage and Family* 79 (5): 1258–1277.

Carpenter, Christopher, and Gary J. Gates. 2008. "Gay and Lesbian Partnerships: Evidence from California." *Demography* 45 (3): 573–590.

Carpiano, Richard M., Brian C. Kelly, Adam Easterbrook, and Jeffrey T. Parsons. 2011. "Community and Drug Use among Gay Men: The Role of Neighborhood and Networks." *Journal of Health and Social Behavior* 52 (1): 74–90.

Everett, Bethany G. 2014. "Changes in Neighborhood Characteristics and Depression among Sexual Minority Young Adults." *Journal of the American Psychiatric Nurses Association* 20 (1): 42–52.

Felson, Jacob, and Amy Adamczyk. 2018. "Effects of Geography on Mental Health Disparities on Sexual Minorities in New York City." *Archives of Sexual Behavior* 47 (4): 1095–1107.

Fischer, Mirjam M., Matthijs Kalmijn, and Stephanie Steinmetz. 2016. "Does Tolerance Matter? A Comparative Study of Well-Being of Persons in Same-Sex and Mixed-Sex Unions across Nine European Countries." *European Societies* 18 (5): 514–534.

Frost, David M., Allen J. LeBlanc, Brian de Vries, Eli Alston-Stepnitz, Rob Stephenson, and Cory Woodyatt. 2017. "Couple-Level Minority Stress: An Examination of Same-Sex Couples' Unique Experiences." *Journal of Health and Social Behavior* 58 (4): 455–472.

Harris, Kathleen Mullan, Carolyn T. Halpern, Eric Whitsel, Jon Hussey, Joyce Tabor, Pamela P. Entzel, and J. Richard Udry. 2009. The National Longitudinal Study of Adolescent Health: Research Design. Carolina Population Center, University of North Carolina at Chapel Hill, Chapel Hill, NC. Retrieved from http://www.cpc.unc.edu/projects/addhealth/design.

Hatzenbuehler, Mark L. 2011. "The Social Environment and Suicide Attempts in Lesbian, Gay, and Bisexual Youth." *Pediatrics* 127 (5): 896–903.

Hatzenbuehler, Mark L. 2014. "Structural Stigma and the Health of Lesbian, Gay, and Bisexual Populations." *Current Directions in Psychological Science* 23 (2): 127–132.

Hatzenbuehler, Mark L., and Bruce Link. 2014. "Introduction to Special Issues on Structural Stigma and Health." *Social Science & Medicine* 103: 1–6.

Joyner, Kara, Wendy D. Manning, and Ryan H. Bogle. 2017. "Gender and the Stability of Same-Sex and Different-Sex Relationships among Young Adults." *Demography* 54 (6): 2351–2374.

Lau, Charles Q. 2012. "The Stability of Same-Sex Cohabitation, Different-Sex Cohabitation, and Marriage." *Journal of Marriage and Family* 74 (5): 973–988.

Lofquist, Daphne, Terry Lugailia, Martin O'Connell, and Sarah Feliz. 2012. "Households and Families: 2010 Census Briefs." Washington, DC: U.S. Census Bureau. Retrieved from http://www.census.gov/prod/cen2010/briefs/c2010br-14.pdf.

Manning, Wendy D., Susan L. Brown, and J. Bart Stykes. 2016. "Same-Sex and Different-Sex Cohabiting Couple Relationship Stability." *Demography* 53 (4): 937–953.

Manning, Wendy, and Kara Joyner. 2018. "Demographic Approaches to Same-Sex Relationship Dissolution and Divorce: Data Challenges and Implications for Research." In *LGBTQ Divorce and Relationship Dissolution: Psychological and Legal Perspectives and Implications for Practice*, edited by Abbie Goldberg and Adam Romero, 35–48. Oxford: Oxford University Press.

McVeigh, Rory, and Maria-Elena D. Diaz. 2009. "Voting to Ban Same-Sex Marriage: Interests, Values, and Communities." *American Sociological Review* 74 (6): 891–915.

Meyer, Ilan H. 2003. "Prejudice, Social Stress, and Mental Health in Lesbian, Gay, and Bisexual Populations: Conceptual Issues and Research Evidence." *Psychological Bulletin* 129 (5): 674–697.

Oswald, Ramona Faith, Courtney Chuthbertson, Vanja Lazarevic, and Abbie Goldberg. 2010. "New Developments in the Field: Measuring Community Climate." *Journal of GLBT Family Studies* 6 (2): 214–228.

Otis, Melanie D., Sharon S. Rostosky, Ellen D. B. Riggle, and Rebecca Hamrin, 2006. "Stress and Relationship Quality in Same-Sex Couples." *Journal of Social and Personal Relationships* 23 (1): 81–99.

Rosenfeld, Michael J. 2014. "Couple Longevity in the Era of Same-Sex Marriage in the United States." *Journal of Marriage and Family* 76 (5): 905–918.

Ross, Helen, Karen Gask, and Ann Berrington. 2011. "Civil Partnerships Five Years On." *Population Trends* 145 (1): 172–202.

Todosijevic, Jelica, Esther D. Rothblum, and Sondra E. Solomon. 2005. "Relationship Satisfaction, Affectivity, and Gay-Specific Stressors in Same-Sex Couples Joined in Civil Unions." *Psychology of Women Quarterly* 29 (2): 158–166.

15

Same-Sex Marriage and Mental Health

The Role of Marital Quality

SARA MERNITZ
AMANDA POLLITT
DEBRA UMBERSON

Lesbian, gay, and bisexual adults are at elevated risk for mental health problems compared with heterosexual adults (Institute of Medicine 2011). More than fifty years of research on heterosexual populations shows that married people have fewer mental health problems than the unmarried, in part because marriage is protective for mental health, providing both direct benefits (e.g., greater socioeconomic resources) and indirect benefits (e.g., social support that acts as a buffer against daily stressors; Umberson, Thomeer, and Williams 2013). While research on the protective effect of same-sex marriage for mental health is still in its infancy, the available evidence demonstrates that same-sex couples in legally recognized relationships, like marriage, report better mental health than those in long-term relationships that are not legally recognized (Wight, LeBlanc, and Badgett 2013), suggesting that marriage is beneficial for mental health in sexual minority populations.

Although marriage may be beneficial for mental health, mental health outcomes are highly dependent on marital quality for different-sex marriages: lower marital quality reduces any mental health benefit (Proulx, Helms, and Buehler 2007) and can negatively alter the pathways through which marriage confers mental health benefits (Williams, Frech, and Carlson 2010). Thus, it is important to consider multiple dimensions of marital quality to understand how marriage affects mental health (Fincham and Bradbury 1987). However, research on the role of marital quality on mental health for same-sex marriages is limited, especially in regard to comparisons between same- and different-sex couples. Using dyadic data from 263 same-sex married couples (157 women with women couples; 106 men with men couples) and 115 different-sex married couples, we examined how multiple dimensions of marital quality compare for same-sex and different-sex couples and how these dimensions were independently associated with depressive symptoms.

Importance of Marital Quality

Marriages vary greatly in overall quality, in terms of both stress and emotional support within the relationship, with implications for physical and mental health (Proulx et al. 2007). Among different-sex couples, low-quality marriages are associated with worse mental health outcomes, ranging from lower psychological well-being to greater depressive symptoms (Proulx et al. 2007). Further, these associations are more pronounced in midlife (Henry et al. 2007), after longer union durations (Umberson et al. 2005), and when marital quality is measured along negative dimensions (e.g., conflict; Proulx et al. 2007). Taken together, these findings suggest that specific dimensions of marital quality (e.g., strain compared to support) matter when predicting mental health outcomes, especially in midlife, with marriages of longer duration.

Marital quality also likely plays a critical role in associations between marriage and health among same-sex couples, yet these associations are relatively unknown. Low-quality same-sex relationships might be directly linked to worse mental health, but most research focuses on the indirect association between relationship quality and mental health through minority stress (e.g., Cao et al. 2017). Because same-sex couples face minority stressors and minority stressors are consistently associated with lower-quality relationships (e.g., Otis et al. 2006), spouses in same-sex marriages could be susceptible to poor mental health indirectly through low-quality unions. However, same-sex cohabiting and married different-sex couples report similar levels of relationship quality (Kurdek 2004), and, unlike different-sex couples, some evidence suggests that relationship quality of same-sex couples is less likely to decline over time (Kurdek 2008), indicating the possible resilience of same-sex couples in the face of minority stressors.

Previous research with different-sex couples shows that multiple dimensions of marital quality are differentially associated with mental health. Positive (e.g., support or satisfaction) and negative (e.g., conflict) dimensions of marital quality are related, but distinct, from each other (Fincham and Bradbury 1987) and each dimension is often independently associated with health (Proulx et al. 2007). For example, negative dimensions of marital quality are more strongly predictive of health than positive dimensions (e.g., Carr and Springer 2010), and high levels of marital strain can be particularly harmful for mental health (Williams et al. 2010).

Compared with different-sex couples, same-sex couples tend to have relationships characterized by better conflict resolution (Kurdek 2004), suggesting that same-sex married couples may have lower scores on negative dimensions of marital quality than do different-sex married couples, and, thus, better mental health. However, because greater minority stress is associated with lower marital quality—measured by having low scores on positive dimensions (Otis et al. 2006), same-sex married couples may have more pronounced associations between positive dimensions of marital quality and mental health compared with different-sex married couples. In this instance, those in a same-sex marriage might have worse mental health than those in a different-sex marriage because their scores on positive dimensions of marital quality are lower. By examining each dimension of marital quality separately, we will be able to determine which dimensions of marital quality are most strongly associated with mental health and establish differences (or similarities) between same- and different-sex married couples.

Empirical Example

We begin with a descriptive analysis of how positive and negative dimensions of marital quality differ for gay, lesbian, and heterosexual couples. Next, we explore how each dimension of marital quality is independently associated with mental health, and whether these associations differ by couple type. We focus on married couples in midlife because declines in marital quality accelerate with age (Umberson et al. 2005) and social networks shrink with age (Luong, Charles, and Fingerman 2011), suggesting that spouses may become more salient sources for intimacy and social support as people age in midlife.

Data

We used dyadic data from a 2015 survey of 378 midlife couples: 115 heterosexual couples, 106 gay couples, and 157 lesbian couples. Each couple was recruited using Massachusetts's vital records and snowball sampling to ensure that same- and different-sex couples were comparable on relationship duration, age, and place of residence. All couples had to be legally married for at least three years, but couples did not have to currently live in Massachusetts to be included in the final sample. Same-sex couples who were married between 2004 and 2012 were sent invitations to participate. Those who participated were asked to refer same- and different-sex married couples of similar age. Additional different-sex couples were recruited through letters and flyers mailed to them based on addresses from publicly available city lists in Massachusetts. Each spouse took a forty-five-minute online survey and received a $50 gift card upon completion. Spouses completed their survey independently of each other.

Descriptive statistics indicate that, in the final sample, participants were between ages thirty-five and sixty-five (average age was 48) and were together on average fifteen years. Relationship duration did not differ between same-sex (M=14.74) and different-sex couples (M=15.89, F=3.39, p=.07). Most participants were college graduates (80%) and white (86%); fewer than half were currently living with children in the household (42%). Compared with different-sex couples, same-sex couples were significantly more likely to be college graduates (84% versus 73%, $\chi^2 = 12.82$, $p < .001$), less likely to involve a person of color (12% versus 18%, $\chi^2 = 5.28$, $p = .02$), and less likely to have children in the household (29% versus 71%, $\chi^2 = 115.98$, $p < .001$). There were no significant differences between same- and different-sex couples on levels of depressive symptoms (M = 16.88 versus M = 17.47, F = 1.98, $p = .16$).

Measures

Marital quality was measured to assess the following multiple positive and negative dimensions: marital well-being, marital support, marital strain, marital conflict, argument frequency, and argument stress. Both spouses independently reported each dimension of marital quality. Marital well-being was measured as the mean of four items ($\alpha = .92$) on a scale from 1 (not at all) to 6 (completely): (1) "I have a warm and comfortable relationship with my spouse"; (2) "I feel I can confide in my spouse about virtually anything"; (3) How rewarding is your relationship with your spouse?" (4) "In general, how satisfied are you with your relationship?" Marital support was measured as the mean of two items asking, on a scale from 1 (not at all) to 5 (a great deal): "In general, how much: (1) Does your spouse make you feel loved and cared for? (2) Is your spouse willing to listen when you need to talk about your worries or problems?" Marital strain was measured as the mean of two items asking, on a scale from 1 (not at all) to 5 (a great deal), "In general, how much": (1) Is your spouse critical of you or what you do? (2) "Does your spouse make too many demands on you?" Marital conflict was measured by four items ($\alpha = .74$), on a scale from 1 (never) to 5 (always), in response to "How frequently does your spouse use each of the following styles to deal with arguments or disagreements with you?" (1) "Explode and get out of control"; (2) "Reach a limit and refuse to talk any further"; (3) "Throw insults and digs"; (4) "Withdraw, act distant or not interested." Argument frequency was measured by one item asking, "About how often do you and your spouse argue with each other?" ranging from 1 (very rarely) to 5 (very often). Argument stress was measured by one item asking, "When you and your spouse argue, how stressful is this for you?" ranging from 1 (not at all) to 5 (extremely).

Depressive symptoms were measured with the Center for Epidemiologic Studies Depression Scale Revised (CESD-R) 11-item scale. Respondents were asked how often, during the past week, they experienced certain feelings or behaviors, coded from 1 (rarely or none of the time) to 4 (most of the time). Example questions included "I felt lonely" and "I did not feel like eating; my appetite was poor." Positive affect or behaviors (e.g., "I was happy") were reverse coded so higher values indicated greater depressive symptoms ($\alpha = .85$).

Control variables included relationship duration (a continuous measure of total years married or living together), whether the respondent was a college graduate, whether the respondent was a racial or ethnic minority, and whether there were children in the household (all dichotomized where 1=yes).

Statistical Methods

To test associations between marital quality and depressive symptoms, we used mixed-effects multilevel modeling with spouses nested within dyads to account for interdependence between spouses. These models included both fixed standard regression coefficients and random variability in couple intercepts. We examined dyad differences in marital quality and depressive symptoms by estimating the interaction between couple type (i.e., same-sex union or different-sex union) with each measure of marital quality. We included both respondents' reports of marital quality (actor effects) as well as their spouses' reports (partner effects) in each model. Each dimension of marital quality was independently associated with depressive symptoms to examine its unique contribution to mental health. All models controlled for relationship duration, educational attainment, race-ethnicity, and the presence of children in the household.

Descriptive Results of Differences in Marital Quality by Couple Type

Descriptive examination of same-sex couples' marital quality across multiple dimensions suggests that same-sex couples generally report higher marital quality than different-sex couples. Same-sex couples reported significantly higher marital well-being (M = 5.18) and marital support (M = 4.38) than different-sex couples (M = 4.89, F = 15.64, $p < .001$ and M = 4.12, F = 19.10, $p < .001$, respectively). Couple differences in negative dimensions of marital quality—marital strain, marital conflict, and argument stress and frequency—were relatively similar to those of positive marital quality. Marital strain was significantly higher for different-sex couples (M = 2.12) than same-sex couples (M = 1.91, F = 9.89, $p = .002$). Couples reported similar marital conflict. Different-sex couples reported significantly more arguments (M = 2.52) than same-sex couples (M = 2.28, F = 10.40, $p < .001$) but did not differ on stress surrounding their arguments. Although we do not distinguish between gay and lesbian couples in tables, gay and lesbian couples did not differ on positive dimensions of marital quality and only differed on the negative dimension of argument stress. Specifically, lesbian couples reported greater stress surrounding their arguments than gay couples.

Results from Mixed-Effects Multilevel Models

For the full sample, respondents who reported better marital well-being had fewer depressive symptoms (see table 15.1). Greater respondent marital support was also associated with fewer respondent depressive symptoms. Respondents who reported greater marital strain, more frequent arguments, and greater stress surrounding these arguments had more depressive symptoms. When spouses reported more marital strain, respondents also had more depressive symptoms, but spouses' reports of arguments and stress surrounding these arguments did not affect respondent depressive symptoms. Lastly, reporting any marital conflict by either the respondent or his or her partner was associated with more respondent depressive symptoms. Notably, most of these associations did not vary by couple type, suggesting that associations between marital quality and depressive symptoms are similar across same- and different-sex couples. We conducted sensitivity analyses to determine whether these associations differed when controlling for minority stress, measured by perceived discrimination; results did not differ from the original analyses.

Discussion

Same-sex couples experience greater minority stress, which is linked with poorer relationship quality (e.g., Cao et al. 2017). Indeed, in our sample, minority stress, in the form of perceived discrimination, was significantly associated with worse marital quality (analyses not shown). However, we found evidence that same-sex couples broadly reported higher-quality marriages than their different-sex counterparts. These results speak to the importance of examining multiple dimensions of marital quality. Prior work has relied primarily on relationship satisfaction to examine associations between minority stress and relationship quality (e.g., Otis et al. 2006), and these associations may differ when marital quality is measured by different dimensions. More affective dimensions of marital quality, such as relationship satisfaction, could be more negatively impacted by minority stress.

Our sample is not representative of same-sex couple types; rather, we look only at married couples. Same-sex couples with access to marriage face less discrimination (and possibly less minority stress) than couples without access to marriage (LeBlanc, Frost, and Bowen 2018). Thus, the association between greater minority stress and lower relationship quality may be less pronounced in our sample than it would be in samples of same-sex couples experiencing higher levels of minority stress. Indeed, in a meta-analysis of minority stress associated with relationship quality, a low effect size in the magnitude of this association was attributed to more privileged sample characteristics (Cao et al. 2017). In addition to being married, our sample was privileged in that it mostly consisted of highly educated and white respondents, suggesting that these couples may be low risk for minority stress and/or poor relationship quality.

Although we found descriptive marital quality differences between same- and different-sex couples, each dimension was similarly associated with

TABLE 15.1

Mixed-Effects Multilevel Regression Models Predicting Depressive Symptoms

	Model 1: marital well-being	Model 2: marital support	Model 3: marital strain	Model 4: marital conflict	Model 5: argument frequency	Model 6: argument stress
	b (se)	b (se)	b (se)	b (se)	b (se)	b (se)
Actor and partner effects[1]						
Actor marital quality	-2.05*	-1.77*	1.25*	1.78*	1.99*	1.31*
	(.38)	(.40)	(.38)	(.42)	(.43)	(.36)
Partner marital quality	.46	-.29	.99*	.90*	-.16	.45
	(.38)	(.40)	(.38)	(.42)	(.43)	(.36)
Same-sex couple	6.11*	5.46*	-1.56	.09	.75	-.25
	(2.32)	(2.53)	(1.28)	(1.42)	(1.36)	(2.14)
Same-sex couple X Actor marital quality	-.14	-.54	.77	.19	-.95	.22
	(.47)	(.51)	(.46)	(.51)	(.51)	(.43)
Same-sex couple X Partner marital quality	-1.06*	-.69	.02	-.35	.62	-.28
	(.47)	(.51)	(.46)	(.51)	(.51)	(.43)

Control variables

Relationship duration	−.03	−.02	−.03	−.03	−.03	−.02
	(.02)	(.02)	(.02)	(.03)	(.03)	(.03)
College graduate	−1.31*	−1.22*	−1.46*	−1.22*	−1.45*	−1.62*
	(.45)	(.46)	(.46)	(.47)	(.47)	(.47)
Nonwhite	.06	.17	−.18	.26	.44	.36
	(.52)	(.53)	(.53)	(.53)	(.54)	(.54)
Children in household	−.24	−.06	−.14	.01	.01	.38
	(.42)	(.43)	(.43)	(.44)	(.46)	(.46)
Intercept	26.72*	27.15*	14.41*	12.88*	14.26*	12.50*
	(1.86)	(1.95)	(1.24)	(1.34)	(1.31)	(1.86)

[1] Marital quality refers to the dimension listed for each model.

depressive symptoms across same- and different-sex couples. Specifically, higher-quality marriages were associated with fewer depressive symptoms, whereas lower-quality marriages were associated with more depressive symptoms. Broadly, these findings suggest that marital quality is important for mental health, regardless of whether the marriage is with a same- or different-sex partner. These results are consistent with studies on different-sex couples (e.g., Proulx et al. 2007), and we extend these findings to same-sex marriages. However, there could be differences between same- and different-sex couples in other relationship types, such as cohabitation. Qualitative research suggests that the meaning of marriage likely differs between same- and different-sex couples, with same-sex couples reporting high levels of commitment prior to marriage (Reczek, Elliott, and Umberson 2009). These qualitative findings suggest that associations between relationship quality and depressive symptoms could differ between same- and different-sex cohabiting couples, and possibly other relationship types. However, such differences may also vary across age cohorts, with greater or less access to legally recognized marriage.

We also found that spouses' reports of marital strain and marital conflict were predictive of a respondent's own depressive symptoms and these associations did not differ by couple type. Marital strain and conflict reflect spousal-specific behaviors (e.g., spouse tendency to criticize), whereas marital well-being and argument stress and frequency measure global couple dynamics (e.g., overall satisfaction or intimacy). When spouses perceive that respondents are treating them poorly, spouses may act negatively toward the respondent (e.g., withdrawing support; Whisman, Uebelacker, and Weinstock 2004), contributing to increased depressive symptoms. Conversely, spouses who perceive that the respondent is highly supportive may act more positively toward respondents, subsequently reducing depressive symptoms. Even though these pathways could operate similarly overall, the context in which individuals evaluate their marital quality could differ by couple type. For instance, among same-sex couples, respondents with higher levels of internalized homophobia perceive their relationship more negatively, and their partner also perceives the relationship more negatively (Otis et al. 2006), suggesting that different factors may alter respondent and/or spousal perceptions of relationship quality.

Future Research

Relationship Biographies

Although we documented links between same-sex couples' marital quality and mental health in midlife, marriage is not the only romantic union to consider. Relationship biographies that collect information for prior relationship and union statuses, including information on relationship type and duration, would be especially valuable for this line of research. Among different-sex couples, scholars have documented significant demographic changes in midlife relationship formation and dissolution, with important implications for health (for review, see Silverstein and Giarrusso 2010). Findings indicate that the prevalence rates of less formalized statuses (i.e., cohabitation) are increasing during midlife and these statuses are also associated with lower relationship quality and worse mental health; relationship dissolution (via divorce or widowhood) was also associated with worse health (Silverstein and Giarrusso 2010). However, same-sex couples who, until recently, had limited or nonexistent access to marriage likely differ in their relationship trajectories compared with different-sex couples. For instance, qualitative research suggests that same-sex couples are highly committed to a relationship prior to marriage and do not view marriage as transformative for their relationship (Reczek et al. 2009), whereas different-sex couples often use a marriage ceremony as a symbolic indicator of status (Cherlin 2004). However, these studies were conducted before marriage equality existed in the United States; differences between same- and different-sex couples seen in past research may reflect the specific opportunities available to couples during that time. Different meanings behind marriage likely have implications for relationship trajectories and, thus, health outcomes, and these meanings may vary across age cohorts and at different points in time.

Additionally, relationship biographies would allow researchers to explore differences within lesbian, gay, and bisexual communities. Among different-sex couples, comparisons of married and cohabiting couples in midlife suggest that cohabiting couples report lower relationship quality and mental health than married couples (Brown, Bulanda, and Lee 2005). However, same-sex cohabitors tend to report similar relationship quality to married different-sex couples (Kurdek 2004), suggesting that same-sex marrieds might not differ in relationship quality from same-sex cohabitors. Yet, having greater access to marital benefits (e.g., health insurance) might be associated with less marital strain, contributing to better relationship quality for same-sex married rather than cohabiting couples. Further, because much of the research on same-sex couples' relationship quality relies on samples consisting of mostly white, highly educated respondents (e.g., Cao et al. 2017), gathering relationship biographies from diverse samples of same-sex couples would allow researchers to examine differences within the lesbian, gay, and bisexual community from different vantage points, such as by race-ethnicity.

Processes across the Life Course

Longitudinal data are needed to gain a comprehensive understanding of the role of marital or relationship quality in associations between relationship status and mental health. Relationship quality is a process that unfolds over time throughout the duration of a relationship (Proulx et al. 2007), and relationship quality at a single time point does not allow researchers to draw causal inferences for these associations. Indeed, experiencing declining health can reduce a couple's marital quality (Yorgason, Booth, and Johnson 2008), and the lack of longitudinal data does not allow researchers to model these potentially causal processes. Longitudinal data for same-sex midlife couples containing detailed information on relationship quality is sparse, yet there are efforts underway to collect this information in existing data sources. Most notably, the Health and Retirement Study has recently begun collecting information on respondents' sexual orientation and gender identity, which will enable researchers to better examine the role of relationship quality in associations between same-sex relationships and health over time.

Longitudinal sources would also allow researchers to explore within-person change in relationship quality and/or mental health among sexual minorities. It may not be the relationship status itself, but rather the *transition* into a different status, that is most strongly associated with mental health. For instance, different-sex couples who transition into marriage from being unpartnered report improved mental health (e.g., Mernitz and Kamp Dush 2016), but they also report diminished mental health when transitioning from marriage into divorce (e.g., Carr and Springer 2010). Further, as many of these studies also document gender differences in these associations, gay couples may fare better or worse than lesbian couples depending on the transition.

Given the relatively recent legalization of same-sex marriage, it is important to examine associations between marital quality and mental health across many relationship types and across time. Dissimilar relationship trajectories between same- and different-sex couples may highlight differences in marital quality, and subsequent depressive symptoms, by couple type. Further, these patterns are likely shaped in part by context—such as the structural constraints and opportunities unique to each couple—providing many opportunities for future research that will allow researchers to better understand specific factors that promote mental health and high-quality relationships.

Conclusions

Mental health problems are more pronounced in lesbian and gay populations (Institute of Medicine 2011), yet same-sex marriage is protective for mental health and may be particularly important to the mental health of same-sex spouses (e.g., Wight et al. 2013). Among different-sex couples, the mental health benefits of marriage are highly dependent on marital quality (Proulx et al. 2007), but the direct effect of marital quality for the mental health of same-sex spouses is largely unexplored. When we consider multiple positive and negative dimensions of marital quality, we find that same-sex spouses report higher-quality marriages compared with different-sex spouses. Further, each dimension of marital quality is similarly associated with depressive symptoms for gay, lesbian, and heterosexual spouses. These findings convey an important message about the broad importance of marital quality for mental health. They also add to growing evidence that same-sex and different-sex married couples are more similar than they are different.

ACKNOWLEDGMENTS

This research was supported by grant R21AG044585 from the National Institute on Aging (awarded to Umberson) and grant P2CHD042849, Population Research Center, and T32HD007081, Training Program in Population Studies, both awarded to the Population Research Center at the University of Texas at Austin by the Eunice Kennedy Shriver National Institute of Child Health and Human Development. This study was also funded in part by the National Institute on Alcohol Abuse and Alcoholism grant number F32AA025814 (awarded to Pollitt). The content is solely the responsibility of the authors and does not necessarily represent the official views of the National Institutes of Health.

REFERENCES

Brown, Susan L., Jennifer Roebuck Bulanda, and Gary R. Lee. 2005. "The Significance of Nonmarital Cohabitation: Marital Status and Mental Health Benefits among Middle-Aged and Older Adults." *Journals of Gerontology: Series B* 60 (1): S21–S29.

Cao, Hongjian, Nan Zhou, Mark Fine, Yue Liang, Jiayao Li, and W. Roger Mills-Koonce. 2017. "Sexual Minority Stress and Same-Sex Relationship Well-Being: A Meta-analysis of Research Prior to the U.S. Nationwide Legalization of Same-Sex Marriage." *Journal of Marriage and Family* 79 (5): 1258–1277.

Carr, Deborah, and Kristen W. Springer. 2010. "Advances in Families and Health Research in the 21st Century." *Journal of Marriage and Family* 72 (3): 743–761.

Cherlin, Andrew J. 2004. "The Deinstitutionalization of American Marriage." *Journal of Marriage and Family* 66 (4): 848–861.

Fincham, Frank D., and Thomas N. Bradbury. 1987. "The Assessment of Marital Quality: A Reevaluation." *Journal of Marriage and Family* 49 (4): 797–809.

Henry, Nancy J. M., Cynthia A. Berg, Timothy W. Smith, and Paul Florsheim. 2007. "Positive and Negative Characteristics of Marital Interaction and Their Association with Marital Satisfaction in Middle-Aged and Older Couples." *Psychology and Aging* 22 (3): 428–441.

Institute of Medicine. 2011. *The Health of Lesbian, Gay, Bisexual, and Transgender People: Building a Foundation for Better Understanding.* Washington, DC: National Academies Press.

Kurdek, Lawrence A. 2004. "Are Gay and Lesbian Cohabiting Couples Really Different from Heterosexual Married Couples?" *Journal of Marriage and Family* 66 (4): 880–900.

Kurdek, Lawrence A. 2008. "Change in Relationship Quality for Partners from Lesbian, Gay Male, and Heterosexual Couples." *Journal of Family Psychology* 22 (5): 701–711.

LeBlanc, Allen J., David M. Frost, and Kayla Bowen. 2018. "Legal Marriage, Unequal Recognition, and Mental Health among Same-Sex Couples." *Journal of Marriage and Family* 80 (2): 397–408.

Luong, Gloria, Susan T. Charles, and Karen L. Fingerman. 2011. "Better with Age: Social Relationships across Adulthood." *Journal of Social and Personal Relationships* 28 (1): 9–23.

Mernitz, Sara E., and Claire Kamp Dush. 2016. "Emotional Health across the Transition to First and Second Unions among Emerging Adults." *Journal of Family Psychology* 30 (2): 233–244.

Otis, Melanie D., Sharon S. Rostosky, Ellen D. B. Riggle, and Rebecca Hamrin. 2006. "Stress and Relationship Quality in Same-Sex Couples." *Journal of Social and Personal Relationships* 23 (1): 81–99.

Proulx, Christine M., Heather M. Helms, and Cheryl Buehler. 2007. "Marital Quality and Personal Well-Being: A Meta-analysis." *Journal of Marriage and Family* 69 (3): 576–593.

Reczek, Corinne, Sinikka Elliott, and Debra Umberson. 2009. "Commitment without Marriage: Union Formation among Long-term Same-Sex Couples." *Journal of Family Issues* 30 (6): 738–756.

Silverstein, Merril, and Roseann Giarrusso. 2010. "Aging and Family Life: A Decade Review." *Journal of Marriage and Family* 72 (5): 1039–1058.

Umberson, Debra, Mieke Beth Thomeer, and Kristi Williams. 2013. "Family Status and Mental Health: Recent Advances and Future Directions." In *Handbook of the Sociology of Mental Health*, edited by Carol Aneshensel, Jo Phelan, and Alex Bierman, 405–431. New York: Springer.

Umberson, Debra, Kristi Williams, Daniel A. Powers, Meichu D. Chen, and Anna M. Campbell. 2005. "As Good as It Gets? A Life Course Perspective on Marital Quality." *Social Forces* 84 (1): 493–511.

Whisman, Mark A., Lisa A. Uebelacker, and Lauren M. Weinstock. 2004. "Psychopathology and Marital Satisfaction: The Importance of Evaluating Both Partners." *Journal of Consulting and Clinical Psychology* 72 (5): 830–838.

Wight, Richard G., Allen J. LeBlanc, and M. V. Lee Badgett. 2013. "Same-Sex Legal Marriage and Psychological Well-Being: Findings from the California Health Interview Survey." *American Journal of Public Health* 103 (2): 339–346.

Williams, Kristi, Adrianne Frech, and Daniel L. Carlson. 2010. "Marital Status and Mental Health." In *A Handbook for the Study of Mental Health: Social Contexts, Theories, and Systems*, edited by Teresa Scheid and Tony Brown, 306–320. New York: Cambridge University Press.

Yorgason, Jeremy B., Alan Booth, and David Johnson. 2008. "Health, Disability, and Marital Quality: Is the Association Different for Younger versus Older Cohorts?" *Research on Aging* 30 (6): 623–648.

16

First Sexual Experience with a Same-Sex Partner in the United States

Evidence from a National Sample

KARIN L. BREWSTER

KATHRYN HARKER TILLMAN

GIUSEPPINA VALLE HOLWAY

Over nearly five decades, social scientists have amassed a substantial body of literature describing what was euphemistically termed the initiation of sexual activity (i.e., first coitus) and its social, behavioral, and physical predictors (NRC 1987; Tolman and McClelland 2011). This research was initially motivated by a concern with teen pregnancy risk (NRC 1987), and the research designs and large-scale surveys that supported it focused on sexual engagement between opposite-sex partners. The conflation of "sexual activity" and coitus rendered nearly invisible sexual engagement between same-sex partners in social science data and research. In recent years, the prevailing paradigm in this area of research has shifted gradually from risk prevention to positive sexual development, opening the door for researchers to consider more inclusive definitions of sexual activity and sexual relationships (Tolman and McClelland 2011).

Concurrent with this paradigm shift has been the inclusion of questions on a broader array of sexual behaviors in several nationally representative surveys, including items about sexual experiences with same-sex partners (SESSP), same-sex attraction, and sexual identity. Analyses of data from these surveys have revealed that SESSP is not limited to those individuals who self-identify as lesbian, gay, or bisexual (LGB; McCabe, Brewster and Tillman 2011), and confirmed that many LGB-identified individuals have had sexual experience with opposite-sex partners (Goldberg and Halpern 2017). Much remains unknown about population-level patterns of SESSP, however, including timing of first SESSP, variation in SESSP risk across population subgroups, and whether SESSP risk has changed over time.

This chapter addresses the timing and correlates of first SESSP using data from a nationally representative sample. We describe how first SESSP risk changes with age, evaluate its variation across the demographic, social, and family characteristics that have well-established associations with first intercourse risk, and assess whether its prevalence has increased over time as attitudes toward sexuality have changed. Because SESSP is not limited to persons who identify as LGB (McCabe, Brewster, and Tillman 2011; Vrangalova and Savin-Williams 2010), our analyses consider individuals who do not self-identify as LGB as well as those who do. We briefly describe our conceptual approach and expectations before describing the data and our findings.

Conceptual Approach and Expectations

Guided by prior research on first intercourse risk, we view first SESSP through a life course lens, framing it as an event that may function as a turning point for some individuals, with implications for their sexual and family-building trajectories. From a life course perspective, event timing—that is, the age at which an event occurs—indicates an individual's progress through key transitions (Giele and Elder 1998). First intercourse, for example, is a signal event that constitutes a key marker in the transition to adulthood (Shanahan 2000). In the United States, average age at first intercourse is seventeen, and its occurrence is strongly age-graded, such that the share of individuals who have experienced coitus increases rapidly through adolescence and the early twenties and more slowly thereafter (Abma and Martinez 2017).

National data collected between 2006 and 2010 show that the share of the population reporting any SESSP nearly doubled between the ages fifteen through seventeen and twenty through twenty-four (Chandra, Copen, and Mosher 2013), suggesting that first SESSP risk increases through adolescence and young adulthood in an age-graded pattern similar to coital risk. At the same time, coital engagement is normative but SESSP is not. Sexual stigma remains embedded in social institutions (Herek 2015); thus, individuals must navigate what may be a difficult process of recognizing and acknowledging same-sex attraction without the guidance of well-established sexual scripts (Simon and Gagnon 1986). It may be, therefore, that first SESSP will occur at older ages, on average, than first coitus and that its occurrence will be less sharply delineated by age.

The life course approach understands event timing within the context of personal history—the unfolding of life experiences that channel and constrain individuals' access to resources and opportunities and shape their perceptions about behaviors and their consequences. These resources, opportunities, and perceptions provide explanatory mechanisms for observed associations between signal events and family background indicators, social and demographic characteristics, and experiences such as schooling and labor force participation (Shanahan 2000).

Family background is particularly important within the life course framework (Shanahan 2000), and the association of family characteristics with coital initiation during adolescence is well established. Compared with their less-advantaged peers, youth from families with better-educated parents and those who live with both parents (birth or adoptive) until age eighteen tend to delay first coitus to later ages (Miller 2002; Waldron et al. 2015), perhaps because they perceive the opportunity costs of nonmarital pregnancy or sexually transmitted infections as too high or are subject to greater parental monitoring. Family religious engagement also is associated with coital initiation: individuals raised in families affiliated with a religious denomination are older at first intercourse and less likely to engage in noncoital sexual behaviors like oral sex (Brewster and Tillman 2008; Manlove et al. 2006).

Our analysis considers three indicators of family background as predictors of first SESSP—mother's educational attainment, living arrangements prior to age eighteen, and family's religious affiliation.[1] That higher levels of parental education are associated with delay of first intercourse raises the likelihood of a negative association between mother's schooling and first SESSP risk; at the same time, education is associated with more tolerant attitudes toward nonmarital sex, teen sex, and sex with same-sex partners (Pampel 2016), suggesting a possible positive association. The likely influence of religion is easier to predict. Although an increasing share of religious denominations are embracing a more tolerant stance toward SESSP, most continue to emphasize the importance of traditional marriage and family life. Thus, we anticipate that being raised within a family claiming a religious affiliation will reduce first SESSP risk. We also expect that individuals who, as juveniles, lived independently of their families for reasons other than schooling will have higher first SESSP risk.

Our models also include indicators of three individual background characteristics: race-ethnicity, nativity, and sexual identity. Racial-ethnic and nativity differences in the timing of first coitus are well documented, with non-Hispanic black youth reporting higher rates of coital experience at every age relative to their Hispanic and non-Hispanic white peers and Asian American and foreign-born youth more likely to remain sexually inexperienced into early adulthood (Zimmer-Gembeck and Helfand 2008). These differences persist in the face of controls for income, schooling, and other measures of family status, leading many life course researchers to regard them as indicators of divergent subgroup norms and structural opportunities (Shanahan 2000). There is some evidence that SESSP prevalence also varies by race-ethnicity and nativity. Compared with their white peers, black and Hispanic youth between the ages of fifteen and twenty-one less frequently reported SESSP, as did foreign-born youth compared with the native-born (McCabe, Brewster, and Tillman 2011). Given these findings, we expect that the timing of first SESSP also will vary by race-ethnicity and nativity. Because of its likely endogeneity relative to SESSP (Diamond 2005; Savin-Williams 1998), sexual identity is included in our models as a control variable, not a covariate of substantive interest.

We also consider two aspects of individual experience: schooling and coital experience. As noted above, a college education is associated with greater tolerance for nontraditional sexual behaviors; moreover, college students may have greater opportunity for sexual experimentation. Thus, we anticipate that SESSP risk will be higher among those with at least some college experience. Based on sexual script theory (Simon and Gagnon 1986), which posits that individuals follow familiar sexual scripts before exploring less-scripted behaviors, we also expect coital experience to predict SESSP. Consistent with this expectation, interviews with LGB individuals suggest that, for many, sexual engagement with opposite-sex partners was an important component of confirming same-sex attraction (Diamond 2005; Savin-Williams 1998). Similarly, virtually all respondents to an online survey of university students who reported SESSP had prior opposite-sex experience (Vrangalova and Savin-Williams 2010).

Finally, consistent with the life course perspective's recognition that event occurrence and timing are contingent on the individual's location in historical time (Giele and Elder 1998), our analyses evaluate cohort differences in first SESSP risk. Over the past several decades there has been a remarkable liberalization of public attitudes toward sexuality and sexual minorities. This shift has been driven largely by the more liberal attitudes of recent birth cohorts (Twenge, Sherman, and Wells 2016). Have these more liberal attitudes been accompanied by a greater propensity to engage in SESSP? Although our models do not include individuals' attitudes toward SESSP, inclusion of birth cohort will provide some insight.

Methods

We use data from the National Survey of Family Growth (NSFG), which gathers information on various aspects of fertility, family formation, and sexual and reproductive health (National Center for Health Statistics 2018). Our analyses draw on data collected continuously over the four-year period from 2011 to 2015. Respondents were selected into a multistage area probability sample designed to be representative of individuals from age fifteen through age forty-four and residing in civilian households in all fifty states and the District of Columbia. Interviews were conducted in-person by trained female interviewers; questions about sexual identity, SESSP, and other sensitive topics were administered using audio-computer assisted self-interviewing (ACASI). Respondents signed consent forms after receiving oral and written information about the survey, and minors participated only with the signed consent of a parent or guardian.

Sample

The 2011–2015 NSFG comprises information from 11,300 females and 9,321 males. We excluded respondents missing information on sexual identity or consensual SESSP (161 females; 132 males), those reporting a sexual identity at odds with their sexual attraction (e.g., identified as a gay male but was attracted only to females; 45 females; 28 males), and those who reported that their first SESSP occurred before age ten (110 females; 79 males). Also excluded were male respondents whose first SESSP and a forced SESSP occurred at the same age ($n=38$)[2] and female respondents with missing data on age at menarche ($n=39$), an item the NCHS uses in constructing its measure of age at first consensual coitus. Respondents' missing data on nativity status, whether they lived alone before age eighteen, and childhood religious affiliation also were dropped (33 females; 31 males), yielding working samples of 10,915 females and 8,996 males.

Timing of First SESSP

Consistent with our life course approach, our analysis uses event-history modeling supported by person-period files constructed from the working samples (Allison 2014). Because year of age is the metric used by the NSFG to report timing of first SESSP, observations in these files represent person-years and each respondent contributes one observation for each year at risk of first SESSP. The observation window starts at age ten and ends at the year of age in which they either reported first SESSP or were interviewed (i.e., right-censored). Female and male respondents were asked different questions about their sexual experiences with same-sex partners: female respondents were asked about the timing of first oral sex or any other sexual experience; male respondents were asked about the timing of first oral or anal sex. Accordingly, the person-year files were constructed separately for females and males.

FEMALES. Female respondents were asked "Have you ever performed oral sex on another female?" and "Has another female ever performed oral sex on you?" Respondents who did not report oral sex with another female were then asked "Have you ever had any sexual experience of any kind with another female?" At a later point in the interview, respondents who had answered yes to at least one of these questions were asked "Thinking back to the *first time* you ever had oral sex or another kind of sexual experience with a *female* partner, how old were you?" Answers, provided in single years, determined the number of person-years contributed to the discrete-time event-history file by each of the 1,928 female respondents with SESSP. The 9,029 respondents who did not report any sexual experience with another female were censored at interview age in the event-history models. The analyses for female respondents were based on a total of 199,896 person-year observations.

MALES. The series of questions for male respondents began with "Have you ever performed oral sex on another male, that is, stimulated his penis with your mouth?" and "Has another male ever performed oral sex on you, that is, stimulated your penis with his mouth?" They were then asked "Has another male ever put his penis in your anus or butt (anal sex)?" and "Have you ever put your penis in another male's anus or butt (insertive anal sex)?" Later in the interview, respondents who had answered yes to at least one of these questions were asked, "Thinking back to the *first time* you ever had oral or anal sex with a *male* partner, how old were you?" Answers, provided in single years, determined the number of person-years contributed to the discrete-time event-history file by each of the 401 male respondents who reported SESSP. The 8,640 male respondents who reported no SESSP were censored at age of interview. The event-history analyses for males were based on 168,142 observed person-years.

Covariate Measurement

Family background indicators were measured as time-invariant dummies. Mother's educational attainment was represented by four dummy indicators, three of which capture the highest educational degree and one that captures respondents who reported not having a mother or maternal figure. Childhood religion was coded one for respondents who reported being raised with a religious affiliation and zero for those who reported that their family had no religious affiliation. Lived on own before eighteen was coded one for respondents who lived apart from their families before age eighteen for reasons other than schooling or similar opportunities, and zero otherwise.

Individual characteristics also were measured as time-invariant dummy variables. Respondents' race-ethnicity was a set of four dummies that distinguished self-identified Hispanics, regardless of race, from non-Hispanic whites, non-Hispanic blacks, and those identifying as either some other race-ethnicity or as multiple races-ethnicities. Nativity status was a single dummy coded one for those born outside of the United States and zero for U.S. natives. Sexual identity was measured as a three-category set of dummy indicators differentiating those who reported a heterosexual or straight identity from persons reporting a lesbian or gay identity, and persons reporting a bisexual identity. Birth cohort was measured as six binary indicators, with five five-year cohorts for persons born from 1966 through 1990 and a single ten-year cohort for respondents born from 1991 through 2000.

The two indicators of individual-level experience were measured as time-varying covariates. The coital experience indicator captures the transition from "virgin" to "nonvirgin" and was coded one for each person-year during which a respondent had no coital experience and zero for the person-year corresponding to a respondent's age at first coitus and for each person-year thereafter. Educational attainment was measured using two time-varying indicators: one capturing the transition to high school graduate and a second capturing the transition to college graduate.

Statistical Analysis

We estimate discrete-time event-history models using logistic regression with a piecewise specification of age. To preserve degrees of freedom, we collapsed the twenty-five-year observation span into seven three-year categories representing ages ten to twelve years through twenty-eight to thirty years, and one fifteen-year category for ages thirty-one to forty-five. Because SESSP measures were constructed differently for male and female respondents, models were estimated separately by sex. All estimates have been adjusted for the complex sampling design of the NSFG and results are representative of the national population ages fifteen through forty-four during 2011 through 2015.

To evaluate potential dependence arising from the use of person-period data, we estimated random intercept and population-averaged models using generalized estimating equations. All three models produced comparable results with no evidence pointing to a need to correct for within-subject dependence. We also evaluated the sensitivity of the results to violating the assumption of noninformative censoring; results provided reassurance that right-censoring of individuals who did not report SESSP is not a concern.

Results

Descriptive analysis indicates that the female and male samples are broadly similar with respect to family background, race-ethnicity, nativity, educational attainment, coital experience, and cohort membership but they differ with respect to sexual identity: More males (97%) than females (93%) identify as straight, and more females (6%) than males (2%) identify as bisexual. Comparisons within gender but across sexual identity categories suggest that LGB respondents are younger, with roughly 55 percent born after 1985 compared with 42 percent of straight respondents, and more LGB-respondents are native-born. Although the distribution of male respondents by race-ethnicity is similar across sexual identity groups, fewer lesbian females than straight or bisexual females identify as non-Hispanic white, and more identify as non-Hispanic black or Hispanic. In addition, fewer lesbian and bisexual females (18% and 16%, respectively) than straight females (23%) have a college degree, but more gay males (32%) than straight or bisexual males (22% and 16%, respectively) do.

Similar shares of females and males report having had coitus (88% and 87%, respectively) or having neither coital experience nor SESSP (12% and 13%, respectively). Experience with same-sex partners differed sharply by gender, however, with four times as many females as males (16% versus 4%) reporting SESSP. Looking within categories of sexual identity suggests that the gender difference in

SESSP is driven largely by the different experiences of females and males who identify as straight. About 11 percent of straight-identified females report oral sex or some other sexual experience with another female; just 1 percent of straight-identified males report engagement in oral or anal sex with another male. Among LGB respondents, more females than males have sexual experience of some kind; just 6 percent of lesbian and 10 percent of bisexual females report no coitus or SESSP compared with 12 percent of gay and 18 percent of bisexual males. More lesbian (56%) and bisexual females (86%) than gay (41%) or bisexual (72%) males report coital experience; more lesbian (92%) and bisexual females (75%) than gay (88%) or bisexual males (68%) report SESSP.

Among those who report coital experience, mean age at first coitus was 17.2 for females and 17.0 for males. Lesbian and bisexual females report slightly younger ages at first coitus (16.9 and 15.9, respectively), on average, than straight females (17.3); compared with straight males (17.0), gay males were older (18.1) at first coitus and bisexual males slightly younger (16.8) on average. Mean age at first SESSP was older than mean age at first coitus among both females (20.4) and males (19.6). It also tends to be somewhat younger for LGB- than straight-identified individuals. Lesbian (19.0) and bisexual females (19.9) were younger, on average, at first SESSP than straight females (20.8), as were gay (19.1) and bisexual (19.5) males compared with straight males (20.2).

Table 16.1 presents adjusted odds ratios (AOR) and 95% confidence intervals (CI) from the discrete-time event-history models, controlling for sexual identity. The age estimates suggest that, net of sexual identity, family background, and individual characteristics and experiences, first SESSP risk is highest at ages sixteen through eighteen for both genders. Among females, this risk subsequently declines until about age thirty. This pattern is broadly consistent with the age-graded transition to first coitus, albeit with a more extended decline in risk. Among males, first SESSP risk drops off through the mid-twenties but then reverses after ages twenty-five through twenty-seven. Additional analysis suggests that this reversal reflects the considerable variability in age at first SESSP, particularly among straight and bisexual males, which is likely a reflection of the small share of men with SESSP.

Overall, results for females are more consistent with our expectations than the results for males. Two indicators of family background are associated with females' first SESSP risk, net of sexual identity: mother's educational attainment and independent living. First SESSP risk is 25 percent higher (95% CI: 5%–48%) for those with a mother who completed high school and 40 percent (95% CI: 10%–78%) higher for those with a mother with at least a college degree relative to those with mothers who did not graduate from high school. Living independently of family members before age eighteen increases first SESSP risk by 59 percent (95% CI: 36%–84%). Although childhood religion is associated with a

TABLE 16.1

Design-Weighted *F*-Tests and Adjusted Odds Ratios for First Sexual Experience with a Same-Sex Partner, by Gender: U.S. Household Residents, Ages 15–44, 2011–2015[a]

	Females	Males
Age [b]	$F_{(7, 108)} = 10.09$ ***	$F_{(7, 108)} = 3.18$ **
10–12 (ref.)	1.00	1.00
13–15	2.40 (1.76–3.27)***	1.78 (1.07–2.94)*
16–18	3.91 (2.68–5.72)***	3.83 (2.18–6.72)***
19–21	2.96 (1.96–4.49)***	3.63 (1.87–7.05)***
22–24	2.57 (1.66–3.98)***	2.53 (1.29–4.98)**
25–27	1.97 (1.19–3.27)**	1.73 (.69–4.35)
28–30	1.84 (1.08–3.13)*	3.46 (1.38–8.70)**
31–45	1.32 (.82–2.14)	2.42 (1.14–5.12)*
Mother's educational attainment:	$F_{(3, 108)} = 2.97$ *	$F_{(3, 108)} = 2.00$
Less than high school (ref.)	1.00	1.00
High school	1.25 (1.05–1.48)**	.81 (0.56–1.18)
College degree or higher	1.40 (1.10–1.78)**	.99 (.62–1.60)
No maternal figure	1.59 (.95–2.66)	3.30 (0.78–13.91)
Any childhood religion	.90 (.74–1.09)	.65 (.44–.96)*
Lived on own before 18	1.59 (1.36–1.84)***	1.35 (.99–1.84)
Race-ethnicity:	$F_{(3, 108)} = 4.05$ **	$F_{(3, 108)} = .59$
Non-Hispanic white (ref.)	1.00	1.00
Non-Hispanic black	.87 (.72–1.05)	.84 (.57–1.23)
Hispanic, any race	.81 (.68–.96)*	1.04 (.66–1.63)
Multiple or other	.72 (.54–.96)*	1.24 (.75–2.00)
Born outside U.S.	.38 (.29–.51)***	.35 (.23–.54)***
No coital experience [c]	.33 (.25–.42)***	.71 (.47–1.08)
Educational attainment: [c]		
High school	1.18 (0.96–1.44)	1.27 (.83–1.93)
College degree or higher	1.24 (1.03–1.51)*	.93 (.62–1.41)

(continued)

Table 16.1. Design-Weighted F-Tests and Adjusted Odds Ratios for First Sexual
Experience with a Same-Sex Partner, by Gender: U.S. Household Residents,
Ages 15–44, 2011–2015[a] (continued)

	Females	Males
Birth cohort:	$F_{(5,\ 108)} = 32.89$ ***	$F_{(5,\ 108)} = 2.65$ *
1966–70 (ref.)	1.00	1.00
1971–75	1.33 (1.00–1.77)*	.83 (.49–1.42)
1976–80	1.37 (.99–1.89)	1.44 (.84–2.47)
1981–85	2.42 (1.80–3.27)***	1.34 (.81–2.20)
1986–90	3.63 (2.77–4.76)***	1.86 (1.04–3.31)*
1991–2000	3.72 (2.72–5.10)***	1.09 (.63–1.89)
N	9,415	8,996
Person-years	199,155	167,401

[a] F-tests of statistical significance for covariates with multiple categories, and
survey-weighted adjusted odds ratios and 95% confidence intervals from
discrete-time logistic regression models, controlling for sexual identity.

[b] Time-varying dummy indicator equal to one at event or censoring.

[c] Time-varying dummy indicators.

* $p < .05$; ** $p < .01$; *** $p < .001$.

10 percent decrease in SESSP risk, the relationship is not statistically significant
($p = .24$).

AOR estimates suggest that individual characteristics and life experiences
also are associated with females' SESSP risk. Relative to non-Hispanic white
females, first SESSP risk is 19 percent (95% CI: 4%–32%) lower for Hispanic females
and 28 percent (95% CI: 4%–46%) lower for non-Hispanic females who identify
as a race other than black or white or as multiple races. First SESSP risk is
62 percent (95% CI: 49%–71%) lower for non-U.S. natives. Coital inexperience and
educational attainment also are associated with first SESSP risk among females.
Each additional year of coital virginity is associated with a 67 percent (95% CI:
58%–75%) reduction in risk. Additional education, on the other hand, is associated with an increased risk of first SESSP: those who have completed a college
degree have a 24 percent (95% CI: 3%–51%) higher risk than their peers with a
high school diploma only.

Results also are consistent with our expectation that SESSP risk is greater
for members of more recent cohorts. First SESSP risk is approximately two to four

times higher for females born after 1980 relative to those born before 1971; additional analysis indicates that the increase across cohorts is approximately monotonic.

The results for males suggest that first SESSP risk is associated with just three covariates. First SESSP risk is 35 percent (95% CI: 4%–56%) lower for males raised in a family with a religious affiliation than for those raised without one and 65 percent (95% CI: 46%–77%) lower for males born outside the United States than for their native-born peers. Although the test statistic ($p = .04$) for birth cohort suggests that it matters for males' SESSP risk, the AOR do not suggest how this risk has changed over time. Pairwise comparisons of the marginal effects (not shown) suggest that the reason is the reference category is too early to capture the increase in males' SESSP risk, which was not evident among cohorts born before 1971–1975.

Conclusions

Sexuality is critical to health and well-being throughout the adult life course, yet scholars' understanding of sexuality remains limited insofar as it draws largely on data describing sexual experience with opposite-sex partners. This chapter uses information from a nationally representative sample of women and men from age fifteen through age forty-four to describe the timing and correlates of first sexual experience with a same-sex partner. Our findings add to both the growing literature on the life course of LGB-identified individuals and the broader literature on sexual experience from adolescence through midlife.

Consistent with prior research, descriptive findings point to substantial differences in the prevalence of SESSP by gender, with women more likely to report SESSP than men (16% vs. 4%, respectively). Findings also confirm that SESSP is not limited to LGB-identified individuals. Eleven percent of straight-identified women and 1 percent of straight-identified men report this type of sexual experience with same-sex partners.

Estimates from discrete-time event-history models suggest that the transition to sexual engagement with same-sex partners is age-graded, much like the transition to first coitus. Among women and men, first SESSP risk peaks from age sixteen through age eighteen and then declines gradually through the young adult years. Consistent with the greater stigma attached to SESSP, the decline in first SESSP risk occurs over a longer age-span than is typical for first coitus risk. As a result, average age at first SESSP is slightly older, regardless of gender or sexual identity.

Results also are consistent with the notion that stigma attached to SESSP is weakening, although perhaps less among men than women. Women born after 1980 were more likely than those born before 1971 to have SESSP, and female's

SESSP risk increased almost monotonically across birth cohorts. Evidence of cohort differences among men was weaker, with those born between 1976 and 1990 being slightly more likely to have SESSP than their peers born between 1971 and 1975.

Not only did straight-identified women report SESSP more often than straight men, but lesbian and bisexual women more often had coital experience than gay and bisexual men. Moreover, among women—but not men—a lack of coital experience was associated with lower first SESSP risk. These findings are consistent with arguments that sexual identity development occurs at somewhat later ages on average among women than men (e.g., Martos, Nezhad, and Meyer 2015). Alternatively, these findings may reflect long-standing gender differences in the nature of opposite-sex relationships. Perhaps men with same-sex attractions are less likely to pursue sexual relationships with women, while women with same-sex attractions may find it easier to succumb to normative pressure to engage in sexual relationships with men.

Our findings also are consistent with prior research suggesting that same-sex sexual engagement is more responsive to social factors among women than men. More of the covariates had statistically significant associations with first SESSP in the models for females. That social factors have little association with men's SESSP risk may reflect greater pressure on them to conform to the expectation of heterosexuality, pressure that is sufficient to obviate differences by social class, race-ethnicity, and family background. At the same time, the greater predictive power of social characteristics in the female models is consistent with other evidence that women's sexuality is less fixed than men's (Baumeister 2000; Diamond 2005).

To our knowledge, the NSFG is the only nationally representative survey to include items about age at first SESSP, along with a sample of LGB individuals sufficient to support analysis. Yet, our ability to describe the transition to sexual activity among LGB individuals, or the same-sex sexual experiences of individuals as they age from adolescence into midlife, continues to be limited by data concerns. Despite a larger sample than is typical, the overall number of respondents identifying as LGB is small, particularly among men. Apparent gender differences in the predictors of SESSP may reflect the smaller sample of men who identify as gay or bisexual and a consequent lack of statistical power within the male subsample. Additionally, the NSFG survey does not ask the same questions of women and men when it comes to first SESSP. The questions answered by women are more ambiguously worded, perhaps leading to the higher levels of reported SESSP among women relative to men and to gender differences in the multivariate findings. Moving forward, surveys designed to provide data on sexual and reproductive health and family-building must include oversamples of sexual minorities and develop more comparable measures of sexual activity for women and men if we are to understand the role of sexual relationships in shaping health and well-being through the life course.

NOTES

1. Selection of specific, conceptually important indicators was guided by availability of data and preliminary analyses.
2. The NSFG female questionnaire does not include items on forced SESSP.

REFERENCES

Abma, Joyce, and Gladys Martinez. 2017. "Sexual Activity and Contraceptive Use among Teenagers in the United States, 2011–2015." *National Health Statistics Reports*, no. 104 (June 2017). Hyattsville, MD: National Center for Health Statistics. Accessed from https://www.cdc.gov/nchs/data/nhsr/nhsr104.pdf.

Allison, Paul. 2014. *Event History and Survival Analysis.* 2nd edition. Quantitative Applications in the Social Sciences, Series 07, no. 46. Thousand Oaks, CA: Sage.

Baumeister, Roy. 2000. "Gender Differences in Erotic Plasticity: The Female Sex Drive as Socially Flexible and Responsive." *Psychology Bulletin* 126 (3): 347–374.

Brewster, Karin L., and Kathryn Harker Tillman. 2008. "Who's Doing It? Patterns and Predictors of Youths' Oral Sexual Experiences." *Journal of Adolescent Health* 42 (1): 73–80.

Chandra, Anjani, Casey Copen, and William Mosher. 2013. "Sexual Behavior, Sexual Attraction, and Sexual Identity in the United States: Data from the 2006–2010 National Survey of Family Growth." In *International Handbook on the Demography of Sexuality*, edited by Amanda Baumle, 45–66. Dordrecht: Springer.

Diamond, Lisa. 2005. "What We Got Wrong about Sexual Identity Development: Unexpected Findings from a Longitudinal Study of Young Women." In *Sexual Orientation and Mental Health: Examining Identity and Development in Lesbian, Gay, and Bisexual People*, edited by Allen Omoto and Howard Kurtzman, 73–94. Washington, DC: American Psychological Association Press.

Giele, Janet, and Glen Elder. 1998. *Methods of Life Course Research: Qualitative and Quantitative Approaches.* Thousand Oaks, CA: Sage.

Goldberg, Shoshana, and Carolyn Halpern. 2017. "Sexual Initiation Patterns of US Sexual Minority Youth: A Latent Class Analysis." *Perspectives on Sexual and Reproductive Health* 49 (1): 55–67.

Herek, Gregory. 2015. "Beyond 'Homophobia': Thinking More Clearly about Stigma, Prejudice, and Sexual Orientation." *American Journal of Orthopsychiatry* 85 (5S): S29–S37.

Manlove, Jennifer, Elizabeth Terry-Humen, Erum Ikramullah, and Kristin Moore. 2006. "The Role of Parent Religiosity in Teens' Transitions to Sex and Contraception." *Journal of Adolescent Health* 39 (4): 578–587.

Martos, Alexander, Sheila Nezhad, and Ilan Meyer. 2015. "Variations in Sexual Identity Milestones among Lesbians, Gay Men, and Bisexuals." *Sexuality Research and Social Policy* 12 (1): 24–33.

McCabe, Janice, Karin L. Brewster, and Kathryn Harker Tillman. 2011. "Patterns and Correlates of Same-Sex Sexual Activity among US Teenagers and Young Adults." *Perspectives on Sexual and Reproductive Health* 43 (3): 142–150.

Miller, Brent. 2002. "Family Influences on Adolescent Sexual and Contraceptive Behavior." *Journal of Sex Research* 39 (1): 22–26.

National Center for Health Statistics. 2018. "About the National Survey of Family Growth." Last modified November 6, 2018. Retrieved from https://www.cdc.gov/nchs/nsfg /about_nsfg.htm.

National Research Council (NRC). Panel on Adolescent Pregnancy and Childbearing. 1987. *Risking the Future: Adolescent Sexuality, Pregnancy, and Childbearing.* Washington, DC: National Academy of Sciences.

Pampel, Fred C. 2016. "Cohort Changes in the Social Distribution of Tolerant Sexual Attitudes." *Social Forces* 95 (2): 753–777.

Savin-Williams, Ritch. 1998. *"... And Then I Became Gay": Young Men's Stories.* New York: Routledge.

Shanahan, Michael. 2000. "Pathways to Adulthood in Changing Societies: Variability and Mechanisms in Life Course Perspective." *Annual Review of Sociology* 26: 667–692.

Simon, William, and John Gagnon. 1986. "Sexual Scripts: Permanence and Change." *Archives of Sexual Behavior* 15 (2): 97–120.

Tolman, Deborah L., and Sara I. McClelland. 2011. "Normative Sexuality Development in Adolescence: A Decade in Review, 2000–2009." *Journal of Research on Adolescence* 21 (1): 242–255.

Twenge, Jean, Ryne Sherman, and Brooke Wells. 2016. "Changes in American Adults' Reported Same-Sex Sexual Experiences and Attitudes, 1973–2014." *Archives of Sexual Behavior* 45 (7): 1713–1730.

Vrangalova, Zhana, and Ritch Savin-Williams. 2010. "Correlates of Same-Sex Sexuality in Heterosexually Identified Young Adults." *Journal of Sex Research* 47 (1): 92–102.

Waldron Mary, Kelly Doran, Kathleen Bucholz, Alexis Duncan, Michael Lynskey, Pamela Madden, Carolyn Sartor, and Andrew Heath. 2015. "Parental Separation, Parental Alcoholism, and Timing of First Sexual Intercourse." *Journal of Adolescent Health* 56 (5): 550–556.

Zimmer-Gembeck, Melanie, and Mark Helfand. 2008. "Ten Years of Longitudinal Research on U.S. Adolescent Sexual Behavior: Developmental Correlates of Sexual Intercourse, and the Importance of Age, Gender, and Ethnic Background." *Developmental Review* 28 (2): 153–224.

17

"Two Sides of a Coin"

Nuances of Maternal Identity for Lesbian Mothers

RACHEL L. HENRY

Motherhood is an expectation for *most* women. Girls in the United States grow up with the cultural expectation that their most important rite of passage is to have children and be nothing less than excited to become mothers (Hare-Mustin and Broderick 1979; Hequembourg 2007; Laney et al. 2014; Mamo 2007; Mezey 2008; Russo 1976, 1979; Shelton and Johnson 2006; Wall 2011). However, this expectation is not necessarily intended to apply to everyone (Epstein 2002; Thompson 2002). The cultural expectation of motherhood is meant for a very specific kind of woman. As Laney et al. (2014) argue, being straight is only one of many expectations for the specific kind of women intended to be mothers; therefore being a lesbian within itself is already a "deviance" (Mamo 2007). Many researchers have found that lesbian mothers struggle with identifying with the "self-concept" of mother because of the exact distinction as both a lesbian and a mother (Hayman et al. 2015; Mamo 2007; Miller 2012; Wall 2011). This struggle to bridge a cohesive understanding of their own "self-concept" between the two identities, lesbian and mother, creates what the current literature establishes as an inherent contradiction in identity. The two identities cannot be understood or embraced within concert with one another. This research aims to examine the different aspects of identity development that contribute to that conclusion and consider whether or not that overarching contradiction is still relevant to lesbian mothers today.

The construction of expectations and boundaries for mothers is clearly defined through Butler's (1990) definition of a heterosexual matrix. Butler argues that the matrix characterizes bodies as sexed, either male or female, and that the sex of a body inherently signifies any sexed body as a specific gender, man/masculine for male sexed bodies and woman/feminine for female sexed bodies. This sex/gender dichotomy requires bodies to uphold heterosexual desire or sexuality, excluding lesbian women from appropriate social constructions of relationship and motherhood boundaries. Mamo (2007) subsequently makes the connection that within women's self-concept the desire is "hetero(sex) [that] leads to their parenthood." These links operate on a set of assumptions about how sex, gender, and desire are all connected and perpetrate such connections as the only right way for them to lead to one another. This binary system establishes a world in which one cannot understand without the other. Mamo (2007) argues that this conflict can even act as a successful barrier to lesbian women making the decision to become mothers.

The cultural dominance of the heterosexual matrix and its connection to parenthood and identity development is also displayed through the binary understanding of biological privilege. Because of the construction that motherhood is the result of being female-bodied and engaging in heterosexual desire, privilege is granted to women who birth their children. By being a co-mother (women who did not birth their children), one is pushed even further outside of the heterosexual matrix by not being linked through a gestational connection. Co-mothers are even more so "outside the normal . . . family construct [which] regulates her as powerless and vulnerable, essentially excluding her from the position of a legitimate mother" (Hayman et al. 2015). Co-mothers do actively work against the delegitimization assigned to them through the heterosexual matrix by doing things such as matching their physical characteristics to that of the sperm donor's (Hayman et al. 2015; Mamo 2007). However, lesbian co-mothers still struggle with biological privilege and a sense of legitimacy (Hayman et al. 2015; Mamo 2007; Miller 2012; Pelka 2009).

In both research with lesbian mothers and heterosexual mothers, community formation is also cited as important to the knowledge distribution and understanding of themselves and their practice as mothers. Without it, lesbian mothers are missing a crucial aspect of identity formation (Hayman et al. 2015; Wall 2011). It is imperative for lesbian mothers to be able to access *alternative* information in regard to their *alternative* way of having children. This becomes a problem when they cannot find that support (Hayman et al. 2015; Wall 2011). In examining connection and support within the heterosexual matrix, historically there were many women invested in second-wave feminism who chose to have nonheterosexual relationships and denounced motherhood as a political act, one considered to be important and crucial to their "liberation" (Wall 2011). From their perspective, this path away from motherhood was the only way to resist the requirement of gender and desire expectations and resulted in many nonheterosexual women who had chosen motherhood to be at a loss of support. While many nonheterosexual partnered women have moved beyond this second-wave feminist movement, the contradictions in discursive understanding of the identity as lesbian and the identity as mother still infiltrate community ideals and relationships, potentially still creating a struggle to find support and knowledge from other lesbian mothers as found in other studies (Hayman et al. 2015; Wall 2011).

Another influence within the challenges of legitimization of identity as a mother is that of language (Gabb 2005; Miller 2012). As Miller points out, there are not two separate terms to identify two mothers equally parenting within the same household. This is because traditionally the parent other than mother is termed father, which discursively holds power only for biologically connected men. Foucault (1978) examines the power of discursive construction and argues that the creation of categories in which names produce and assign power as well as knowledge. Creation of categorical words such as "mother," "mom," "mommy," or "mama" are not discreetly understood. "Mother" and all variations of it identify the woman who gave birth to a child or who is the sole woman raising the child within a two-parent, heterosexually coupled family. These categories help to legitimize those whom they apply to (Foucault 1978). The legitimacy resonates with how a mother is to understand her own positionality as well as how laws are legitimized. Miller (2012) argues that these complications around language and the power that they strip co-mothers of inhibits identity development. Miller states that "the limitations . . . further exacerbate problems of recognition perpetuated by legal disenfranchisement and general social homophobia or heterosexism." Even in regard to documented parental status, while the federal laws recently passed for same-sex marriage (*Obergefell v. Hodges* 2015) have helped co-mothers gain legal rights to their children, what they are now entitled to pursue with minimal cost or challenges is a "stepparent" adoption. Thus, even their legal entitlement to rights over their children is loaded with discourse that conveys particular elements of power as to just how legitimate they are as rightful parents.

This research among different disciplines discusses the experiences of lesbian women who have children. As has been examined, there are issues of power, legitimacy, and cultural frameworks at play, shaping these experiences, influencing the ways in which lesbian women develop their identity as mothers. However, how do each of these different influences come together and shape how lesbian mothers experience their maternal identity formation when they have children? The present student extends this prior research to examine the many different influences for lesbian motherhood identity and to explicitly ask if being a lesbian and being a mother is still an inherent contraction as past research and queer theoretical analysis suggests.

The Present Study

Regarding the terminology for this study, I utilize the term "gestational mother" in reference to the mother who gave birth to the child. "Co-mother" is utilized in reference to the mother who did not give birth to the child. Co-mothers may still be biologically connected to their child if they donated their eggs to their partner who is the gestational mother. "Lesbian couple(s)" or "women in lesbian relationships" will be utilized to describe two women in a relationship who made the decision to have a child together. These are research terms only and not part of the legal nomenclature where moms are made by biological, gestational, and social ties. The terminology that I employ in this study is not to signify that this is the terminology that all women choose to utilize in their own lives, and each individual's choice of language is to be respected.

Methods

Participants

The participants of the present study (N=11) were women who planned for and brought their children into their family within a same-gender or same-sex relationship and identified as a mother. At least one of their children had to be between the ages of two and eighteen and living with them.

Of the mothers included in this study, eight self-identified their sexual orientation as lesbian (72%), two self-identified as queer (18%), and one self-identified as asexual (9%). All of the eleven participants self-identified as cisgender woman (100%). Not all participants were still with the partner that they had their child with (N=2) but both participants who were no longer with the partner they had children with had remarried. None of the participants were partnered to each other. Six of the mothers had one child (55%), four of the mothers had two children (36%), and one mother had three children (9%). Four participants were gestational mothers to all of their children (36%), six participants were co-mothers to all of their children (55%), and one participant was both a gestational mother and a co-mother (9%). The average age of participants was forty years old (range 32–50). All participants had high levels of education; each participant had an associate's degree or more education. All eleven participants self-identified as white. All eleven participants were located in California. It is important to note that the findings are not generalizable beyond the sample demographics, which notably includes a very specific makeup of white, well-educated, partnered mothers. See table 17.1 for a detailed chart of participants.

Procedure

Recruitment. Participants were recruited through a variety of methods. E-newsletters were posted with community resource centers for LGBTQ members as well as fertility and midwifery offices that serve LGBTQ families. Snowball sampling was also utilized, as some participants referred their contacts after participating. This produced a convenience sample of mothers for the present study.

Interviews. All interviews were conducted via video chat (N=10) or in person (N=1). The length of the interviews lasted from thirty-four to eighty-two minutes. A pseudonym was given to each participant in order to protect

TABLE 17.1

Participant Chart

Pseudonym	Age at time of interview	Race	Education	Number of children at time of interview	Positionality with child (children)
Andy	36	White	Professional degree	2	Gestational mother
Carmen	35	White	Professional degree	1	Co-mother
Hayden	33	White	Associate's degree	1	Gestational mother
Riley	43	White	Master's degree	2	Gestational mother
Quinn	34	White	Master's degree	3	Gestational mother and co-mother
Sam	39	White	Master's degree	2	Gestational mother
Alex	32	White	Doctoral degree	1	Co-mother
Charlie	49	White	Bachelor's degree	1	Co-mother
Morgan	50	White	Bachelor's degree	1	Co-mother
Drew	44	White	Bachelor's degree	1	Co-mother
Kerry	40	White	Professional degree	2	Co-mother

confidentiality. Participants were given a $15 gift card as a thank you for their time. The semistructured interviews for this study allowed mothers to reflect on their experiences of maternal identity formation. The semistructured questions were modified based on the positionality of what this research categorized as the participant being a gestational mother or a co-mother. Questions traced the mothers' experiences with identity from prior to having children, to the present, and what they imagine the future to be like. A few examples of the questions asked include the following: How did you feel when your child joined your family? Can you tell me what the identity of being a mom means to you? How supported did you feel in becoming a mother? Can you share with me the first experience in which you felt like a mother? How has becoming a parent changed your identity?

Data Analysis

Process. The qualitative data analysis for this study was guided by modified grounded theory (Charmaz 2017) in order to explore themes that exist in current literature as well as leave room for other findings to emerge, as they exist.

Thematic Categories Definitions. The four thematic categories that emerged from data analysis are defined as follows; contradiction in identities was coded any time a participant indicated that was or is challenging to integrate her self-concept as a lesbian and her self-concept as a mother. However, upon additional analysis of the data, this code expanded to also include any time a participant discussed the integration of her self-concept as a lesbian and her self-concept, regardless of if she expressed it as challenging or not. Biological connection was coded any time a mother's biological connection to her child, or lack thereof, was discussed. Legal access was coded any time legal rights, action, or lack of legal access was mentioned. Finally, any reference to feelings of delegitimization or legitimatization of identity through the language use of others or self was coded as language use.

Results

Qualitative data analysis was utilized to explore the various nuances that may impact lesbian mother's identity development as informed by prior research through the modified grounded theory approach. By examining these four thematic categories as detailed here, consistencies and differences among the mothers were analyzed. The experience of contradiction in identities as well as the circumstances in which the delegitimization of identity were experienced was utilized to understand how lesbian mothers ingrate both identities into their self-concept.

Contradiction in Identities

Lesbian mothers are expected to experience a contradiction in their identities because they struggle to integrate their self-concept as a mother and as a lesbian (Hayman et al. 2015; Mamo 2007; Miller 2012; Wall 2011). Four of the mothers in this study did express some barriers to situating their self-concept within motherhood because of their identity as a lesbian. However, the seven other mothers did not experience a contradiction in their identity at all. Some of them recognized their "lesbian motherhood" as always apparent, but they still experience positive aspects to integrating those two identities.

Of the four mothers who did experience a contradiction in their identities, two of these mothers felt this contradiction before they had children because they thought that their identity as a lesbian limited their options to have children. As Sam stated: "I don't think I ever really thought about what would it be like to be in a—be a gay parent. I mean once I came out, I still thought about having kids, but I don't think I ever put the two together. I don't think I thought about being a lesbian and having kids. They were kind of like these separate thoughts" (Sam, gestational mother). As she states about her experiences, Sam felt as though her identity as a mom and as a lesbian could not fit together. As previous research suggests, these women could not put themselves within the model of what it means to be the "right" kind of mothers, and therefore struggled to see themselves holding both identities at the same time.

However, there were also four moms who explicitly felt that their two identities, as a lesbian and as a mom, "seamlessly integrated." Each of these moms also talked about what it is that contributed to the easy integration of these two identities. Kerry, a co-mom, felt that once her kids were born, her identities were like "two sides to a coin"; both identities are a part of her, but neither one impacts the other's ability to be present and an active part of her self-concept. Although their two identities are manifested because of different experiences, these mothers show that there are also lesbian women who do not struggle with integrating their two identities; their identity as a mom and identity as a lesbian are not contradictory at all.

Biological Connection

Five of the six women who were exclusively co-mothers worried about the impact not being a birth mother would have on outsiders' perceived connection with their child and how it would or would not validate their identity. While describing an outing with her child's birth mom and donor, Carmen stated, "We all went somewhere together. It was just sooo obvious who his biological parents are. And he looks so much like both of them. That it was like, wow, I wonder if people think that I'm the nanny." Carmen felt that her lack of biological connection might lead others to not seeing her as a part of the family. So in order to work through those feelings, she had to find meaning in her positionality as a mother: "I actually had this really important role. I think by [my wife's] not acknowledging that, it didn't give me the space to realize what I was going to gain by not being related or not being a gestational parent" (Carmen, co-mom). Once Carmen felt that her personal experience into motherhood was valid and given space, she could come to understand her own role as a mom, find meaning in her positionality as a co-mother, and build that relationship with her child. Several other mothers also pursued alternative ways to make meaning of their position as the nongestational parent and forge a connection as a co-mother.

Language Use

During the process to have a child, the language use of others deeply impacted the experience of many mothers. How others referenced them as an individual or a family could easily delegitimize a mother's sense of maternal identity or right to be a part of the process. Mothers cited the out-of-date language use of birth classes, a place parents-to-be normally turn to for support and guidance. Andie said that when she and her partner went to a birthing class, "the teacher was always diving us into groups. Like, 'Okay well so moms you go over here and dads and [Andie's partner] go over here . . . *moms* over here and *partners* over here' and I said, 'Well actually, I mean she's a mom too'" (Andie, gestational mom). Andie discussed that she actually had a very hard time self-identifying as mother while she was pregnant because it hurt her to see that her partner was not being respected in the same way. The hospital was also a common place for co-mothers to be delegitimized because of others' language use. When touring the hospital that her wife was supposed to give birth in, Dawn said that the guide was walking a large group through the tour saying: "'Now father's you'll park here. And fathers you'll come here. And then father, this is what you'll do.' And so I looked at the other lesbian couple [on the tour] and I said, 'So where do we park? Where do we sit? (laughs) What do we do?'" (Dawn, co-mom). While able to joke about the experience with another couple that was going through the same thing, Dawn still did not see herself being represented in the language use by the hospital practitioners. This experience led Dawn and her partner to making the decision to find a different hospital to give birth at.

Legal Access

Nine out of the eleven mothers discussed the legal steps they took to establish both mothers' relationship with their child. All nine of these mothers cited being on the birth certificate as an important aspect of that establishment. As Charlie stated, "We were legally married and we were like, oh we do have protections. I will be on the birth certificate, thank God we live in California." The co-mothers' being able to put their names on the birth certificate was meaningful because it assisted in validating their identity and rights as a mother. However, Charlie then went onto say: "Until Donald Trump got elected. And last Monday we met with a lawyer to start the second parent adoption process, which is—Really hurts me in my heart but I know I have to do it. I mean philosophically, I shouldn't have to adopt my own daughter" (Charlie, co-mom). While two of the mothers in this study began the adoption process for the co-mother right after their children were born, five of the co-mothers had begun the process to adopt their children as a result of the 2016 presidential election of Donald Trump, like Charlie.

Prior to this election, the mothers felt confident in their name on their child's birth certificate and the political progress LGBTQ families have made in recent history. It felt like enough to validate and legitimatize their motherhood. However, the 2016 election had shaken that confidence that the co-mothers' right to their children would not be threatened. In regard to now pursuing an adoption postelection, Morgan stated: "It makes me very, very angry. I'm on the birth certificate; I shouldn't have to go through a 'stepparent adoption.' Which I think is offensive. It's an offensive word for who I've been. And there's nothing wrong with stepparents . . . but I'm not a stepparent. I'm that child's parent. . . . And it angers me that other people don't understand that I do have to do this and reason that I have to" (Morgan, co-mom). Morgan brought up the fact that the adoption does not accurately portray her role as a mother and delegitimizes her experience and position as a mother.

Conclusions

In many ways, the findings of this study support some aspects of previous research. Particularly when considering forms of connection, either with their child or with support systems, the participants in this study echoed the findings of previous work that signifies the substantial importance of finding pathways of support (Hayman et al. 2015; Wall 2011). Additionally, many co-mothers discussed intentional thought around how their child came into the family and the dynamics once their child joined the family to ensure that there were alternative ties or connections between them and their child beyond biological connection (Hayman et al. 2015; Mamo 2007).

However, these findings begin to depart from the other literature on lesbian mothers' identity development by suggesting that their motherhood identity is not inherently contradictory because of their lesbian identity, as is so intensely characterized in past literature (Hayman et al. 2015; Mamo 2007; Miller 2012; Wall 2011). While there were a few mothers who did struggle to navigate the integration of their two identities, just as many expressed that their identities integrated without any struggle or concern. This is important because it suggests that perhaps lesbian motherhood is not as much of a contradiction as it once was. It is possible that lesbian mothers are becoming more integrated into society and therefore are able to integrate their identities more readily. In the other areas of salient experiences, the most common reason for a mother to feel that her identity was invalidated, ignored, or in contradiction with her lesbian identity was because of *external* circumstances. When it comes to biological connection, many of the co-mothers wanted to be visibly understood and validated as a part of the family when out in public, and if that was denied to them, that was when they felt that their identity as a mother was invalided. For language use, these experiences typically had to do with a lack of inclusion for both moms in parenting spaces, or if they were both recognized as mothers then the invasive inquiry about their family makeup that often followed. Additionally,

the legal rights that these mothers have to fight for, as well as the political climate in which they were entering at the time of the study, was impactful as a
result of the imposition of others onto their families.

This clear element of external impact challenges how the heterosexual
matrix operates within lesbian mothers' identity development. The previously
argued "deviance" from the motherhood standard supported by the heterosexual matrix has historically been understood as the source for lesbian mothers'
internalized contradictions in identities that creates challenges to bridging both
into her self-concept. This study shows that that should no longer be assumed
as the typical experience of lesbian mothers, but instead simply one experience.

The impact of discursive power (Foucault 1978), on the other hand, has
remained consistently salient. Gabb (2005) and Miller (2012) both analyzed the
powerful effect that the access to language and how language is utilized toward
lesbian mothers can be inhibiting in lesbian mother's identity development. This
study shows that investment in this contradiction in the identities between "lesbian" and "mother," explained through the reinforcement of the heterosexual
matrix, is coming from people who are not lesbian mothers themselves. It is then,
when these other people impose their struggle to understand a cohesive "lesbian mother," that these moms feel that their identity may be invalid, illegitimate, or a contradiction.

There are limitations to this study, namely, that the sample size was eleven
and several of the participants were recruited through word of mouth. Additionally, all participants included in the analysis were mothers who brought their
child into their family through conception and /birth, which excluded mothers
who adopted their children and may have different experiences with their identity. Finally, all participants were also based in California, a socially liberal and
relatively LGBTQ friendly state to live in. Many of the mothers felt that they experienced little to no discrimination because of where they lived; this may have
impacted the extent to which they felt that others accepted their identity. However, these limitations do not undermine the findings here. The findings of this
study offer alternative narratives that should be included and considered in the
conversation of lesbian mothers' maternal identity.

The experiences of identity integration for lesbian mothers are indeed
nuanced. However, these nuances are not necessarily negative, nor do they automatically create tension and a contradiction in the identities of "lesbian" and
"mom" for these lesbian mothers themselves. The power of language, what lesbian mothers call themselves, how lesbian mothers and families are referred to
by others, and the questions asked of lesbian mothers all had profound effects
on the mothers in this study when discussing their feelings of legitimacy. Challenging discursive power by using inclusive language on legal documents or
when referring to co-mothers and refraining from asking invasive questions

about a lesbian mother's family would decrease these incidents that make lesbian mothers feel illegitimate in their role and identity as a mother.

REFERENCES

Butler, Judith. 1990. *Gender Trouble: Feminism and the Subversion of Identity.* New York: Routledge.

Charmaz, Kathy. 2017. "Constructivist Grounded Theory." *Journal of Positive Psychology* 12 (3): 299–300.

Epstein, Rachel. 2002. "Butches with Babies: Reconfiguring Gender and Motherhood." *Journal of Lesbian Studies* 6 (2): 41–57.

Foucault, Michel. 1978. *The History of Sexuality: An Introduction.* Vol. 1. New York: Vintage Books.

Gabb, Jacqui. 2005. "Lesbian M/Otherhood: Strategies of Familial-Linguistic Management in Lesbian Parent Families." *Sociology* 39 (4): 585–603.

Hare-Mustin, Rachel T., and Patricia C. Broderick. 1979. "The Myth of Motherhood: A Study of Attitudes toward Motherhood." *Psychology of Women Quarterly* 4 (1): 114–128.

Hayman, Brenda, Lesley Wilkes, Elizabeth Halcomb, and Debra Jackson. 2015. "Lesbian Women Choosing Motherhood: The Journey to Conception." *Journal of GLBT Family Studies* 11 (4): 395–409.

Hequembourg, Amy L. 2007. "Becoming Lesbian Mothers." *Journal of Homosexuality* 53 (3): 153–180.

Laney, Elizabeth K., Lisa Carruthers, M. Elizabeth Lewis Hall, and Tamara Anderson. 2014. "Expanding the Self: Motherhood and Identity Development in Faculty Women." *Journal of Family Issues* 35 (9): 1227–1251.

Mamo, Laura. 2007. *Queering Reproduction: Achieving Pregnancy in the Age of Technoscience:* Durham, NC: Duke University Press.

Mezey, Nancy J. 2008. *New Choices, New Families: How Lesbians Decide about Motherhood:* Baltimore: JHU Press.

Miller, Katrina L. 2012. "What Will They Call You? Rhetorically Listening to Lesbian Maternal Narratives." *International Journal of Listening* 26 (3): 134–145.

Obergefell v. Hodges, 135 S. Ct. 2071, 576 U.S., 191 L. Ed. 2d 953 (2015).

Pelka, Suzanne. 2009. "Sharing Motherhood: Maternal Jealousy among Lesbian Co-mothers." *Journal of Homosexuality* 56 (2): 195–217.

Russo, Nancy Felipe. 1976. "The Motherhood Mandate." *Journal of Social Issues* 32 (3): 143–153.

Russo, Nancy Felipe. 1979. "Overview: Sex Roles, Fertility and the Motherhood Mandate." *Psychology of Women Quarterly* 4 (1): 7–15.

Shelton, Nikki, and Sally Johnson. 2006. "'I Think Motherhood for Me Was a Bit like a Double-Edged Sword': The Narratives of Older Mothers." *Journal of Community & Applied Social Psychology* 16 (4): 316–330.

Thompson, Julie Marie. 2002. *Mommy Queerest: Contemporary Rhetorics of Lesbian Maternal Identity.* Amherst: University of Massachusetts Press.

Wall, Misty. 2011. "Hearing the Voices of Lesbian Women Having Children." *Journal of GLBT Family Studies* 7 (1–2): 93–108.

Conclusion

Future Directions for Research on Health of Sexual Minority Couples

CORINNE RECZEK

HUI LIU

LINDSEY WILKINSON

The study of health and well-being of sexual minority couples became a bourgeoning field in the 1990s, cross-cutting several disciplines including sociology, demography, public health, psychology, family studies, human development, and economics. One of the reasons that this topic has blossomed in recent decades is the perceived puzzle same-sex marriage presents for research that assumes heteronormativity—the notion that all unions are monogamous partnerships comprised of cisgender, heterosexual partners. Namely, if heterosexual union status matters for health, as is shown in hundreds of academic studies, does marriage also matter—and in the same way—for those in sexual minority unions? In this book, we begin to bring together a consensus on this question, finding that marriage and other union statuses do indeed matter for sexual minority couples, although sometimes in different ways for sexual minorities. In this concluding chapter, we consider the future of research on this topic in order to engender new research questions alongside new data collection efforts. In doing so, we imagine our movement forward through new research questions and new data collection methods.

Past research has provided significant insight into the dynamics of sexual minority families and well-being, in part due to a drastic proliferation of data sources at the population level, community level, and individual level that are reflected in the chapters of this book. This collection of studies provides new clues in our quest to understand whether, and if so, how, sexual minority unions shape the health of individuals. For example, the data sources presented in this book, including the National Health Interview Surveys, the National Longitudinal Study of Adolescent to Adult Health, the National Survey of Family Growth, and the Social Justice Sexuality Project, provide opportunities for researchers to understand large-scale, generalizable patterns in how we think about same-sex unions and health. Moreover, the smaller-scale qualitative data sources presented in this book show the importance of focusing on the nuance of family ties and health—in all its complexity. Although these data sources represent a movement forward in studying sexual minority families and health, each has significant limitations that lead us to call for better data, better questions, and more sophisticated analytical techniques. Indeed, data limitations—both qualitative and quantitative—represent the major obstacle in moving this line of research forward. Below, we outline what is needed in the next stage of research on this topic, which all require serious efforts in data collection, with the hopes to inspire future researchers as they undertake this area of study.

Longitudinal and Population-Level Studies

One unique contribution of this book is that a majority of the chapters are quantitative studies based on large-scale population-based representative data. This type of research represents an emerging trend, yet represents a minority of research on this topic. Moreover, studies of population-based data in this area, inclusive of most chapters in this book, are primarily based on cross-sectional data. One of the hallmarks of late twentieth- and early twenty-first-century research on marriage and well-being was the emergence of population-level data that tracked individuals over time, or longitudinally. With this type of data, scholars are able to assess causal relationships from transitions into and out of marriage, and speak to broader population-level trends that could be generalized to the United States as a whole. This allowed scholars to test whether the protective effects of marriage were a consequence of selection effects (e.g., healthier people marrying), as well as to examine the specific aspects of marriage that promoted health (e.g., marital protection). Over this research period, scholars consistently found conclusive evidence for both, informing the ways in which we discuss marriage and the consequences of marriage policy for heterosexuals today. The collection of longitudinal data that include sexual minority couples would allow us to similarly articulate whether marriage is related to better health among sexual minority couples due to a selection effect (i.e., healthier LGBTQ people marrying) or due to a protective effect (e.g., a benefit for sexual minority couples by virtue of their marriage). New longitudinal, population-based data would further allow us test whether this causal effect is generalizable to the population level.

One example of the use of longitudinal, population-based data presented in this book is Joyner and colleagues' examination of social context and the stability of same-sex and different-sex relationships (chapter 14), which uses data from the National Longitudinal Study of Adolescent to Adult Health (Add Health). Yet Add Health is one of a minority of data sets that allows for any longitudinal or contextual analysis, and it itself has many limitations, including its dated nature and lack of emphasis on couples. Future creation and use of longitudinal, population-based data that focus on family and couple-level processes is key if scholarship on sexual minority families and health is to reach the same level of scientific consensus as is found for heterosexual families and health.

Using a Life Course Perspective to Examine Sexual Minority Relationships, Health, and Well-Being

The use of longitudinal, population-based data has also provided researchers the ability to use the life course perspective to examine heterosexual families and health. According to the life course perspective, the developmental tasks and challenges of life change from childhood through young adulthood and middle and older ages. Each person meets these challenges within a specific social, cultural, and economic context that influences health and well-being. For example, recent research on heterosexual marriage shows that marital quality, marital transitions, and marital histories are key to understanding health outcomes over time. However, we know very little about how these longitudinal factors matter for sexual minorities (Reczek, Liu, and Brown 2014). In taking a life course perspective on sexual minority families and health, the presence or absence of a same-sex partner, the transitional processes into and out of marriage or cohabitation, and relationship quality within marriage or cohabitation become central to understanding health outcomes. Yet, most current research on sexual minority couples falls short in considering a full life course picture of relationship transitions or relationship quality, primarily due to data limitations. This represents a major obstacle to fully applying a life course approach to the analysis of health and well-being of sexual minority couples. For example, being previously married (divorced) is shown to negatively affect health, but is this true for a man who was previously married to a woman, and is now dating a man? This is an important question, as older cohorts of individuals were often married to a different-sex partner prior to coming out as LGBTQ. And as Goldberg (chapter 4 in this volume) demonstrates, sexuality is fluid over the life course, with some sexual minorities more or less visible at different points across the life course depending on current relationships status and gender of partner. Such a life course history may yield a very different relationship with, and effect of, marriage. Moreover, relationship quality appears to be central to obtaining the health benefits of marriage, especially among women in different-sex relationships. Yet, we know very little about how relationship quality differs for sexual minority couples, nor how relationship quality will shape health over time among sexual minority cohabiting and married individuals. Mernitz's results (chapter 15 in this volume) suggest that same-sex couples report higher marital quality than different-sex couples; this finding deserves more research and attention with population-level data given the implications for both same-sex and different-sex couples.

In terms of dissolution, research on heterosexual marriage suggests that divorce contributes to worse health, at least in the short term, largely through the stress of relationship dissolution and the loss of resources associated with marriage. However, we do not yet know if the health consequences of relationship dissolution among same-sex couples are similar or different for different-sex couples (Goldberg 2010). Some research suggests that same-sex couples break up and divorce at similar rates as different-sex couples, while other research shows that same-sex couples have higher rates of dissolution than those in different-sex unions (e.g., Lau 2012; Manning, Brown, and Stykes 2016), perhaps because there are unique challenges faced by same-sex couples due to their stigmatized status. Moreover, while a growing body of research shows that relationships involving two women are more likely to dissolve than relationships with two men, Joyner and colleagues (2017) demonstrate that, actually, male same-sex couples appear to have a higher dissolution rate than both female same-sex couples and different-sex couples. Nevertheless, it is not clear how the processes of relationship dissolutions and transitions shape the health and well-being of same-sex couples. Moreover, given variation in heteronormativity across time and space, a contextual component to this analysis is necessary, as Joyner and colleagues' (chapter 14) and Alston-Stepnitz's (chapter 3) chapters in this volume suggest. To answer these questions, future studies should apply a life course approach using longitudinal data on union history, transitions, and relationship quality among same-sex couples, integrating contextual analysis when possible.

Linked Lives between Sexual Minority Partners

Previous research on marriage and health further draws on the life course perspective to direct attention to the linked lives between spouses. This body of research suggests that spouses' health risks are linked through shared environment and life experiences, as well as through the influence of the other's health behaviors. Previous investigations of heterosexual marriage and health have fallen short of capturing the complexities of marital relationships by overlooking the dyadic nature of marriage due to a continued focus on the individual rather than the dyad as the unit of analysis (Carr and Springer 2010). Recent studies, mostly laboratory based, find evidence of correlated risks of chronic illness (e.g., cancer and cardiovascular diseases) between spouses. However, our understanding of how spouses in sexual minority unions affect each other's health is far from complete, as nationally representative dyadic studies are rare (Carr and Springer 2010). In an attempt to address this dearth of research, a small number of studies have utilized dyadic data to show the interconnected nature of health for individuals in same-sex and different-sex couples. For example, in a series of studies using qualitative dyadic data, Reczek and colleagues find that same-sex and different-sex spouses strongly influence one another's health behavior—for better or worse—by using social control tactics, environmental influence, and social pressure (Reczek and Umberson 2012). Additionally, a quantitative daily diary study that followed 808 same-sex and different-sex spouses over the course of five days and measured health and relationship factors found that individuals in same-sex couples provide instrumental and emotion work in response to a sick partner in distinct ways relative to individuals in different-sex couples (Umberson et al. 2017). An analysis of this same data set also reveals that individuals in same-sex couples have more concordant health behaviors than those in different-sex couples (Holway, Umberson, and Donnelly 2018). These studies demonstrate the importance of the linked lives approach, wherein one partner's lifestyle and circumstance are salient to the other partner. While research in this volume makes creative use of individual-level data, including time use data from the American Time Use Survey (ATUS) to address quality of time spent with partner (chapter 2 by Flood and Genadek) and survey data from the National Health Interview Surveys (NHIS) to assess conjoint work hours and health behaviors of couples (chapter 6 by Fan), true couple-level analysis is still lacking. We call on future studies to collect dyadic data that follows both partners over time at the population level in both different- and same-sex unions to assess possible health effects of these linked lives.

Heterogeneity of Sexual Minority Couples

The majority of chapters in this volume focus on same-sex unions. This in part reflects the current research, which is limited because most existing population-level data sources rely on household rosters (i.e., via the reported relationship of each household member with household head and their reported sex). However, same-sex dyads are but one of a number of family formations sexual minorities make. Previous work, including most chapters in this book, does not consider the substantial heterogeneity of sexual minorities and does not include gender minorities, such as transgender couples. This is a remarkable oversight in the broader literature, primarily due to data limitations, that limits our understanding of unions and health.

Most notably, the categories of "same-sex" and "different-sex"—which we have used across this volume—reinforce the sex/gender binary wherein men and women are different or opposite. Doing so erases nonbinary identities and configurations (e.g., trans, gender queer) that have important implications for health and well-being among the broader sexual minority as well as the gender minority population. For example, most studies ignore or erase bisexual, pansexual, asexual, queer, transgender, genderqueer, and nonbinary individuals. For example, transgender and gender queer people are one of the least understood and most stigmatized gender and sexual minority groups. The literature on transgender couples and health is limited, with a primary focus on transgender people in relationships with cisgender people (e.g., transgender men coupled with cisgender women) (Moore and Stambolis-Ruhstorfer 2013; Pfeffer 2017). This literature shows that transgender people appear to receive the social support benefits of being in an intimate relationships relative to those who are not (Pfeffer 2017). Our recent work further suggests that transgender married people report lower levels of perceived discrimination than cohabiting or previously married transgender people in multiple life domains such as work, family, medical care, and public accommodations (Liu and Wilkinson 2017). Other studies show, however, that trans individuals partnered to cis people also experience unique relationship strains and possible negative health consequences (Pfeffer 2017). This early research is only a starting point for understanding relationship and health dynamics among trans families, and future work should continue to uncover how trans relationships shape health.

Sexual minority populations have experienced heightened heterogeneity in other ways due to rapid social, cultural, and legal changes across age and cohorts. For example, in relation to cohort change, more people identified as a gender or sexual minority in 2016 than ever before—by some estimates, 7.3 percent of millennials reported that they were lesbian, gay, bisexual, or transgender (Gates 2017). New questions arise with increases in these identifications, such as, how does a transgender identity matter in forming a relationship and for how that relationship shapes health and well-being, and how does having both a sexual minority and gender minority identity shape relationship formation and health? These relationships are largely invisible in our current research, which is problematic given that bisexual, transgender, and queer people are at heightened risk for mental and physical health problems (Institute of Medicine 2011). Future studies should give fuller consideration to heterogeneity within sexual minority families and how this heterogeneity further complicates existing union formation and health disparities (Institute of Medicine 2011).

These drastic changes in the sexual minority population, alongside other social, legal, and cultural changes that have occurred over the last few decades, need to be examined. Chapters in this volume begin to address important questions about the impact of changes across time (e.g., chapter 16 by Brewster et al.) and across space (e.g., chapter 14 by Joyner et al.) on the health of sexual minority couples, with particular emphasis on legal changes impacting sexual minority families (e.g., chapter 12 by Kazyak and Finken). It is likely that the health consequences of sexual minority unions depend on age and cohort, requiring future scholars to use careful age-period-cohort analysis to parse the health impacts of our changing social contexts. Likewise, gaps in our understanding of the role played by regional and geographic variation should be addressed in future research, perhaps through the use of quasi-natural experiments and multisite comparative studies. Only using these more innovative techniques will we fully understand the relationship between gender and sexual minority populations and health.

Intersectionality

Related to the concept of heterogeneity is the theoretical perspective of intersectionality. An intersectional perspective posits that sexuality interacts with other social identities such as race, class, and gender to impact health outcomes. Past research shows that within heterosexual marriage, race, class, and gender all shape health outcomes in unique ways. However, most research on gender and sexual minority families and health has neglected racial, ethnic, and socioeconomic differences. Given the well-known disparities in health and family across race and class, this constitutes an urgent gap for future research.

Currently, it is unclear how existing findings on health of sexual minority couples, mostly based on white, middle-, and upper-class families, do or do not apply to nonwhite and non-middle-class gender and sexual minority individuals and families. In her study on black queer mothers, Moore shows how, for individuals who identify as black, being in a same-sex couple results in different dynamics than is typically experienced by whites in same-sex families (Moore 2011). These racial dynamics, including notions of self-identity, racial discrimination in the workplace, and racism in family and community life, likely have serious consequences for health and well-being. However, very few population-based surveys are able to address racial differences. In one of our recent studies (Liu et al. 2017), we work from the intersectional perspective to analyze health disparities across union status at the intersection of the sex composition of a couple, race-ethnicity, and gender, and our analysis of the NHIS data suggests that same-sex cohabitors face substantial health disadvantages relative to the different-sex married, with little variation by race-ethnicity and gender. Fewer health differences are found for same-sex cohabitors in comparison with both different-sex cohabitors and unpartnered singles, yet there is greater variation by gender and race-ethnicity. In addition to a lack of understanding about the diverse experiences of LGBTQ people of different socioeconomic and demographic groups, the intersection of additional sources of diverse experiences should be addressed in future research. While chapters in this volume begin to address this intersectionality among same-sex couples using available data sources (e.g., chapter 1 by Brown et al., chapter 5 by Denney et al.), more work needs to be done to ensure the diversity of the LGBTQ population is represented in research on family and health.

Conclusions

The legalization of same-sex marriage and the increased acceptance and prevalence of sexual minority families have fostered a substantial shift in how we understand and study the consequences for family life on health. Because family health is shaped by public policy, including but not limited to marriage policy, the quickly changing legal and social landscape provides a significant charge for scholars, researchers, and policy makers to better understand the relationship between gender and sexual minority families and health. The ability to participate in marriage may promote health behavior, better mental health, and reduce social stigma in the gender and sexual minority population. However, there may still be unequal access to some of the benefits of marriage for sexual minorities. For example, marriage promotion programs that are meant to promote marriage—especially among low-income individuals with children—do not appear to be utilized to promote same-sex marriage, creating unequal access to potential resources. Moreover, the U.S. Supreme Court recently decided in favor of allowing businesses the right to deny same-sex wedding services, such as a wedding cake or venue, while federal and some state laws allow for the firing of employees for being gay or gender nonconforming. These policies may greatly restrict access to income, health insurance benefits, and job security. Thus, it is clear that the benefits of marriage are still not equally distributed, with social stigma tempering the potential effects of legal rights, but that in many ways policy, law, and public perception do not treat sexual minorities as equals to heterosexuals.

Research on sexual minority families and well-being provides opportunity to transform how family is defined, to refine our methods for examining the processes through which family shapes health, and to bolster the health of all Americans across the sexual and gender minority spectrum. Our approach in this book, and in this chapter, reveals the contributions and critiques of the science on sexual minority families and well-being, including interdisciplinary work that focuses on the lived experiences and narratives of sexual minority adults and their families. Further, we provide directives for future work to utilize dyadic, longitudinal, population-based data with adequate measurement of all forms of gender and sexual identity. As our politics, policies, and data continue to change in the twenty-first century, new frontiers will be broken in research on sexual minority family health. Although all chapters in this book focus on evidence in the United States, the topics on same-sex unions, health, and well-being appeal to audiences all over the world, given the worldwide trend in the rising numbers of sexual minority families. The estimates of the sexual minority population and same-sex household worldwide will continue to increase given ongoing social and political changes and increasing rights for sexual minority people. We hope this chapter serves as a starting place for the next generation of scholars who are interested in sexual minority unions worldwide.

REFERENCES

Carr, Deborah, and Kristen W. Springer. 2010. "Advances in Families and Health Research in the 21st Century." *Journal of Marriage and Family* 72 (3): 743–761. https://doi.org/10 .1111/j.1741-3737.2010.00728.x.

Gates, Gary J. 2012. "Same-Sex Couples in Census 2010: Race and Ethnicity." *UCLA: The Williams Institute.* Retrieved from https://escholarship.org/uc/item/66521994.

Goldberg, Abbie E. 2010. *Lesbian and Gay Parents and Their Children: Research on the Family Life Cycle.* Washington, DC: American Psychological Association.

Holway, Giuseppina Valle, Debra Umberson, and Rachel Donnelly. 2018. "Health and Health Behavior Concordance between Spouses in Same-Sex and Different-Sex Marriages." *Social Currents* 5 (4): 319–327.

Institute of Medicine. 2011. *The Health of Lesbian, Gay, Bisexual, and Transgender People: Building a Foundation for Better Understanding.* Washington, DC: National Academies Press.

Joyner, Kara, Wendy Manning, and Ryan Bogle. 2017. "Gender and the Stability of Same-Sex and Different-Sex Relationships among Young Adults." *Demography* 54 (6): 2351–2374.

Lau, Charles Q. 2012. "The Stability of Same-Sex Cohabitation, Different-Sex Cohabitation, and Marriage." *Journal of Marriage and Family* 74 (5): 973–988.

Liu, Hui, Corinne Reczek, Samuel CH Mindes, and Shannon Shen. 2017. "The Health Disparities of Same-Sex Cohabitors at the Intersection of Race-Ethnicity and Gender." *Sociological Perspectives* 60 (3): 620–639.

Liu, Hui, and Lindsey Wilkinson. 2017. "Marital Status and Perceived Discrimination among Transgender People." *Journal of Marriage and Family* 79 (5): 1295–1313.

Manning, Wendy D., Susan L. Brown, and J. Bart Stykes. 2016. "Same-Sex and Different-Sex Cohabiting Couple Relationship Stability." *Demography* 53 (4): 937–953.

Moore, Mignon. 2011. *Invisible Families: Gay Identities, Relationships, and Motherhood among Black Women.* Berkeley: University of California Press.

Moore, Mignon R., and Michael Stambolis-Ruhstorfer. 2013. "LGBT Sexuality and Families at the Start of the Twenty-First Century." *Annual Review of Sociology* 39: 491–507.

Pfeffer, Carla A. 2017. *Queering Families: The Postmodern Partnerships of Cisgender Women and Transgender Men.* New York: Oxford University Press.

Reczek, Corinne, Hui Liu, and Dustin Brown. 2014. "Cigarette Smoking in Same-Sex and Different-Sex Unions: The Role of Socioeconomic and Psychological Factors." *Population Research and Policy Review* 33 (4): 527–551.

Reczek, Corinne, and Debra Umberson. 2012. "Gender, Health Behavior, and Intimate Relationships: Lesbian, Gay, and Straight Contexts." *Social Science & Medicine* 74 (11): 1783–1790.

Umberson, Debra, Mieke Beth Thomeer, Rhiannon A. Kroeger, Corinne Reczek, and Rachel Donnelly. 2017. "Instrumental- and Emotion-Focused Care Work during Physical Health Events: Comparing Gay, Lesbian, and Heterosexual Marriages." *Journals of Gerontology: Series B* 72 (3): 498–509. https://doi.org/10.1093/geronb/gbw133.

NOTES ON CONTRIBUTORS

ELI ALSTON-STEPNITZ is a graduate student currently working toward his PhD in sociology at the University of California, Davis. His primary research interests are gender and sexuality, particularly the ways gender and sexuality intersect with law, science and technology, and popular culture.

KARIN L. BREWSTER is professor of sociology and research associate at the Center for Demography and Population Health at Florida State University. Her research addresses two areas of inquiry from a social demographic perspective: sexuality in adolescence and early adulthood and contemporary family change.

DUSTIN BROWN is an assistant professor of sociology and a research fellow at the Social Science Research Center at Mississippi State University. He is a social demographer with research interests in population health, aging and the life course, family, and social stratification. His recent research primarily examines race-ethnic, educational, and marital status differences in morbidity, disability, and mortality risk.

JUSTIN T. DENNEY is an associate professor of sociology and the William Julius Wilson Distinguished Professor in the College of Arts and Sciences at Washington State University. His research focuses on how the characteristics of families and places influence individual health outcomes and has received support through the Health Disparities Scholar Program at the National Institute on Minority Health Disparities, the University of Kentucky Center for Poverty Research, and the Foundation for Child Development.

CHRISTINA DRAGON has worked in sexual and gender minority health since 2011, with a focus on federal data systems and health disparities. She is a career health scientist for the federal government and has followed research opportunities across several agencies. She holds a masters' of science degree in public health from Johns Hopkins Bloomberg School of Public Health, and a double major from Smith College in Neuroscience and Woman and Gender Studies.

WEN FAN is an assistant professor of sociology at Boston College. Her research focuses on the ways in which social factors—especially family dynamics, work environments, and gender norms—intersect to shape health and well-being over the life course, in different historical moments, and across social contexts. Her research has appeared in *Advances in Life Course Research*, *American Sociological Review*, *Social Science Research*, *Social Science & Medicine*, *Society and Mental Health*, and elsewhere.

ANDREW FENELON is an assistant professor of public policy and sociology at Penn State University. Previously, he was an assistant professor at the University of Maryland and the acting associate director of the Maryland Population Research Center. His work focuses on social inequalities in health, and his recent project examines the impact of federal housing assistance programs on health and well-being of U.S. children. His research has been featured in the *New York Times*, on *NPR*, and in the *Washington Post*, the *Guardian*, and *Politico*.

EMMA FINKEN is a graduate student at the University of Nebraska–Lincoln. She is pursuing her master's degree in sociology and a graduate certificate in women's and gender studies. Her research interests include sexuality and social psychology.

SARAH MARIE FLOOD is director of U.S. Survey Projects at the Institute for Social Research and Data Innovation at the University of Minnesota, where she oversees projects funded by the National Institutes of Health to develop, support, and improve population data infrastructure. Her research is at the intersection of gender, work, family, life course, and time use. She has published work on the time use and well-being of parents, couples, and older adults.

DAVID M. FROST is an associate professor in social psychology in the Department of Social Science at University College London. His research interests sit at the intersections of stress, stigma, health, sexuality, and close relationships. His primary line of research focuses on how stigma, prejudice, and discrimination constitute minority stress and, as a result, affect the health and well-being of marginalized individuals. He also studies how couples psychologically experience intimacy within long-term romantic relationships and how their experience of intimacy affects their health. His research has been recognized by grants and awards from the National Institutes of Health, the Society for the Psychological Study of Social Issues, and the New York Academy of Sciences.

KATIE R. GENADEK is a research associate at the Institute of Behavioral Science at the University of Colorado Boulder. She is a demographer and labor economist with research focusing on work, family, and well-being for individuals, couples, and parents. She also analyzes historical and contemporary policy impacts on employment and time use.

ABBIE E. GOLDBERG is a professor of psychology at Clark University. Her research examines diverse families, including adoptive parent families and lesbian and gay parent families. She is the author of over 110 peer-reviewed articles and three books, including *Gay Dads: Transitions to Adoptive Fatherhood*, and is the editor of three books, including the *SAGE Encyclopedia of LGBTQ Studies*.

BRIDGET K. GORMAN is professor of sociology and dean of undergraduates at Rice University. Her research examines how morbidity, physical functioning, and medical care use vary based on gender, sexual orientation, race-ethnicity, and nativity among U.S. adults.

RACHEL L. HENRY is a Cultural Humility Training Institute director in Northern California. Her research explores the intersections of queer identity and parenthood. She holds a bachelor's degree in psychology from University of California, Santa Cruz and a master's degree in sexuality studies from San Francisco State University.

GIUSEPPINA VALLE HOLWAY is an assistant professor of sociology at the University of Tampa. Her research interests include family, intimate relationships, and sexual and reproductive health. Her current research explores the sociodemographic factors that shape individuals' sexual trajectories, with a particular focus on adolescent and young adult populations. Her work also considers how romantic partners shape each other's health-related behavior and mental health. Recent work appears in the *Annual Review of Sociology*, *Journal of Adolescent Health*, and *Social Currents*.

NING HSIEH is an assistant professor of sociology at Michigan State University. Her research examines how social, cultural, and institutional factors contribute to health disparities faced by sexual minority and aging populations.

KARA JOYNER is a professor of sociology at Bowling Green State University. She has published research in the *American Journal of Public Health*, *American Sociological Review*, *Demography*, *Journal of Marriage and the Family*, *Population and Development Review*, *Social Forces*, and *Social Psychology Quarterly*. Her current research addresses the formation of interracial friendships and romantic relationships, the effects of structural stigma on the health and well-being of sexual minorities, and the measurement of family formation in surveys.

EMILY KAZYAK is an associate professor of sociology and women's and gender studies at the University of Nebraska–Lincoln. Her research agenda focuses on the cultural and legal meanings of sexuality and how these meanings change, particularly with regard to increasing recognition of LGBTQ identities and families. Her recent research investigates American public opinion of religious freedom laws that reference LGBTQ people.

PATRICK M. KRUEGER is associate professor of health and behavioral sciences at the University of Colorado Denver. His research focuses on race-ethnic and socioeconomic disparities in health, health behaviors, and mortality.

NAVYA R. KUMAR recently graduated from Rice University with a B.A. in sociology and a certificate in civic leadership. She is currently a first-year medical student at Baylor College of Medicine.

ALLEN J. LEBLANC is the Health Equity Institute Professor of Sociology at San Francisco State University. His research has generally concerned societal and individual responses to chronic illness and disability, the etiology of social stress and health, and government programs relating to disability and health care for low-income Americans. His past and present projects include National Institutes of Health–funded studies of social stress, psychosocial resources, and health among sexual- and gender-minority persons, with a particular focus on the relational context of stress experience.

HUI LIU is a professor of sociology at Michigan State University. Her recent research, funded by the National Institutes of Health, investigates the social-biological interactions in linking marriage and health as well as the well-being of same-sex families. Her research on marriage and health has been widely reported in prominent national and international news outlets including the *New York Times*, the *Washington Post*, CNN, *US News and World Report*, the *Sydney Morning Herald*, and *China Daily*.

WENDY MANNING is the Dr. Howard E. and Penny Daum Aldrich Distinguished Professor of Sociology, director of the Center for Family and Demographic Research, and co-director of the National Center for Family and Marriage Research. She was the lead researcher on the American Sociological Association's Amici Briefs in 2013 and 2015 on marriage equality (*Hollingsworth v. Perry* and *Obergefell v. Hodges*). Her research focuses on the health and well-being of young adults as well as family formation and stability.

SARA MERNITZ is a postdoctoral fellow at the Population Research Center at the University of Texas at Austin. Her research broadly focuses on romantic relationships and their longitudinal associations with mental health and substance use.

JARRON M. SAINT ONGE is associate professor of sociology and population health at the University of Kansas. His research investigates the role of social determinants on health behaviors and health outcomes. He is particularly interested in understanding how residential context, race-ethnicity, and socioeconomic status influence health lifestyles and the subsequent impact on health disparities.

AMANDA POLLITT is a postdoctoral fellow in the Population Research Center at the University of Texas at Austin conducting research on lesbian, gay, bisexual, and transgender mental and physical health. She aims to understand how gender, sexuality, and family provide contexts for stigma in the lives of LGBTQ people and how this stigma influences health. She received her PhD in family studies and human development from the University of Arizona.

BARBARA PRINCE is an assistant professor of sociology at Lebanon Valley College. She has published research in *Population Research and Policy Review*, *Journal of Marriage and Family*, and *Teaching Sociology*. Her research focuses on the effects of social context on outcomes of sexual minorities and the scholarship of teaching and learning.

CORINNE RECZEK is an associate professor of sociology at the Ohio State University. Her research, funded by the Eunice Kennedy Shriver National Institute of Child Health and Development, examines the relationship between union status and health among sexual minorities. Her most recent project investigates how gender and sexual minority young adults navigate the transition to adulthood.

LACEY J. RITTER received her PhD in sociology with an emphasis on health and aging from Florida State University in 2017. Following graduation, she became an associate professor of sociology at Wingate University in North Carolina. She currently serves as director of the Long Term Care Administration minor at Wingate University and as a member of a coalition focused on food insecurity and poverty in various low-income North Carolina counties. She researches and presents on various issues related to health and health care access, gerontology, dying and death, and sexuality.

LORI E. ROSS is an associate professor in the Social and Behavioural Health Sciences Division of the Dalla Lana School of Public Health, University of Toronto, and leader of the Re:searching for LGBTQ2S Health Team (www.lgbtqhealth.ca). Lori conducts community-based, mixed methods research in partnership with communities that experience marginalization, with a particular focus on LGBTQ2S communities.

MATT RUTHER is an assistant professor of urban and public affairs at the University of Louisville. His current research looks at health disparities between sexual minorities and heterosexual populations, and the role of neighborhood effects in explaining these disparities.

RICHARD K. SCOTCH is professor of sociology, public policy, and political economy at the University of Texas at Dallas. His research interests include social policy reform and social movements in disability, health care, education, and human services; he has a forthcoming book, *Allies and Obstacles*, coauthored with Allison Carey and Pamela Block, on social movements of parents of children with disabilities to be published by Temple University Press in 2020. In 2017 he completed a community needs assessment of the LGBTQ population in Texas with Kara Sutton for the Texas Pride Impact Funds.

JULIANNA Z. SMITH is an independent research methodologist who specializes in the application of advanced statistical methods to analyze dyadic and longitudinal data. Her work focuses on better understanding the experiences of LGBTQ individuals and members from a range of family types, including multiracial, adoptive, LGBTQ parented, low income, and dual earner.

RUSSELL L. SPIKER is a postdoctoral scholar at the Vanderbilt University LGBT Policy Lab. Their recent research examines the health concordance of same-sex partners and the role of couple-level health outcomes in sexual minority health disparities. Their other research on sexual minority health investigates marital status, alcohol use, and children of same-sex parents and has been published in *Demography*, *Journal of Marriage and Family*, and *Social Science Research*.

KARA SUTTON is a visiting lecturer at Southern Methodist University, where she teaches courses on community development, contemporary social issues, and nonprofit evaluation. Her research interest lies at the intersection of public policy, human services, and community-based interventions, with a particular focus on underserved and marginalized populations. She has worked as a researcher and consultant on a diverse array of topics including early childhood education for disadvantaged youth, offender reentry support services, and workforce opportunities for individuals with disabilities.

KATHRYN HARKER TILLMAN is a professor of sociology at Florida State University. She studies the social and health-related outcomes of adolescents and young adults, with a particular focus on the influence of family and interpersonal relationships for individual development, health and risk-taking behaviors, and overall well-being. Her most recent research includes examinations of sexual behavior and romantic relationship formation during adolescence and emerging adulthood, the association between youth sexual behavior and psychological, behavioral and reproductive health outcomes, and the social and psychological well-being differences between youth engaged in romantic relationships with same-race and different-race partners.

ZELMA OYARVIDE TUTHILL is a doctoral student in the Sociology Department at Rice University. Her research examines how race and sexual orientation intersect to shape the health status and lived experiences of men and women. Her mixed-method dissertation examines how sexual minority black and Latino men and women utilize their community ties and social networks to garner health-promoting behaviors.

KOJI UENO is professor of sociology at Florida State University. He engages in both quantitative and qualitative research to examine the impact of sexual orientation on mental health, friendships, and status attainment by drawing on life course and social psychological perspectives. His work has been funded by National Science Foundation and Social Science Research Council and published in sociology journals such as *Social Problems*, *Social Forces*, *Journal of Health and Social Behavior*, and *Work and Occupations*.

DEBRA UMBERSON is professor of sociology and director of the Population Research Center at the University of Texas–Austin. Her research focuses on social determinants of health across the life course, with attention to social ties, health disparities, and the use of blended research methods. Much of her work considers how spouses influence each other's health-related behavior, mental health, and health care and how these processes vary across gay, lesbian, and heterosexual unions. She is an elected Fellow of the Gerontological Society of America, recipient of the American Sociological Association's 2015 Matilda White Riley Distinguished Scholar Award for research on aging, and the 2016 recipient of the Leonard I. Pearlin Award for Distinguished Contributions to the Sociological Study of Mental Health.

LINDSEY WILKINSON is an associate professor of sociology at Portland State University with research interests in gender and sexuality, education, and health. His work has been published in journals such as *Gender & Society*, *Journal of Marriage and Family*, and *Social Science Research*.

INDEX

Note: The letter t following a page number denotes a table